THE
POLITICS
OF
GRATITUDE

Also by Mark T. Mitchell

Michael Polanyi: The Art of Knowing (author)

The Humane Vision of Wendell Berry (coeditor)

Related Titles from Potomac Books

New Common Ground: A New America, a New World
—Amitai Etzioni

The Mythology of American Politics:
A Critical Response to Fundamental Questions
—John T. Bookman

Divided America on the World Stage:
Broken Government and Foreign Policy
—Howard J. Wiarda

Getting Immigration Right: What Every American Needs to Know
—David Coates and Peter Siavelis, editors

The Cure for Our Broken Political Process: How We Can Get
Our Politicians to Resolve the Issues Tearing Our Country Apart
—Sol Erdman and Lawrence Susskind

THE
POLITICS
OF
GRATITUDE

Scale, Place & Community
in a Global Age

MARK T. MITCHELL

Potomac Books
Washington, D.C.

Library of Congress Cataloging-in-Publication Data
Mitchell, Mark T.
  The politics of gratitude : scale, place & community in a global age /
Mark T. Mitchell. — First edition.
      p. cm.
  Includes bibliographical references and index.
  ISBN 978-1-59797-663-3 (hardcover : alk. paper)
  ISBN 978-1-59797-738-8 (electronic)
  1. United States—Politics and government. 2. Social values—United States. I. Title.
  JK275.M58 2012
  306.20973—dc23

                                                    2012027664

Printed in the United States of America on acid-free paper that meets the American National Standards Institute Z39-48 Standard.

Potomac Books
22841 Quicksilver Drive
Dulles, Virginia 20166

First Edition

10 9 8 7 6 5 4 3 2 1

To my parents, *Delvin and Patty Mitchell*
who, by example, showed me
how to love and how to grow things

CONTENTS

ACKNOWLEDGMENTS

A s no man is an island, so no book is the product of one person, even if the title page suggests otherwise. Thus it is fitting—especially in a book about gratitude—to take a moment and discharge, if only partially, the debts of gratitude owed by the author.

The first glimmers of this book took shape when the late George A. Panichas invited me to write a piece for a symposium in the journal *Modern Age*. The symposium, titled "Why I Am Conservative," offered participants the opportunity to explain the factors contributing to their intellectual journeys. The essay I wrote focused on the ideas of limits, gratitude, and human scale—concepts that are ignored by most contemporary conservative writers—and left me wondering exactly how well I fit with what today passes for conservatism. I was given the opportunity to explore these ideas in greater depth when I received a sabbatical year at Princeton University under the auspices of the James Madison Program in American Ideals and Institutions. For a singularly delightful year, I had the privilege of thinking and writing without the demands of teaching. The bulk of this book was written in the upstairs office of a home we rented in the beautiful farming county outside Princeton. I am grateful to Robert P. George, Bradford P. Wilson, and the rest of the folks at the Madison Program for making that year in Princeton such a wonderful and productive time.

The administration of Patrick Henry College has continually encouraged my writing projects, and for that I am grateful. Additionally, I must thank my students, especially those in the political theory program, past and present. Their intellectual curiosity, eagerness to engage, and propensity to ask hard questions make teaching a delight. I would especially like to thank Rachel Blum, who graciously read and commented on the entire manuscript. In addition to good students, I am grateful for good colleagues, especially the wry Canadian humor and wise advice of Les Sillars.

My friend and literary agent, Jeremy Beer, has been a great source of encouragement, wisdom, and counsel throughout the long process required for making a book. Thanks, Jeremy.

Although I don't know him well, I owe a great debt of gratitude to Wendell Berry, whose work was first introduced to me by a student who thought I would enjoy his poetry. Indeed, I did. I then continued on to his essays and novels. The ideas and ideals described by Berry continue to influence me in ways I am only beginning to understand.

Finally, and closer to home, I must thank my wife, Joby, for her constant support and good judgment. Much of what follows here began in conversations with her and was refined in the same way. My boys, Seth, Noah, and Scott, and daughter, Tana Rose, give me four concrete reasons to hope.

INTRODUCTION

Amerian politics is broken. One of the few things most Americans agree on is that Congress is an ineffectual body proficient in pandering to special interests while glibly spending money borrowed against our grandchildren's future. The presidency oscillates between Democrats and Republicans, but nothing really seems to change. The near collapse of the banking industry in 2008 indicated that the corruption is not limited to the public sector, and the subsequent government bailout of certain entities deemed "too big to fail" suggests that we have forgotten how to think and act in terms of human scale.

The so-called culture wars have increased in rancor, even as the lines have become more fixed and the warriors more intransigent. Voices of decency, propriety, and wisdom are drowned out by those who specialize in vitriol and who take delight in demonizing their opponents. Somewhere in the process we have abandoned any conception of the common good.

The political landscape is dominated by "liberals" and "conservatives" who often seem both illiberal and downright hostile to conserving much of anything. For instance, the word "conservative" is used—indeed overused—to describe a political and cultural position as broad as it is nebulous. While most conservatives embrace some version of market capitalism and some limits on the size and scope of government, self-identified conservatives don't agree on the substantive contents of the term. As a result, the word has become so elastic that it can be used to describe anything from a minimalist "night-watchman state" to so-called compassionate conservatism, which looks to government to facilitate, if not deliver, social services. Many who express an enthusiasm for foreign military adventures in the name of universal democracy call themselves conservative, but so do the relative few who support a restrained foreign policy that is skeptical of nation building. Evangelicals championing "family values" call themselves conservative as do business executives whose advertising campaigns seem hell-bent on undermining those same values. Is a concept that is so watered down that it can be credibly used to describe this range of views really worth much at all? Is the word itself worth conserving?

Likewise, the concept of liberalism has undergone changes of its own, for initially it had little to do with a steadily expanding welfare state. Liberalism derives, etymologically, from the Latin *liberalis*, which means liberty. Liberalism is a relative newcomer on the political scene. For liberals, the primary political unit is the individual and the primary concern is individual liberty. Entailed in this is the notion that humans are beings with the capacity to choose. Liberalism, then, is the political school of thought that emphasizes the free choices of individuals. The language of human rights goes hand in hand with liberalism, for these rights refer primarily to the moral status of individuals. Along with the notion of human rights goes the idea of human equality: all humans equally possess certain rights. When Thomas Jefferson wrote that "all Men are created equal, and that they are endowed by their Creator with certain unalienable Rights, that among these are Life, Liberty, and the Pursuit of Happiness," he was giving voice to concepts firmly rooted in the liberal tradition. In this sense, a major strand—and perhaps *the* major strand—of the American founding stems from liberalism.

At this point, an obvious problem emerges. According to this definition of liberalism, it seems that Americans, both Republicans and Democrats, are liberals. That is, they emphasize individual liberty, and political discourse is framed in terms of individual rights.

But Republicans, when they hurl the word "liberal" as an epithet, are not accusing Democrats of their love of liberty and rights. Instead, they are suggesting several things depending on the context. If the subject at hand is fiscal policy, then liberalism means a propensity to increase taxes—especially on the wealthy—and to increase state spending on social programs. If the subject is defense, liberalism means antimilitarism and a propensity to coddle the enemy. In the area of sexual ethics, liberals are libertines who want to destroy the sanctity of marriage between one man and one woman and instead permit marriage between any two consenting adults. Liberals are pro-choice on abortion and against capital punishment. Liberals, so goes the rant, are soft on crime. They love the poor and resent the rich. They are convinced that global warming will destroy us all and that the state should take drastic measures to stop it. When "conservatives" call their opponents liberals they mean, at root, that they are irreligious god-haters or at least Unitarians. Liberals tend to drink pinot noir and concoctions with funny little umbrellas. In short, a liberal, in this colloquial sense, emphasizes expansive personal liberties and favors state solutions to social ills. The high rate of taxation and state intervention that makes the latter possible may, in fact, truncate the former, but that is beside the point.

When Democrats hurl names at Republicans, words like "fundamentalist" and "warmonger" merge to create an image of a gun-toting, Bible-thumping radical, a sort of John Brown for our times. Because some Democrats believe that the so-called Christian Right, secretly or not, has designs on turning the United States into a Christian fundamentalist theocracy, the term "conservative" sometimes carries these connotations. At the very least it is used to designate a group of people who have a particular set of moral beliefs that they want to impose on the rest of society. Furthermore, conservatives tend to be selfish and unconcerned about the poor and destitute. Conservatives are against capital gains taxes and for capital punishment. They oppose inheritance taxes, corporate taxes, and any kind of progressive taxes, which has the effect of funneling more money to the rich at the expense of social programs that help the poor, whom conservatives resent as shiftless drags on society. Conservatives, so goes the rant, are selfish partisans of big business who, at the same time, want to impose a strict morality on the rest of us. They see the natural world as a resource to be strip-mined and deny that human activities have anything to do with climate change. They also tend to be flag-waving jingoists who love war, thrive on militarism, and own at least one handgun. Conservatives tend not to read books; they watch NASCAR and drink beer from a can (unless they are Baptists in which case they drink Mountain Dew). Big business's use of salacious themes in advertizing may not be compatible with the moralizing rhetoric of the culture warriors, but that is beside the point.

Both of these descriptions are caricatures used by one group to discredit the other. And while they don't get us far, they can give us some hints about what each side deems most dangerous. Those on the right are concerned about the libertinism and statism of the left, while those on the left worry about the moralism and social apathy on the right. Liberals want the right to be left alone in the bedroom, and they highlight the rights of the poor and disadvantaged. Conservatives demand the right to keep their own money and the freedom to raise their children in a decent society. Both generally recur to the language of individual rights to make their claims. In this sense, partisans on both the right and the left drink deeply of the well of liberalism.

Many liberals are progressives. Progressives believe that things are getting— or at least can get—progressively better. They are optimistic about human nature and the human capacity for good. They understand human progress to consist of, at least in part, progress toward greater individual freedom. Progressives tend to be optimistic about the human capacity to solve problems. They look forward to the possibility, perhaps in the distant future, of a world without wars, famine, or sickness. Some progressives look for a future without government or private property, but in America most look forward to one characterized by democracy and plenty for all.

American leaders on both the right and the left have, at various times, expressed their conviction that things are progressively improving, even as they lament the slippage that occurs when the opposition is in power. Ronald Reagan famously claimed that it is "morning again in America." Talking heads on the right regularly equate progress with economic growth and argue that if the federal government would simply step aside, a new era of prosperity would dawn. Commentators on the left argue that if conservative culture warriors would stop prying into the private lives of others, peace and happiness would advance significantly. In recent years, it is impossible not to hear politicians, on both the left and the right, speak of "moving forward" or "moving ahead." Apparently, they all assume that forward is the only reasonable direction and that things will get better if we continue to press onward in the same direction. In other words, the doctrine of progress seems deeply embedded in American political discourse.

If partisans on both the left and right express themselves primarily in terms of individual rights and think of politics in terms of an underlying and open-ended progress, then we don't really need the term "conservatism" at all. Both sides are firmly rooted in the soil of progressive liberalism. They agree about the purpose of government (to protect individual rights) and the direction of history (progress). They may disagree about which individual rights to privilege and what specifically constitutes progress, but these are really in-house debates among liberals.

We are at this point confronted with a startling question: is conservatism a term that is useful or meaningful in the American context? At best "conservatism," as it is generally used today, seems to represent merely one shade of liberalism. When the issue is framed in this manner, the raging debate between "conservatives" and "liberals," while dealing with important matters, is really a series of tempests in one particular political teapot. The foundational questions have, it seems, been laid to rest. All sides are committed to the fundamental ideas of individual rights and progress.

In this book, I want to explore an alternative that I call the politics of gratitude. It attempts to move beyond the timeworn liberal-conservative dichotomy that has reduced our political and cultural discourse to clichés, vitriol, and downright silliness. While this narrative will not be recognized as either liberal or conservative by the chief spokespersons of either camp, I would like to poach the word "conservative" for its etymological bounty. The word "conserve" comes from the Latin *conservare*, which is a verb meaning to watch over, preserve, and protect or to continue to dwell in. This term describes stewards, people who commit themselves to preserving the good things of this world. Together they dwell in their various places, watching over those places and the goods inherent therein as they tend them in trust for the next generation. Stewardship gives birth to acts of responsibility and care that are oriented toward the long-term preservation of the natural, cultural, and institutional goods we have inherited, even as it seeks to improve them in the process.

This book attempts to develop an account of politics and culture rooted in gratitude and giving birth to responsible lives characterized by stewardship and a commitment to community. In the first half of the book, I discuss four concepts that are often neglected in our contemporary discourse but that are essential to a politics of gratitude. The four build upon one another and, hopefully, culminate in something that resembles coherence. They are as follows: (1) creatureliness, (2) gratitude, (3) human scale, and (4) place. In the second half, I employ these concepts in thinking about five different areas: (1) politics, (2) economics, (3) the natural world, (4) family, and (5) education. The outcome, perhaps already suspected, will be a political and cultural vision that is at once local, limited, modest, republican*, grateful, and green.

In a climate of increasingly shrill and partisan debates, where the words "liberal" and "conservative" are used as terms of abuse, where important matters are torpedoed by special interests seeking to aggrandize their power, Americans are

---

* By "republican" I mean a form of government based on regular elections and representation in the context of the rule of law.

looking for a better way. They are seeking a political and cultural direction that is authentically different and not simply the retreads of shortsighted ideas born of partisan politics and failed ideologies. Fortunately, there is hope. Many, on both the left and the right, are coming to the conclusion that neither the conservatism of the Republicans nor the progressivism of the Democrats offers long-term solutions to the many challenges besetting us. This book does not attempt to beat the same old drum or the same old heads. What follows is an alternative political and cultural vision rooted in gratitude, common sense, and a deep affection for the sheer goodness of life.

PART I.
THE CONCEPTS

1

Creatures:
Limits and Dependence

What is man, that thou art mindful of him? And the son of man,
that thou visitest him? For thou hast made him a little lower than
the angels, and hast crowned him with glory and honour. Thou
madest him to have dominion over the works of thy hands.

Psalm 8:4–6

Human beings are creatures. But what exactly does that mean, and why does it matter? We use the term "creature" easily and unthinkingly, yet if we pay some attention to the word, we can begin to grasp some important truths about ourselves and the world we inhabit.

Consider first the etymology. "Creature" is tied to the word "create," which suggests that creatures are the handiwork of a creator. Our English word "creator" comes to us unchanged from the Latin word, which can also mean procreator, father, founder, or one who appoints. Our word "creative" derives from the Latin *creatrix*, which is in the feminine gender and implies a female creator or mother. A creature, then, is the work of a creator who exercises creativity to bring something new into the world.

Since these words come to us from the Latin, it should not surprise us that they are infused with religious connotations. Regardless of whether one was a Roman pagan who worshipped a variety of anthropomorphized deities or a Christian who worshipped a single God, the language of creator and creatures clearly implied that the visible world, including human beings, was the product of some nonhuman creative power. The world did not create itself. Humans, being part of the world, owed their existence to something other than themselves.

Today we live in a world from which the old pagan gods have fled. The great monotheistic religions have not died, although large numbers have grown suspicious of claims about miracles, burning bushes, and creation *ex nihilo*. More than a hundred years ago, Friedrich Nietzsche declared that God was dead; more recently scientists, journalists, and other opinion makers have joined the chorus.[1]

Nevertheless, we inhabit a God-haunted language. Because the great majority of our history has transpired in the context of religious belief, it should not be surprising that the various facets of our natures have been articulated in explicitly religious terms. Thus, in tracing some of the aspects traditionally ascribed to the human condition, the use of religious terms and connotations is unavoidable.

The claim that humans have natures implies that there is a given structure within which humans are compelled to operate. At the very least it implies that there is a structure within which humans, acting normally, ought to remain. There are, of course, differing views about what constitutes human nature. In the Hebrew tradition, the concept is rooted in the belief that humans are created in God's image. It also has something to do with a longing for knowledge, which, as the story goes, was fatally exploited by the crafty serpent. When the humans ate from the tree of knowledge, their eyes were opened and they knew good from evil. The consequence of this act of disobedience was expulsion from paradise, followed by a life of pain and eventual death. Embedded in this account is the concept of free will, which has often been cited as the quality that makes us uniquely human.

In the Greek tradition, emphasis is placed on human rationality. Humans, Aristotle argued, are rational creatures, and this is precisely what separates humans from all other animals. That is not the same as saying that we are completely separated from the rest of the natural world. Humans, like plants, grow and need nutrition. Like other animals, humans ingest food, move around, and reproduce. But the ability to reason, to follow an argument from premise to conclusion, to deliberate about various alternatives and settle on one for clear reasons, is an exclusively human prerogative. According to Aristotle, reason is the faculty that makes us most godlike. He conceived of god as pure reason, and when we exercise our rational faculties, we are imitating the divinity.

The longing for knowledge and the ability to reason make possible social and political organization according to law. Moses is the lawgiver (or perhaps better, the law receiver) in the Hebrew tradition. He went to the mountain and received the commandments written on tablets of stone. Through Moses, God instituted a moral and legal system by which the Hebrew people were governed. The law regulated behavior, and obedience to that law brought divine blessing, while disobedience incurred divine punishment. The Talmudic tradition is an extended exercise in close reasoning about the content of the law and its application to particular cases. As such, the law of Moses could not be implemented apart from human reason. Law provides principles, but principles must be applied, and reason is needed to bridge the gap. In short, law requires judgment, and judgment implies reason.

While it doesn't ignore law, the Aristotelian tradition emphasizes virtue. Virtues are excellences of character that are proper to human beings. In the same way that any person familiar with trees can identify a healthy tree from an unhealthy one, so too it is possible to distinguish an excellent human from one who is something less. An excellent person possesses a variety of virtues, including courage, justice, self-control, moderation, friendliness, and generosity. These virtues are unique to humans because they are derived from the natural ends suited specifically to human beings.

For both the Hebrew and the Greek traditions, human nature is tied to notions such as reason, free will, law, and morality. In the scholastic tradition of the medieval world, these categories continued to be central—albeit with considerable discussion and some disagreements—to the definition of human nature. Most Western thinkers, at least into the fourteenth century, were united in the belief that humans shared a nature that was given to them by God. Or to put the matter in another way, human creatures were created by God with certain attributes that made uniquely human action possible, and they were restrained by moral standards that could be grasped through reason.

This unwritten moral law is clearly seen in Greek drama. In his *Antigone*, the Greek playwright Sophocles, for example, has his heroine appeal to the "law of the gods" in defending her actions that violated a direct edict of the king. There are, she insisted, laws that are prior to those made by kings, and we are obligated to them before any other law. Plato appealed to what he called The Good, a moral reality that humans can know and ought to follow. Aristotle also acknowledged that there are certain actions—adultery, for instance—that are simply wrong. Cicero speaks of the laws of nature, which ultimately derive from God.

This collection of ideas was organized in various ways in the Christian centuries, primarily in the form of natural law theory. Perhaps best articulated by the churchman Thomas Aquinas, natural law consists of moral principles that can be known through reason. According to Thomas, natural law is the participation by the rational creature in eternal law. Eternal law is the governing will of God over all creation. Humans, being finite creatures, cannot directly and fully comprehend the eternal law. Instead, they can participate in it through reason. Thomas is quick to admit that reason is limited and therefore humans cannot, by reason alone, grasp the full purpose of human existence. Holy Scripture—what Thomas calls divine law—is necessary for grasping the truth that the proper end of human existence is unity with God. In short, while natural law provides a useful, even indispensable guide, it is not sufficient for a fully successful life.

While they did not deny natural law, the leading lights of the Reformation downplayed its importance and emphasized instead the revealed word of God, which conveys moral truths rooted ultimately in God's nature and will. Such figures as Luther and Calvin emphasized the effects of the Fall and argued that human reason was not immune from the damage. While both at times speak favorably of natural law (Calvin more than Luther), they prefer to appeal to the guidance offered by Holy Scripture and its direct interaction with conscience.

Since the Reformation, a variety of moral theorists have, in different ways, attempted to shed the strictures of both divine commands and natural imperatives. Immanuel Kant, for instance, attempted to derive moral imperatives directly from reason itself with no appeal to eternal law, without which Thomas's system would fall apart. Kant, appealing directly to the logical structure of moral commands, sought also to rid moral theory from its long entanglement with nature. In contrast, John Stuart Mill's utilitarianism attempted to speak of morality in terms of the amount of pleasure (or pain) a certain action is likely to produce. In both thinkers, we see an attempt to throw out the twin babies of God and nature while preserving the bathwater of moral truth.

In more recent times, other thinkers have pushed the ideas of Kant and Mill in a variety of directions, but apart from a few throwbacks who still cling to natural law theory and others who have attempted to revive Aristotle's ethics of virtue, the descendants of Kant and Mill hold the field along with those who have attempted to go a step further and dispense altogether with the idea of moral norms that guide or limit human will.

In the American context, the language of moral order is couched primarily in the vocabulary of rights. The Declaration of Independence refers to the equality of all humans by virtue of certain rights endowed by a creator and possessed by all. The notion of natural rights grew out of the natural law tradition. Rights can be thought of as moral cushions that surround the individual. Each person has certain God-given rights, which is one way of saying that each person possesses inherent dignity that ought to be respected. Rights are often thought of as liberties, so that when I claim to have a right to do something, I am claiming that I am at liberty to do it. But rights also imply duties. If all humans are equal and possess certain rights, then each person is morally obligated to respect the rights of others. It is inconsistent to insist that my natural rights be respected while I am simultaneously infringing on the rights of others.*

Although the language of natural rights emerged from the natural law tradition, the modern world witnessed a separation of the two so that the idea of rights was divorced from the idea of natural law and the theism on which natural law depended. Once this separation occurred, there was little to prevent rights from expanding so that today the language of individual rights dominates our political discourse, while notions like God-given dignity, duty, and responsibility have receded to the background. When rights become detached from natural law, they open the door to individuals and groups claiming various freedoms without any attempt to justify those freedoms in terms of natural law or universal moral truth. Freedom itself becomes the one imperial value against which all others are measured. Thus, if a particular law inhibits my freedom (limited only by the freedom of others), then it is an unjust law.

When rights devolve merely into claims to freedom, without reference to any notion of duty or responsibility or the common good, something has gone awry. Ultimately, the isolation of rights from a broader context of human nature and moral truth represents a bold attempt to assert the autonomy of the human will over all else. It is an attempt to deny the limits within which human creatures were intended to live. This expansive and untethered conception of rights lies at the heart of modern liberalism.

---

* It is important to distinguish between natural rights and conventional or civil rights. For example, all people have a natural right to life, but the right to vote in a U.S. presidential election is one granted only to people who meet certain qualifications set out by law: U.S. citizen, eighteen years old, etc. The former right is universal; the latter is limited to a particular group of people.

CREATURES AND LIMITS

Because we are embodied, human beings inhabit a particular space. Our interests, concerns, and awareness extend outward from the particular space we occupy. We cannot in the truest sense be cosmopolitans, for we cannot extend our physical selves, or even our mental or emotional selves, to inhabit, understand, or empathize with the entire world. If all politics is local, this is because all humans are local. That is to say, we are confined in space and limited—more than we sometimes like to admit—by that confinement.

We also find ourselves confined by time. Death and taxes are said to be sure things, but while the tax man may occasionally be outsmarted, death always wins. We all live under the dark cloud of mortality. However, even under this species-wide death sentence, we can act, and we do so only within time. Time is that mysterious and fleeting locus of human action. Ironically it may be our very mortality that imbues our actions with meaning. The gods of the Homeric world, for instance, lived lives of empty frivolity. They may have been immortals, but they possessed all the vices found in human beings. The serious characters in Greek myth, the characters whose lives are suffused with meaning, are not the gods but the humans. They suffer. They make sacrifices for comrades. They grow old. They die. The tragic element attending our mortality makes our time on earth pregnant with meaning. We can use our time to help others, to enjoy a sunset, to worship the divine—or we can destroy life, ignore the beauty that appears as an unexpected gift, denounce God as a tyrant, or ignore him as a fable. Our choices matter because they are finite in number, and the time within which we can choose is ever shrinking as we slowly but inexorably fade to dust. Time limits us. But without it, human action is unintelligible.

We are limited in other ways, of course. The Judeo-Christian tradition speaks of a fall from grace. Theologians have used up plenty of ink (not to mention midnight oil) attempting to grasp exactly what was lost at this inauspicious event, but most seem to agree that the story of the Fall represents a way of coming to grips with the fact that humans are imperfect. We are not self-sufficient, we are not omniscient, and our thoughts as well as our actions are subject to error. Part of what motivates human striving is an attempt to recover, if but in a dim way, that goodness, stability, and health that exists only in our collective memory.

In classical Greece, the idea of a fall from original grace does not play a central role (although the story of Pandora and her box echoes in interesting ways the story of Genesis 3). Plato, for example, thought human error, both moral and intellectual, was a problem that could be solved through education. Unlike later Christian theologians, Plato denies that a person could know the right course of action and then do otherwise. The solution to immoral action, therefore, is proper education. Plato realized, however, that only a few are capable of achieving the highest form of education, one suited to the philosopher. The result, in practical terms, is much the same as in the Jewish, Christian, and Muslim traditions: humans (or the vast majority of humans) are doomed to error. They will suffer from poor judgment, and they will often commit vicious deeds. For the Jew, the remedy is adherence to the Torah; for the Christian, it is the gospel of Christ; for the Muslim, it is a life of faithfulness and submission. But setting religious solutions aside, in the mundane world of human affairs, human imperfectability requires a political structure capable of enforcing laws for those who refuse to obey freely. Of course, there is an immediate related problem: if humans are morally imperfect and inclined at times to do wrong, and if political structures are necessary to enforce the laws, why should we think that those running governments will be more inclined toward virtuous action than their subjects? Who will guard the guardians? This question lies near the heart of political philosophy.

To recognize our imperfectibility is crucial. To grasp our contingency is no less necessary. That we are contingent means that we are not self-sufficient. At its most rudimentary, we are not responsible for our own existence. We are, as Martin Heidegger put it, thrown into the world, and we must proceed from there. We do not plan our own entrance, and we don't, short of suicide, plan our own exit. We are also contingent insofar as we depend on others. From the moment of our birth, we depend on our parents to feed and clothe us; without the care of others, we would soon perish. After childhood, we still need others for companionship, economic relationships, and a multitude of other cooperative endeavors. Humans are also reproductively contingent (at least until we realize the dream of severing sex completely from reproduction). Only God is noncontingent.

A world of contingency and finitude is also a world of mystery. The kind of mystery of which I speak is something more fundamental than merely a bit of knowledge that has yet to be discovered. We need, then, to distinguish between a mystery and a puzzle. Humans are naturally drawn to puzzles. We instinctively want to put the pieces in the right order. The disorder bothers us, and we derive a sense of satisfaction when the pieces fall into place. This urge to solve puzzles has provided the motivation for great discoveries and advances in science and the exploration of our world.

A mystery is something different. A mystery is a limit beyond which a contingent being cannot go (at least without divine assistance). To believe in mystery is to hold that there are verities that we cannot fully grasp even though we believe they exist. The being of God is an obvious example. If God exists, and if He is something like the being described in Holy Writ, then although we can catch glimpses of Him, we can never wholly grasp His being or nature. Finite creatures can no more grasp an infinite creature than they can ingest the universe, for to do so they would have to swallow themselves. This is not merely a problem of scale. It is more fundamentally a problem of being. To be content with the mystery inherent in human existence is to be content with our creatureliness. It is to recognize the limitations of creatures and the prerogatives of the creator.

Yet we chafe against limits. This has always been a human trait, but it has become especially acute in the modern world. We can bring this characteristic to light by considering some formative moments in the emergence of the modern world and how those moments illustrate our urge to break free from that which limits us.

THE BIRTH OF THE MODERN

According to Hannah Arendt, the modern world was formed by a dynamic collection of factors, including the rise of the new science, the fragmentation of the church during the Reformation, and the sense of endless possibilities opened up by the age of exploration.[2] These three factors provide a useful starting point for our discussion.

The New Science

The new science emphasized empirical investigation. In so doing, it attempted to extricate itself from the confines of Aristotelian categories filtered through the work of medieval scholastics. The possibilities for new discoveries seemed endless. New tools, including the scientific method, were created to aid humans in their renewed quest for knowledge. The invention of the telescope allowed the scientist to gaze into the heavens and witness the movement of the planets. Earth, far from being at the center of a series of concentric spheres, was seen to be merely one planet among others. The telescope made it conceptually possible to imagine observing Earth from a distant point. It unloosed the imagination from terrestrial confines and made the possibility of exploring the heavens conceivable. At the same time, this new perspective produced doubts about the significance of human existence in a universe of unimaginable magnitude, millions of flaming suns, and empty space.

The age of science unleashed a flood of energy and excitement. Scientific advances were made not only in the interest of primary knowledge but in the service of commerce and industry as well. The age of science became the age of technology. The steam engine, the internal combustion engine, the telegraph, and the computer advanced in stunning ways the potential for humans to control the world and improve standards of living. Those old limitations of space and time were constantly pushed back as faster communication and travel made the world smaller. The rush to seize nature and wring her secrets from her eventually led to, among other things, the development of the atomic bomb. The irony is significant: We plumbed the atom and found a way to destroy the world.

Scientists have now successfully mapped the human genome, and this has led to the hope of truly astonishing advances in medical science. The possibilities, we are told, are breathtaking. Hitherto incurable diseases will be eradicated. Genetic abnormalities will be corrected. All well and good. But as with splitting the atom, we may find at the heart of the human genome an irony rather than an answer: we may find that in manipulating the very stuff of humanity, we compromise what it means to be human.

The Reformation

The fragmentation of the church during the Reformation opened the door for new ecclesiastical forms that emphasized the individual's relationship with God. The Reformers were concerned that centuries of accretions had compromised the authenticity of the Roman church and that a restoration was desperately needed. Luther's initial desire was to reform the church from within, but when church leaders proved less than enthusiastic, he was excommunicated and the Protestant Reformation began. Luther emphasized the centrality of Holy Scripture and the responsibility of each man before God. Religion, of course, was not wholly separated from politics. Kingdoms were ruptured and wars were fought as the unifying force of Rome was broken. New kingdoms and new loyalties were born as the idea of the individual and his or her unmediated relationship with God came into full view.

When the spirit of Protestantism encountered the growing secular impulse, the fully autonomous individual began to take shape. What might be termed "secular Protestantism" produced individuals bound by neither social or natural constraints nor even by the divine. This new emphasis on the individual, among other things, helped to give birth to the idea of individual rights, which has served as the center-piece for much of modern political thought. It is no accident that thinkers such as Thomas Hobbes and John Locke—in whose work we see the development of the ideas of natural rights, the state of nature, and the social contract—were Protestants.

The New World

The so-called New World, opened up by European explorers searching for a shorter trade route to India, provided the blank canvas upon which intrepid individuals could imagine finding wealth, power, and adventure. In a society just waking to the idea of progress, the New World provided the ideal venue for expansion and development. Europeans saw America as a quintessential example of the state of nature waiting to be tamed, settled, and developed—waiting for the hand of progress to begin its work. The expanse of this new landmass was beyond what most Europeans could conceive. The vast stretches of land, the visible resources of timber and cropland, and the potential (mostly fabled) promise of gold and silver created a sense of limitless possibilities and endless progress. Given this aura of limitlessness, Europeans who settled in America, as well as those who stayed behind, came to see the New World as a place to get rich and as a place where conventional limits on using and acquiring were suspended. Exploitation often accompanied exploration and continued long after the land was settled. The idea of infinite progress in a land beyond measure led to practices that were not sustainable. Although it took generations for the realization to sink in, the alleged infinitude of resources was an illusion. And even though today we know that our resources are limited, the habits and practices born of this early burst of optimism have profoundly shaped the way we think and behave.

To the European mind, the New World was a place where limits were suspended, or at least so far expanded that it amounted to the same thing. The idea of progress was nurtured and grew in this context. Discovery and invention went hand in hand. The scientist and the explorer were cut of the same cloth. They sought to uncover that which had been hidden by the mists of superstition, ignorance, and fear. They boldly sailed uncharted waters with the confidence that nature would yield her secrets to those who brooked no coy refusals. And yield she did. With almost breathtaking swiftness, when one considers the rate of previous disclosures, the natural world was disrobed and her secrets penetrated. One advance served only to encourage further investigation, the success of which brought even more confidence and energy. The age of progress gave rise to the notion that old limits could confidently be jettisoned in a new and thrilling push to know, to understand, to control.

The progress of this new era was in part made possible by the abandonment of old ways of thinking. To the extent that this progress resulted from discarding old associations linking official teachings of the church with Aristotelian cosmology, doubt about the verities of religion began to be voiced. This was not a universal reaction, but for many thinkers, as human understanding of the workings of nature increased, the mysterious workings of God seemed to decrease. The physical universe could, it was thought, be understood in terms of a smoothly working machine. The parts were in place, the energy was present, and although God had perhaps wound up the works in the beginning, after that single divine intervention the machine hummed along without assistance.

It is no surprise that the idea of progress in the physical world should also bleed into the moral world. Indeed, if humans could improve their lot through science and technology, wasn't this evidence that humans themselves were getting better? There was little reason to imagine that the improvements were limited to the physical sphere. Human nature, so long thought to be a static reality, now came under the probing hand of the spirit of progress.

In theological terms, this meant that the doctrine of the Fall had to be discarded. After all, the story of the Fall amounts to a description of the permanent human condition. To overcome the effects of the Fall, one must be saved. And although salvation has different meanings in various religious traditions, at the most generic level it means wholeheartedly submitting to the divine. But if the putative effects of the Fall can be overcome through human effort and intellect, then divine means of salvation are not necessary. The salvation that was once thought to lie in divine grace now presented itself—when the accretions of ignorance and superstition were scraped away—as the work of human hands. The old Platonic idea that understood error as merely a product of poor education returned to the fore. Only this time, it was infused with the idea of equality.

While Plato thought that only a few were capable of achieving intellectual and therefore moral perfection, modernity's new democratic impulse opened the door to everyone. Education could, if properly conceived and applied, lead all people toward moral perfection. A perfect world, inhabited by perfect citizens, seemed possible. Of course, no one imagined or suggested that this new world would come about soon or automatically. It would require hard work and time, but with the early scientific and technological successes providing reason for enthusiasm, the project was under way.

This perfect world was one in which the uncertainties that plagued premodern people would be eradicated, even as the certainties those same premoderns held were tossed aside. The verities that in an earlier time limited imagination, and therefore action, were broken down. A new world was emerging, and limits were no longer seen as protective boundaries but rather as offensive impositions to be broken and transcended or—in the pre- and (ironically) postmodern idiom—transgressed. What was once seen as a sin against God or an offense against nature was now seen as the rightful prerogative of the human species. And while the prerogative belonged to the species as a whole, the engines of desire and action were individuals who had been unshackled from the constraints of religious communities through the fragmentation of the church and freed from obligations to society by the dissolution of the medieval social structure. Now all individuals were equal before God and man—and God's existence was questionable.

What this amounted to was the birth of the autonomous individual. No longer, at least in the Protestant world, was a priest necessary to serve as an intermediary between God and the individual. And while the Reformation did not extend throughout Europe, the spirit of the Reformation was pervasive, so that even the church in Rome, that bastion of medieval intellectual and spiritual prejudices, found itself slowly succumbing to the powerful forces in play. In the social realm, no longer was a serf attached to a particular piece of land and obligated to a particular nobleman or lord. Each man was the master of his own fate. Social mobility became a possibility. And while wealth often did remain in certain families, formal restraints to upward mobility were dissolving. These forces were nowhere more powerful than in America, where Protestantism was the dominant religion and feudalism never existed.

The emergence of the autonomous individual had important implications for the related ideas of authority and community. The autonomous individual regards authority as offensive. If all men and women are equal, then no one should be able to dictate my actions. Seen in this light, all authority is illegitimate—unless, of course, I choose it myself. With this emerges the doctrine of the consent of the governed. Authority is the product of my will. It is not natural and is surely not a divine prerogative. It is, rather, rooted in my willingness to forfeit a piece of my autonomy in exchange for certain perceived benefits.

Because communities represent a kind of authority, the autonomous individual is suspicious of communities as well. Many natural communities—the family, the church, the town—were more or less difficult to exit in the premodern world, where social mobility was even more elusive than physical mobility. But as both types of mobility became increasingly possible, the binding force of community correspondingly diminished. Communities of choice came to be seen as more respectful of an individual's autonomy. Easy exit was seen as an asset to the individual rather than as a liability to the community. As with authority in general, the binding force of the community was seen to be rooted in individual will: I belong to this community because I have chosen it, and I can leave any time I please. While this shift was a boon for the autonomous individual, it served to weaken the structures of many communities, as membership came to be rooted in desire and will rather than tradition, longstanding practice, geography, and nature.

As we will see, the dissolution of the idea of natural authority and the communities embodying that authority has not, as might have been expected, led to the dissolution of authority per se, nor the diminution of power. The irony is great, for as authority has been seized by the autonomous individual, the most powerful form of government the world has ever seen—the centralized nation-state—has emerged. Furthermore, the death of God has not led to the death of authority. The modern bureaucratic state, in collusion with giant, seemingly impersonal economic forces, represents a stunning consolidation of power. The modern autonomous individual, therefore, finds himself confronted with secular powers that in an earlier age were not even imagined. It is no coincidence that totalitarianism (as opposed to garden-variety tyranny) emerged only in the modern world.

A collection of attitudes coalesce in this war against limits that characterizes our age. First, there is an enthusiasm for the possibilities latent in the natural world, which can be unlocked by the scientific method. With this comes the urge to dominate the natural world, both for the sake of knowledge and to benefit humanity. Second, there is the emergence of secularism, whereby an understanding of dependence and contingency is replaced by notions of independence and self-assertion. Third, there is the rise of the autonomous individual who insists that all attachments be rooted in an act of individual will.

But now many have begun to suspect, at least in moments of honesty or fear, that the dream of human perfection and mastery of nature is impossible. Perhaps a perfectly happy world of autonomous individuals is not achievable. To be sure, the twentieth century was not kind to those dreaming of a perfect and peaceful future. The earlier optimism of the modern age has, for many, turned into despair, and modern politics oscillates between these two extremes.

The virtue that allows us to avoid the extremes of both optimism and despair is humility. Humility impels us to recognize our dependence and is the opposite of pride, or what the Greeks called hubris, the fatal weakness that in Greek drama destroys the protagonist and his plans. All ages have their characteristic vices, and a particular kind of social hubris is our era's tragic flaw. Hubris, as we shall see, is fundamentally incompatible with a politics of gratitude.

2

Gratitude:
A Creature's Love

I hate ingratitude more in a man than lying, vainness, babbling, drunkenness, or any taint of vice whose strong corruption inhabits our frail blood.

Shakespeare, *Twelfth Night*

When we start to grasp what it means to be a creature and what might be lost if we neglect to root our self-understanding in this truth, we begin to see the ways we have steered off course. If we are in fact creatures who are contingent and dependent, then at least one disposition we ought to possess is gratitude. If we are creatures who owe debts to others, both living and dead, we must consider the nature of those obligations both individually and corporately. We must consider what a disposition of gratefulness would mean for building and sustaining a culture, organizing ourselves socially, and conducting our politics.

Yet we tend to be an ungrateful lot. As early as 1930, the Spanish philosopher José Ortega y Gasset observed that modern men and women are, among other things, characterized by "radical ingratitude."[1] Such a claim, though, will be met with obvious objections. There will be those who think primarily of etiquette: "I taught my children to say please and thank you, and they usually do." There will be those who think in personal terms: "I have a nice house, a new car, and a boat. Sure, I'm grateful." Or there will be those who think in terms of the nation: "We live in the greatest nation on earth! Damn right, I'm grateful." But although the language of gratitude is not dead—far from it—something is amiss. Our modern, affluent, technological, well-fed society oscillates between smug self-satisfaction and hand-wringing despair—the latter, admittedly, a minor note that is heard with each new economic, political, or natural disaster but then gradually fades. But gratitude means more than good manners; it means more than the pleasure associated with possessing plenty of nice things; and it surely means more than mere relief that we have managed to escape, or at least survive, the latest crisis. These may be manifestations of gratitude or shadowy reminders of the real thing, but they do not lie at the heart of gratitude.

As soon as we begin to plumb the meaning of gratitude, we are led to consider its object. I can and should be grateful to my parents for the care and nurture they provided for me (assuming they did). I can and should be grateful to the friend who was willing to help me during a difficult time. I can and should be grateful to be part of a community of people who care about each other and seek the best for each other. I can even be grateful to a God who may have more to do with my existence and subsistence than is readily apparent.

What passes for gratitude today is often a vague sense of well-being. It is a sense of goodwill with no clear object. But can we say "thank you" when there is no one, living or dead, to whom the words are directed? Without an object, gratitude seems prone to slide into self-satisfaction. Like little Jack Horner, we pull out the proverbial plum and congratulate ourselves for our cleverness, intelligence, work ethic, or even our good luck. This is a perverted form of gratitude, and it is indicative of our condition that we cannot distinguish authentic gratitude from such a debased facsimile.

So what exactly is gratitude? According to Merriam-Webster, gratitude is "the state of being grateful." Grateful is defined as "appreciative of benefits received." Gratitude is derived from the Latin *gratia*, which has a variety of meanings, including grace, charm, loveliness, love, favor, thanks, and, of course, gratitude. In our contemporary English, most of the Latin meanings have disappeared. We are left with gratitude and a word that is quite similar in modern usage: thankfulness, which has its roots in the Old English *thanc*.

In the first instance, gratitude is a disposition toward the world that reminds us that we are not alone. We are not solitary creatures owing nothing to anyone. Rather, gratitude points to our dependence. It points to our contingency. When our thoughts are characterized by gratitude, they are outward looking. Gratitude breaks us out of the cocoon of self-satisfaction and self-concern that is a constant temptation and impels us to think about the ways our lives are related to others. Gratitude is quintessentially relational.

But gratitude is not simply a disposition we can choose to exhibit. We can choose to be friendly, for instance, regardless of how others treat us. We can choose to act justly even if we have been wronged. But gratitude is different. It is a disposition that is the result of goodness. It is a response to an act of beneficence. We are grateful when a stranger helps us find our way in a strange city. In such a case, a person who stood to gain nothing stopped to give us directions. She gave us something we needed. Why? Because of goodness. And we are right to be grateful. When a friend presents us with a gift, we feel grateful. Again, we are responding to an act of goodness. Gratitude, then, is not the same as friendliness or generosity, for those dispositions can exist regardless of how another person behaves toward us. Gratitude requires the action of another before it can come into being. Without an initial act of goodness from another, gratitude is only potential.

If we push this analysis a bit further, something interesting emerges. Gratitude is not tied directly to the success or failure of an attempted act of goodness. For example, we can be grateful to a person who in good faith gives us directions in a strange city, even though, because the helpful stranger does not know about a construction site downtown, the directions lead us astray. In the same way, if a friend gives us a necktie that we despise, a disposition of gratitude is still warranted. We capture this truth in the saying "it's the thought that counts." We are right to be grateful even if the outcome of the act itself is not desired. In short, gratitude exists in a relationship between two or more people and is a response to an act that is motivated by a desire to benefit the other.

A MORAL DUTY

Gratitude is a disposition of thankfulness that is an appropriate response to an act of goodness. But is there a moral duty to be grateful? Does ingratitude indicate a moral failure? The discussion of gratitude as a moral duty was common in the eighteenth century. David Hume, for one, argued that there are some moral duties "to which men are impelled by a natural instinct or immediate propensity." Hume ranked gratitude to benefactors, along with love of children and pity for the unfortunate, as moral duties to which humans are naturally impelled.[2]

It seems somewhat odd, though, to suggest that gratitude is a moral duty because it appears to be of a different category than, say, the moral duty to tell the truth. Truth telling is an action originating in the speaker. Like gratitude, it requires another person (unless we think of telling oneself the truth as a moral duty). But unlike truth telling, gratitude involves not an overt act but merely a subjective disposition. One can be grateful and do nothing (although gratitude can and often does imply some notion of reciprocity).

Immanuel Kant argued that there are several duties that we owe to other humans simply because they are human. These include beneficence, gratitude, and sympathy. These are similar to the duties Hume thought arose from natural instinct. According to Kant, gratitude is "the venerating of another on account of a benefit we have received from him." Gratitude is not merely a duty among others but a "sacred duty." To violate that duty would be "to extinguish the moral principles of benevolence, even at their source." Why does Kant place such an emphasis on gratitude? He argues that the person who is indebted remains always under obligation to the benefactor. This, Kant believed, is true even if the receiver of the benefit pays back the benefactor in kind. No matter what the receiver subsequently does, it always will be the case that the benefactor acted first when nothing but goodness impelled him. This original, uncoerced act forever obligates the receiver. To be ungrateful is to forget or ignore this initial act of goodness.[3]

It is little wonder that Nietzsche regarded gratitude as a terrible burden. As he put it, "The man who gives a great gift encounters no gratitude; for the recipient, simply by accepting it, already has too much of a burden."[4] If, as Nietzsche suggested, the will to power is the central motive force of human existence, then gratitude would indeed be a burden, for it highlights the relative powerlessness of the recipient even as it points out the relative power of the benefactor. In short, gratitude highlights our dependence, not our independence, and to the extent that all people have been on the receiving end of beneficence, all people have a duty to be grateful.

Perhaps this obvious acknowledgment of our weakness is also an indication of the possibility of goodness in human relationships, for gratitude, as we have seen, requires antecedent goodness. Thus, goodness and neediness go together. Our neediness, our various weaknesses and dependencies, are the necessary condition for acts of goodness. A god, on the other hand, has no need of beneficence and consequently has no duty to be grateful.

A MORAL VIRTUE

Is it also appropriate to think of gratitude as a virtue, an excellence of character? Cicero, for one, included gratitude among the virtues and its opposite, ingratitude, among the vices. Aristotle, in contrast, spoke of the virtue of generosity but not of the virtue of gratitude. The excellences of character that Aristotle wrote about are active and initiating and not passive and responsive like gratitude. Furthermore, for Aristotle, the most virtuous man is the most self-sufficient man. Gratitude, while proper in the wake of generosity, is a signal of need, of apparent weakness. As Aristotle put it, "Excellence consists in doing good rather than in having good done to one, and in performing noble actions rather than in not performing base ones."[5]

Aristotle applied the ideal of self-sufficiency both to the individual and to the state. In his mind, the *polis*, or city-state, was oriented toward self-sufficiency, and any other organization—say, the family or the village—was an inferior part of this complete whole. In the same way, a dependent person is not a fully excellent person. A person of excellence is, among other things, a person of means, for to practice the virtue of generosity requires money, and to give on a large scale (a virtue Aristotle distinguishes from generosity) requires significant sums. Not surprisingly, then, gratitude is not included among Aristotle's list of virtues. It is instead a sign of dependence.

By Cicero's day, the polis was no more. Rome was a republic that included much of the known world and with ambitions extending even farther. The notion of a self-sufficient city-state was no longer the ideal. All roads led to Rome, and Roman influence extended along those roads to encompass the formerly independent city-states that served as Aristotle's ideal. The idea of the self-sufficient man disappears in Cicero along with the idea of a self-sufficient city-state. There is a sense of interdependence in Cicero that is not readily evident in Aristotle. According to Cicero, the virtues (or a good share of the virtues) "proceed from a natural inclination to love and cherish our associates." Nature confirms the law that gives birth to and supports the virtues. Without the ratifying power of nature, "what becomes of generosity, patriotism, or friendship? Where should we find the desire of benefiting our neighbors, or the gratitude that acknowledges kindness?"[6] Gratitude, for Cicero, is a virtue rooted in nature itself. To act ungratefully to a benefactor is to act unnaturally. Gratitude, then, is not a sign of weakness but of moral character. It represents an understanding of natural relationships. It exhibits a sense of propriety.

Even in Aristotelian terms, gratitude might be seen as a second-tier virtue, for although it signals relative weakness, gratitude is properly given to a benefactor. If, as we have seen, gratitude can be understood as a moral duty, it is something that the receiver owes to the benefactor. Rendering to another what is owed him is a question of justice. For Aristotle, justice, in one of its forms, pertains to the just distribution of goods among people. If gratitude is, indeed, something that the receiver owes the benefactor, then in being grateful, the receiver is exhibiting the virtue of justice, and to act ungratefully is to be unjust. When seen in this light, while gratitude is not a virtue anyone would want to need to exhibit, when a person finds himself indebted to another, gratitude is precisely the disposition a virtuous person will possess.

Aristotle's view, of course, assumes that it is possible and desirable for an individual to be completely self-sufficient. In the previous chapter, we discussed some of the ways humans are naturally dependent on others. If these dependencies are, in fact, reflective of the human condition, then perhaps Aristotle is overstating his case. If we all necessarily owe debts of gratitude that we will never be able to pay, perhaps gratitude is not so much a sign of our weakness as of our common humanity.

GRATITUDE AND FREEDOM

Gratitude is an appropriate disposition, then, that some writers have referred to as a moral duty and others as a virtue. Whether we consider gratitude in either light, a necessary element for the exercise of gratitude is freedom. One cannot act dutifully or virtuously unless one is free to act otherwise. If this is the case, then gratitude cannot be forced. It cannot be demanded. It must be freely given.

In his gospel, St. Luke records a story that depicts gratitude, ingratitude, and the freedom that accompanies both:

> And it came to pass, as he went to Jerusalem, that he passed through the midst of Samaria and Galilee. And as he entered into a certain village, there met him ten men that were lepers, which stood far off: And they lifted up their voices, and said, Jesus, Master, have mercy on us. And when he saw them, he said unto them, Go shew yourselves unto the priests. And it came to pass, that, as they went, they were cleansed. And one of them, when he saw that he was healed, turned back, and with a loud voice glorified God, And fell down on his face at his feet, giving him thanks: and he was a Samaritan. And Jesus answering said, Were there not ten cleansed? But where are the nine? There are not found that returned to give glory to God, save this stranger. And he said unto him, Arise, go thy way: thy faith hath made thee whole.[7]

Lepers were social outcasts. They were not allowed to approach nonlepers for fear of contagion. That is why these ten stood off at a distance and called to Jesus. They had, apparently, heard stories of his healing powers and sought him out. They desperately wanted to be healed and to rejoin their families. Until they heard of this healer, their hopes of a normal life were gone. Contracting leprosy signaled the end of one's freedom to live a life among one's own. Instead, one lived among other lepers, a community of social outcasts awaiting death. It was a life without hope.

These ten lepers called out to Jesus, and he told them to go to the priest, who could declare them clean and therefore free to return to their homes. They had nothing to lose and everything to gain, so they went, and on the way they were healed. The question Jesus asks indicates the goodness of gratitude. It was right that the one returned to give thanks. The other nine were healed, but in their head-long rush to the priest and then to their homes, they forgot to express gratitude. We intuitively recognize that the one did what was right, and the nine, while perhaps feeling gratitude, could have done better by showing it. Here we can also see the centrality of freedom. Jesus did not demand that the other nine return to express gratitude. Gratitude, as we have seen, is a disposition that is the result of benefi-cence, but it cannot be coerced. The receiver must give it freely, just as beneficence is not real unless it too is a product of free choice. One man, exercising his freedom to express this gratitude, returned, and Jesus commends him and, by implication, judges the nine. Because gratitude is a moral act deeply rooted in the nature of human relationships, we can immediately see that the act of the one was morally superior to the inaction of the others.

GRATITUDE TO GOD

Not surprisingly, many believe that God is a being who deserves our gratitude. While reflecting on the physical goodness of the natural world, Cicero remarked, "In truth, we can hardly reckon him a man, whom neither the regular courses of the stars, nor the alterations of day and night, nor the temperature of the seasons, nor the productions that nature displays for his use, do not urge to gratitude towards heaven."[8] St. Paul instructed his fellow Christians to "in everything give thanks."[9] It is hard to imagine how we could give thanks in everything unless the object of that thanks is God. If God is the author of life, the source of all goodness, then surely continual thanks are in order simply because we possess life and enjoy breath.

The notion of gratitude to God is explicitly laid out in Psalm 100, a song of praise to God for his goodness:

1   Make a joyful noise unto the Lord, all ye lands.

2   Serve the Lord with gladness: come before his presence with singing.

3   Know ye that the Lord he is God: it is he that hath made us, and not we ourselves; we are his people, and the sheep of his pasture.

4   Enter into his gates with thanksgiving, and into his courts with praise: be thankful unto him, and bless his name.

5   For the Lord is good; his mercy is everlasting; and his truth endureth to all generations.[10]

The first verse is in the imperative mood. It is a command to all people to address the Lord. Verse two is an imperative as well. Serve him. And do it with gladness. Why? Verse three tells us: the Lord is God. He made us, and as a corollary, we did not make ourselves. We are the products of divine intelligence and power, and as a result we are His. How, then, should we respond? Verse four: be thankful. Praising God is a vocal expression of thanksgiving that is fitting for voiced creatures in the presence of the creator. But God is not simply our creator. He is not simply a powerful force that brought us into existence. According to verse five, we ought to thank God not only because he created us, but because he is good and merciful and true. He exemplifies creating power as well as moral goodness. As creatures, it is fitting that we express our gratitude to the creator. As moral creatures, it is fitting that we express our gratitude to God for the moral structure of the creation and the probity with which he governs.

The "Prayer of General Thanksgiving" in the Anglican Book of Common Prayer expresses well the kind of gratitude that is properly due to God:

Almighty God, Father of all mercies, we, thine unworthy servants, do give thee most humble and hearty thanks for all thy goodness and loving-kindness to us and to all men; We bless thee for our creation, preservation, and all the blessings of this life; but above all, for thine inestimable love in the redemption of the world by our Lord Jesus Christ; for the means of grace, and for the hope of glory. And, we beseech thee, give us that due sense of all thy mercies, that our hearts may he unfeignedly thankful; and that we show forth thy praise, not only with our lips, but in our lives, by giving up our selves to thy service, and by walking before thee in holiness and righteousness all our days; through Jesus Christ our Lord, to whom, with thee and the Holy Ghost, be all honour and glory, world without end. *Amen*.[11]

Gratitude is due not only for our creation but also for our preservation and all the blessings that come to us each day. Additionally, for the Christian, gratitude is due to God for the redemption in Christ, for it is an act of grace. Grace, of course, denotes unmerited favor, so grace is a kind of gift that is undeserved. (Grace is also one of the largely forgotten meanings of the Latin word *gratia*.) This divine gift properly elicits our gratitude. How is our gratitude displayed? In words and in deeds. We can speak our gratitude, as does the psalmist, and we can show our gratitude to God by living lives characterized by service to others.

GRATITUDE TO PARENTS

Another obvious object of gratitude is our parents. While God is the ultimate giver of life, in a more proximate sense, we owe our lives to our parents. Assuming our parents raised us, we owe them a debt of gratitude for providing us with food and shelter and educating us to know right from wrong. The Latin word *pietas*, from which we get our word "piety," has a variety of meanings including a sense of duty, devotion, kindness, tenderness, and loyalty to the gods, to one's parents, and to one's country. When a son acts dutifully toward his father, he is demonstrating pietas. Gratitude is tied up with this duty, for if the outward act is performed without the inward disposition of love and gratitude, it is not one of pietas. Pietas consists of proper action born of proper motivation. In the classical world, as in some contexts today, pietas for one's father was tied inextricably to pietas toward the gods, for knowledge and devotion to the gods is acquired directly from one's father. We honor the gods because we honor our father and he honors the gods. Thus, we can see a generational transmission of pietas that extends from son to father and ultimately to God.

This multigenerational duty that includes both one's father and his gods is no better illustrated than in the character of Aeneas, the legendary founder of Rome and the subject of Virgil's epic *The Aeneid*. Aeneas was, of course, a Trojan warrior who fought to defend his city against the invading Greek army. After ten long years of war, the Trojans fell for a ruse in the form of a horse, and Troy was sacked by the Greek army. Through the anguished eyes of Aeneas, we witness the carnage. As the city goes up in flames, Aeneas first attempts to marshal the Trojan soldiers; however, he soon realizes there is no hope of victory. His mother, the goddess Venus, appears to him and encourages him to leave the fight and return to his wife, son, and father. Aeneas narrates the story:

> Now I descended where the goddess guided,
> Clear of the flames, and clear of enemies,
> For both retired; so gained my father's door,
> My ancient home. I looked for him at once,
> My first wish being to help him to the mountains;
> But with Troy gone he set his face against it,
> Not to prolong his life, or suffer exile.[12]

Aeneas refuses to even consider leaving his father in the doomed city. He declares that if his father stays to be slaughtered by the Greeks, he will remain as well. Aeneas prepares to return to the hopeless fray and at least die a warrior's death if escape is not an option. His wife begs him not to go. She holds up their young son, Iulus, to remind him of what will soon be lost. In the midst of this confusion, the gods send a sign. A tongue of flame appears on the young boy's head. This moves the old man. He knows this is a portent. He lifts his eyes to heaven and asks Jupiter for another sign to confirm that this flame really is divine. Immediately, with a crack of thunder, a star falls from the sky and disappears into the darkness of the mountain beyond the city. This is enough. He is now ready to go. The gods, despite the destruction of Troy, appear to have a plan for Aeneas and his little band. But the old man is feeble. He cannot walk quickly, let alone run. Aeneas realizes what must be done:

> "Then come, dear father. Arms around my neck:
> I'll take you on my shoulders, no great weight.
> Whatever happens, both will face one danger,
> Find one safety. . . .
> Father, carry our hearthgods, our Penatës.
> It would be wrong for me to handle them—
> Just come from such hard fighting, bloody work—
> Until I wash myself in running water."

> When I had said this, over my breadth of shoulder
> And bent neck, I spread out a lion skin
> For tawny cloak and stooped to take his weight.
> Then little Iulus put his hand in mine
> And came with shorter steps beside his father.[13]

Here we see a profound example of pietas. Aeneas flees the burning city with his father on his back and his young son at his side. He willingly shoulders the burden of his father, for that is what duty demands. His pietas does not allow him to touch the household gods, so the old man carries them. Thus, Aeneas bears the burden of his father and their gods. He is literally, and figuratively, bearing the weight of the past as a good son must. His gratitude, as displayed in his pietas, makes any other option unthinkable. He will not leave his father or the gods of his father. But Aeneas is a father himself. He has duties not only to the past and to heaven but to the future as well. Thus, he takes little Iulus by the hand, and together they leave the city. Aeneas, the man of pietas, does his duty, and in the process, teaches Iulus, through the example of his actions, how to be a man.

GRATITUDE TO ANCESTORS

Gratitude to one's father opens the door of the imagination to see that our existence is not merely the result of one father. We are a part of a long line of fathers and mothers who have passed down to us not only the physical traits we exhibit but practices and stories, ways of living and of dying. In short, they have given us the culture we inhabit, which is to say, they have given us a world that is specifically human. As soon as we see this, we can realize that our debt is truly beyond comprehension, let alone beyond repaying. Our gratitude will be born of love for those who have gone before us. But we do not love without discernment or criticism. We can love them for the example they have set (both good and bad); we can love them as fellow travelers on this road of beauty and pain; and we can love them even as we love ourselves.

Kant writes, "As to the extent of gratitude, it is not by any means confined to contemporaries, but goes back to our ancestors, even to those whom we cannot certainly name. And this is the reason why it is considered indecorous not to defend the ancients as much as possible against all attacks, invective, and slights—the ancients being considered here as our teachers."[14] As Aeneas bore the burden of his father and his father's gods, so too we bear the burden of those who have gone before. We carry a debt of gratitude that can never be repaid, and we do so as an act of virtue and as a moral duty. We seek to preserve that which has been entrusted to us, carrying it for a time, and if we have raised our Iulus well, he may assume that burden of gratitude when our time is past. In this way, our responsible actions are born of gratitude, and with luck or grace, one day many years hence our children and theirs in turn may express their gratitude to us by shouldering the burden of their inheritance and carrying it for the time allotted to them. In this way, and no other, culture is transmitted.

At the end of the long winter at Valley Forge, George Washington praised the steadfastness of the American soldiers in the face of difficult circumstances. These soldiers, he wrote, "will despise the meanness of repining at such trifling strokes of Adversity, trifling indeed when compared to the transcendent Prize which will undoubtedly crown their Patience and Perseverance, Glory and Freedom, Peace and Plenty to themselves and the Community; The Admiration of the World, the Love of Country and the Gratitude of Prosperity!"[15] Yes, the world would admire them and their country would love them, but generations yet unborn would rise and call them blessed. Their sacrifice was for only a few months, but the debt of gratitude would extend down through the generations as free men and women reaped the bounty of the sacrifices made in that frozen place. Washington thought in those terms. His rhetoric suggests he believed his men thought the same. That one of the most significant things we are passing on to our children is a national debt of breathtaking size suggests, perhaps, that we have lost the perspective shared by the general and his men.

GRATITUDE TO THE STATE

According to Edmund Burke, the state is a gift given to us for our benefit. It is the product of generations of accretions and modifications. It is not perfect and thus change is surely possible and often necessary. When we seek to alter that which we have inherited, however, we must do so with circumspection lest we find that in our enthusiasm to modify we mar, and in our rush to perfect we destroy. Accordingly, "no man should approach to look into its [the state's] defects or corruptions but with due caution; that he should never dream of beginning its reformation by its subversion; that he should approach to the faults of the state as to the wounds of a father, with pious awe and trembling solicitude."[16]

Burke, writing about the abuses he witnessed in Jacobin France, was concerned that the spirit of revolution in the name of abstract ideals—which is to say, in the name of the perfectibility of man and the state—would lead not to an earthy paradise but to a literal hell. Thus, he urged caution, and he couched his advice in terms of filial piety. Just as one must treat one's father gently—all the more so if he is wounded and wanting care—so too must one approach the modification of the state with due caution. "By this wise prejudice we are taught to look with horror on those children of their country who are prompt rashly to hack that aged parent in pieces, and put him into the kettle of the magicians, in hopes that by their poisonous weeds, and wild incantations, they may regenerate the paternal constitution, and renovate their father's life."[17]

GRATITUDE TO THE NATURAL WORLD

There are others who suggest that the natural world is a proper object of our gratitude. To be sure, without soil, we would die. Without clean air and clean water, our health is impossible to maintain. The simple beauty of a sunrise or a bird's song testifies to those "unbought graces" of which Burke writes. The poetry of Wendell Berry is replete with expressions of gratitude. He is a farmer who lives close to the land and also a poet who can express well the manifold dimensions of gratitude that naturally emerge from a soul rightly attuned to the creation. Here is an example:

> When despair for the world grows in me
> And I wake in the night at the least sound
> in fear of what my life and my children's lives may be,
> I go and lie down where the wood drake
> rests in his beauty on the water, and the great heron feeds.
> I come into the peace of wild things
> who do not tax their lives with forethought
> of grief. I come into the presence of still water.
> And I feel above me the day-blind stars
> waiting with their light. For a time
> I rest in the grace of the world, and am free.[18]

Unlike some nature writers whose gratitude begins and ends with nature, and thus devolves into a cult of nature, Berry realizes that gratitude to nature is ultimately directed to God. We can express gratitude to God by noticing the creation and living in harmony with it. Living in harmony with nature implies a life characterized by responsible action. In the same way that the past is a burden handed down to us by our fathers, so too care for the natural world is something that requires thoughtful attention and careful and sustained effort. If we care well for the natural world, our descendents, if they are wise, will be grateful to us, but woe to our memories if we abuse that which has been entrusted to us.

INGRATITUDE

If we see gratitude as a moral duty, then ingratitude is a failure to live as duty requires. If, however, we see gratitude as a moral virtue, ingratitude reveals a flawed character. In either instance, ingratitude is a moral failure that we easily recognize and condemn. But although ingratitude is universally condemned, it is not the kind of moral failure that we usually punish. In fact, to punish a person for ingratitude would seem, in most cases, to be an overextension of law. While legal punishment for ingratitude may not be possible or wise, social punishment is certainly possible in the form of scorn or censure. So too is the kind of punishment meted out by the ruler depicted in the parable of the ungrateful servant:

> Therefore is the kingdom of heaven likened unto a certain king, which would take account of his servants. And when he had begun to reckon, one was brought unto him, which owed him ten thousand talents. But forasmuch as he had not to pay, his lord commanded him to be sold, and his wife, and children, and all that he had, and payment to be made. The servant therefore fell down, and worshipped him, saying, Lord, have patience with me, and I will pay thee all. Then the lord of that servant was moved with compassion, and loosed him, and forgave him the debt. But the same servant went out, and found one of his fellowservants, which owed him an hundred pence: and he laid hands on him, and took him by the throat, saying, Pay me that thou owest. And his fellowservant fell down at his feet, and besought him, saying, Have patience with me, and I will pay thee all. And he would not: but went and cast him into prison, till he should pay the debt. So when his fellowservants saw what was done, they were very sorry, and came and told unto their lord all that was done. Then his lord, after that he had called him, said unto him, O thou wicked servant, I forgave thee all that debt, because thou desiredst me: Shouldest not thou also have had compassion on thy fellowservant, even as I had pity on thee? And his lord was wroth, and delivered him to the tormentors, till he should pay all that was due unto him.[19]

To be sure, we live in a different world today; nevertheless, readers naturally condemn this ungrateful servant and believe he is getting his just deserts in the end. Furthermore, if this is a story about gratitude, then it appears that in certain cases the actions born of gratitude can be properly expressed not to the benefactor himself, who has no need of reciprocity, but to another whose needs are analogous to those alleviated by the benefactor. In this sense, gratitude is truly a social virtue and ingratitude is a social vice.

Writers throughout history have condemned ingratitude in the strongest terms. George Washington, for instance, was unambiguous: "Nothing is a greater stranger to my breast, or a sin that my soul more abhors, than that black and detestable one, ingratitude."[20] Thomas Aquinas argued that ingratitude is a sin because its opposite, gratitude, is a "moral debt required by virtue," and if that moral debt is not paid, the negligence is sin.[21] Kant, for his part, argued that "ingratitude towards one's benefactor is, according to the judgment of mankind, one of the most odious and hateful vices."[22] Finally, the ninth circle of hell, in Dante's *Inferno*, is reserved for the ungrateful: for those who betray kin, hosts, and benefactors. At the center of hell, in the very maw of Satan himself, is Judas Iscariot, the betrayer of Christ.[23]

INGRATITUDE TO GOD

Of course, as there are a variety of persons to whom gratitude is properly due, so too there are a variety of ways that the vice of ingratitude is manifested. Ingratitude to God is one. In *Paradise Lost*, John Milton vividly depicts the fall of Satan from his heavenly position of honor. Satan admits that he rebelled against God because of his pride and his ambitious desire to rule. As a result, he was expelled from heaven and cast down to a fiery lake, where he long lay, dazed upon its surface. When his senses returned, he made his way to the world that God had only recently formed. There he hatched a plan to wreak havoc in that world to spite the heavenly creator and ruler. His motive was hatred born of pride, and thus he even hated the new sun whose rays reminded him of the glory of heaven and the happiness he once enjoyed. In this moment of reflection, tinged by regret, Satan admitted that serving God was not at all onerous and that his rebellion was not justified on that score. But presaging Nietzsche's comment about gratitude two centuries later, this fallen angel acknowledged the burden:

> Ah wherefore! he deserved no such return
> From me, whom he created what I was
> In that bright eminence, and with his good
> Upbraided none; nor was his service hard.

> What could be less than to afford him praise,
> The easiest recompense, and pay him thanks,
> How due! yet all his good proved ill in me,
> And wrought but malice; lifted up so high
> I 'sdained subjection, and thought one step higher
> Would set me highest, and in a moment quit
> The debt immense of endless gratitude,
> So burthensome, still paying, still to owe;
> Forgetful what from him I still received,
> And understood not that a grateful mind
> By owing owes not, but still pays, at once
> Indebted and discharged; what burden then?[24]

Satan, according to Milton, is guilty of the sin of ingratitude. Because the debt he owed to God was greater than he was willing to bear, he sought to overthrow God and thereby expunge the debt. But even this cosmic rebel acknowledges that a grateful mind relieves the burden of gratitude though the debt remains. It seems that a grateful mind is something that Satan cannot, or better, will not, muster. In that light, he could not but rebel, for the revolt had already occurred when he chose to withhold his gratitude.

The Torah suggests that material prosperity can lead to the sin of ingratitude to God. In making his covenant with Israel, God repeatedly warns the people that if they come to enjoy the blessings of the promised land but forget to thank God for providing the bounty, they will be cursed:

> When thou hast eaten and art full, then thou shalt bless [thank] the LORD thy God for the good land which he hath given thee. Beware that thou forget not the LORD thy God, in not keeping his commandments, and his judgments, and his statutes, which I command thee this day: Lest when thou hast eaten and art full, and hast built goodly houses, and dwelt therein; And when thy herds and thy flocks multiply, and thy silver and thy gold is multiplied, and all that thou hast is multiplied; Then thine heart be lifted up, and thou forget the LORD thy God, which brought thee forth out of the land of Egypt, from the house of bondage; Who led thee through that great and terrible wilderness, wherein were fiery serpents, and scorpions,

and drought, where there was no water; who brought thee forth water out of the rock of flint; Who fed thee in the wilderness with manna, which thy fathers knew not, that he might humble thee, and that he might prove thee, to do thee good at thy latter end; And thou say in thine heart, My power and the might of mine hand hath gotten me this wealth.[25]

This, of course, is the perennial temptation of abundance. In ages of marginal or even scanty provisions, it is easier to think in terms of gratitude, for nothing is taken for granted. One might even find oneself praying earnestly for daily bread and then thanking God when it arrives. In an age of plenty, comforts are taken for granted, and how much more the daily bread upon which we subsist? Could it be that gratitude is more difficult precisely because we have so much for which to be thankful?

INGRATITUDE AND THE NATURAL WORLD

That in an age of plenty we can take our bounty for granted is an obvious hazard. But equally, in an age when we are increasingly insulated and isolated from the natural world, we can become blind to the gifts all around us. When we come to think of our milk, meat, and vegetables as mere products of the grocery store, we have lost sight of reality. We have lost sight of the simple fact that we are sustained physically by the earth, by animals, by plants, by the soil, all of which are nourished by the sun. This is no small oversight, for if we take the time to observe the natural world around us, we come to see one measure of our debt. Berry writes of the giftedness of the natural world when he notes,

Outdoors we are confronted everywhere with wonders; we see that the miraculous is not extraordinary but the common mode of existence. It is our daily bread. Whoever really has considered the lilies of the field or the birds of the air and pondered the improbability of their existence in this warm world within the cold and empty stellar distances will hardly balk at the turning of water into wine—which was, after all, a very small miracle. We forget the greater and still continuing miracle by which water (with soil and sunlight) is turned into grapes.[26]

Gratitude manifests itself in care and responsible action whereas ingratitude toward the natural world leads, perhaps invariably, to carelessness and exploitation. This is not a significant problem in a world of limitless resources, and this is precisely how many perceived the New World when it was first discovered. In reality, though, the natural world is finite. While no one denies this today, we tend often to be so far removed from a daily conscious interaction with the natural world that we are blind to careless acts born of inertia.

KING LEAR

Perhaps one of the most striking literary examples of the tumultuous effects of ingratitude is Shakespeare's *King Lear*. Lear is an aging king who decides to divide his kingdom between his three daughters and relinquish the throne. As a condition for inheriting her third, each daughter is asked by Lear to express her love for him. He promises to bestow the largest portion on the one who loves him best. The two eldest, Goneril and Regan, do their best to win his favor and do not shy from the obsequious. The youngest, Cordelia, speaks last. She cannot bring herself to speak in the lofty (and insincere) phrases of her sisters, yet she acknowledges that

> I am sure my love's
> More ponderous than my tongue.[27]

When called to speak, she is silent. When pushed by her father, she acknowledges her duty to him and does not shrink from all that it implies. Yet in affirming the propriety of her love, she also criticizes the fawning words of her sisters, who had boldly declared that all their love belonged to their father. What, Cordelia asks, of their husbands?

> Good my lord,
> You have begotten me, bred me, loved me. I
> Return those duties back as are right fit,
> Obey you, love you and most honour you.
> Why have my sisters husbands, if they say
> They love you all? Haply when I shall wed,
> That lord whose hand must take my plight shall carry
> Half my love with him, half my care and duty.
> Sure I shall never marry like my sisters
> To love my father all.[28]

Cordelia does not lack filial piety. At the same time she understands that propriety demands a variety of loyalties. Thus, she refuses to pledge all her love to her father in a way that would compromise her love for her future husband. She is steadfast even though the price of her decision is her share of the kingdom as well as her father's love. Lear, in his rage, splits the kingdom between Goneril and Regan and disowns Cordelia.

A central theme in this play is the disorder created by unnatural acts. In relinquishing his throne, Lear voluntarily parcels out the inheritance that ordinarily would follow his death. The act is unbecoming of a king and defies the nature of legitimate royal authority. Lear, in making this unnatural abdication, throws the kingdom into turmoil. He is shocked when, in short order, Goneril treats him not as king but as a doddering old man. In his rage, he accuses her of ingratitude, which, in Lear's mind, is an offense not only against the parent but against nature itself.

> Ingratitude, thou marble hearted-fiend,
> More hideous, when thou show'st thee in a child,
> Than the sea-monster.[29]

He retires to the home of Regan, hopeful that she will treat him as he thinks he deserves.

> Thou better knowest
> The offices of nature, bond of childhood,
> Effects of courtesy, dues of gratitude.[30]

He soon discovers that Goneril and Regan are colluding against him, and he curses them both, calling them "unnatural hags."[31] Yet, the disarray of the kingdom, the discord, the machinations, the filial loves turned to hatred, are all brought about, or at least set loose, by the unnatural act of the king forfeiting his crown and dividing his kingdom. The Duke of Gloucester, musing about these troubled times, is forced to admit, "Tis strange, strange."[32]

Ironically, Lear's fool sees matters most clearly. In the way of fools, he speaks in riddles with plenty of nonsense, but this is only to soften the target. After responding to a silly query with an apparently correct answer, the fool congratulates Lear: "Yes indeed, thou wouldst make a good fool." Lear, obsessed with his mistreatment at the hands of his daughters, contemplates taking the throne back by force:

Lear: To take't again perforce—monster ingratitude!
Fool: If thou wert my fool, nuncle, I'd have thee beaten
for being old before thy time.
Lear: How's that?
Fool: Thou shouldst not have been old till thou hadst been wise.[33]

Here we see the full significance of Lear's act. He has grown old but not wise. In his foolishness he unnaturally forfeited the crown and brought misfortune to himself and chaos to the realm. His unnatural act unleashed other unnatural acts, including the ingratitude of Goneril and Regan. The reader can immediately recognize the sin of Goneril and Regan. Their callous disregard for their father, their lack of deference to his desires, is clearly a reflection of their impiety. But it takes no more than the words of a fool to help us focus on the true root of the problem. Filial ingratitude is only the symptom of Lear's impiety. In dividing the realm and relinquishing the throne he has treated cheaply that which had been entrusted to him. Lear is guilty of ingratitude, not simply to his father, as are Goneril and Regan, but to his fathers, who in a line of succession guarded the prerogatives of royal authority and handed an intact kingdom on to the next generation at the proper time. Like Esau, Lear has treated his inheritance as a thing to be casually given away, and ironically his colossal act of ingratitude is rendered invisible to his mind by the glaring light of his daughters' ingratitude. The beam in his eye makes him blind to the speck in theirs. The results are, of course, tragic. Lear dies but not before he is forced to gaze upon the bodies of his three daughters, all violently slain.

The tragedy of King Lear shows us that the effects of ingratitude are not simply personal and private. Instead, ingratitude can shake a kingdom to its very core. If gratitude is a moral duty or a virtue, then it is not simply a matter of private individual concern. When one shirks a duty, one becomes culpable in the eyes of others. When one's character is vicious and not virtuous, others suffer. The effects are magnified when the ingratitude begins in the hearts of those entrusted to lead the state. Through the power of a bad example as well as the ripple effect of negligent policies, the nation is thrown into disarray. When leaders fail to acknowledge the debts of gratitude they owe, wise judgment is impossible, for good judgment requires an accurate perception of the world. Ingratitude is the product of a distorted view of reality, and the decisions that emerge from such a view will invariably carry that distortion.

This, of course, leads us to the obvious question: do we as a society see the world through the lens of gratitude, or do we suffer from the astigmatism of ingratitude? If our society is characterized, to some extent, by the disposition of ingratitude, what are the effects? Might it be possible to trace the lines of ingratitude through some of the social and political problems that vex us? Might there be a connection between achieving a proper sense of gratitude and admitting our creatureliness?

Gratitude is the result of beneficence, and our gratitude to our benefactors will tend to produce responsible actions, for gratitude forces us to think beyond our immediate concerns. It requires us to see the manifold ways we are joined with others in complex relationships of owed and owing, of debt and debtor, where we all, at different times, take a turn playing the benefactor even as we find ourselves in need of beneficence. A full-orbed understanding of gratitude moves beyond human beings to both the supernatural and to the natural: to the God who created us and the natural world by which we are sustained.

Gratitude gives birth to acts marked by responsibility, for in expressing our gratitude, we acknowledge our dependence beyond ourselves, which, if we are honest, is ongoing. To acknowledge our dependence is to deny our independence. It is to admit of our contingency and our creatureliness. To be grateful, in short, is to be humble. Ingratitude, on the other hand, is a manifestation of hubris. It is a pride that dooms us to a false conception of the world and therefore renders wisdom impotent and judgment faulty. To recover a better vantage point requires, on this account, a recovery of that sense of gratitude by which we acknowledge, through our dispositions and actions, the giftedness of the lives we live and the world we inhabit.

3

Human Scale:
Propriety in Our Lives

I am calling also for an end to giantism, for a return to the hu-
man scale—the scale that human beings can understand and
cope with; the scale of the local fraternal lodge, the church con-
gregation, the block club, the farm bureau. . . . In government,
the human scale is the town council, the board of selectmen, and
the precinct captain. It is this activity on a small, human scale
that creates the fabric of community, a framework for the cre-
ation of abundance and liberty.

Ronald Reagan, speech to the Executive Club of Chicago, 1975

So far we have discussed the notion of creatureliness and the disposition of gratitude. A third concept—a practical outgrowth of the first two—is the idea of human scale. We have seen that both a denial of our creatureliness and ingratitude find their roots in hubris, or in a kind of pride that skews one's view of reality and brings disorder to what it touches. One of the practical outworkings of this hubris is the loss of an appropriate sense of scale. We have in our day come, in many respects, to adore the massive, to aspire to the giant, to favor the super-sized. This represents an unnatural view of reality, and the practical results are striking, obvious, and, well, big.

Right at the beginning, it is important to make clear that I am not simply agitating for a "small is beautiful" aesthetic. Neither, in fact, was E. F. Schumacher, who coined the phrase. According to Schumacher, the modern world is positively obsessed with all things huge; therefore, to recover a correct sensibility, it is necessary to champion the small, the modest, the human scale. Today we live in an atmosphere charged with giantism, and for that reason we need to consider with care the implications of that disposition. We need to give serious thought to the ways our culture has become intoxicated with the big, and we need to explore the reasons this has come to pass.

In the middle of the twentieth century, the Swiss economist Wilhelm Röpke wrote of what he termed "the cult of the colossal." Röpke's description of this phenomenon can help us to think about the various ways our world has become enamored with size.

> The cult of the colossal means kowtowing before the merely "big"—which is thus adequately legitimized as the better and more valuable—it means contempt for what is outwardly small but inwardly great, it is the cult of power and unity, the predilection for the superlative in all spheres of cultural life. . . . To this style of the time correspond, in equal degree, the unexampled increase in population, imperialism, socialism, mammoth industries, monopolism, statism, monumental architecture, technical dynamism, mass armies, the concentration of government powers, giant cities, spiritual collectivism, yes, even Wagner's operas. Since the cult of the colossal reduces qualitative greatness to mere quantity, to nothing but numbers, and since quantity can only be topped by ever greater quantity, the intoxication with size will in the end exceed all bounds and will finally lead to absurdities which have to be stopped. Since, moreover, different quantities of difference species can only be reduced to a common denominator by means of money in order to render them comparable in the race of outdoing each other, the result is a tendency to measure size by money pure and simple—as, for instance, in the American seaside resort, Atlantic City, where in 1926 I found a gigantic pier simply being christened "Million Dollar Pier." Thus we find very close bonds of kinship between the cult of the colossal and commercialism.[1]

For his part, Röpke thought that, as the twentieth century wore on, the predilection for the colossal would fade, unable to bear its own weight. Sadly, he was wrong. In some ways, the momentum has even increased. Nevertheless, his description stands as a powerful indictment that must be grasped if the problems he identifies are to be wisely addressed.

Before turning to a description of this unnatural trend in our society, it might first be useful to describe what I take to be normal. If the colossal is abnormal, the normal, as I already indicated, is not the tiny. Rather, the scale that is suitable to humans is the human. Human scale is suited to human flourishing.

Why exactly is human scale important? The ancient Greek philosopher Protagoras once remarked, "Man is the measure of all things." While he no doubt overstated the case, Protagoras does get at an important truth. Much of what humans do must be tied to the measurement of the human being. If that connection is broken, human artifacts and institutions become unnatural monstrosities ill equipped to serve well the purpose for which they were created. Take, for example, a simple chair. Carpenters cannot build good chairs without first considering the human form and size. If they paid attention only to form and not size, they could construct a chair twenty feet high or three inches tall. The form would suit, but the size would not. If, however, they considered human size but not form, there is every chance that the "chair" would be unsittable or at least terribly uncomfortable. Obviously, carpenters must attend to the needs of human beings before they commence building chairs. Only then will the products have a chance of being good chairs. The same principle applies to the construction of buildings. While the varieties are endless, there are certain principles that must be followed when, for instance, building a home. Doors must be within a certain range of size and manageability. Steps cannot be too high lest they act as barriers rather than facilitators. Vertical windows dignify the human form whereas horizontal slits at waist level make seeing out difficult and, from the perspective of the street, appear to cut off legs and heads. The same kinds of arguments apply to streets, cities, schools, farms, technologies, and businesses. The principle of human scale applies to politics and economics as well. A political or economic structure that pays no heed to the natural requirements of a human being will invariably be in tension with the humans it is intended to serve.

In what follows, I want to discuss a variety of factors contributing to our modern affection for giantism. As we will see, many of the factors that serve as foundational assumptions of our modern way of thinking do, at the same time, urge us onward to colossal dimensions in both our ideas and our artifacts.

SECULARISM

In chapter 1, we touched on some aspects of secularization, but in the context of our discussion of human scale, it is necessary to return to this phenomenon. With secularization we come to forget our creatureliness. We come to neglect the debt of gratitude we owe to God. When we forget (or ignore) that we are contingent creatures, we inadvertantly create an enormous metaphysical void. In ages of belief, God, among other things, served as a cosmic ordering principle. His presence oriented the various particulars of reality into a coherent whole. His existence made possible the so-called unity in diversity witnessed in, for example, medieval philosophy. With the rise of secularism this ordering principle was lost. The manifold particulars came unmoored from the orienting fact of God's existence. Without the unity that God's existence provided, particulars lost their orientation to the whole. Only multiplicity remained.

No one understood this better than Nietzsche. In his parable of "The Madman," Nietzsche famously announces the death of God. Giving voice to this momentous event,

> The madman jumped into their midst and pierced them with his eyes. "Wither is God?" he cried; "I will tell you. *We have killed him*—you and I. All of us are his murderers. But how did we do this? How could we drink up the sea? Who gave us the sponge to wipe away the entire horizon? What were we doing when we unchained this earth from its sun? Whither is it moving now? Whither are we moving? Away from all suns? Are we not plunging continually? Backward, sideward, forward, in all directions? Is there still any up or down? Are we not straying as through an infinite nothing?[2]

God's existence provided a sort of metaphysical ordering principle by which individual lives and, indeed, entire societies could be arranged. With the demise of God, that ordering principle was removed. The world was cut loose and threatened to fly into pieces. Nietzsche recognized the mind-boggling implications. People would come slowly to grasp "what this event really means—how much must collapse now that this faith has been undermined because it was built upon this faith, propped up by it, grown into it; for example, the whole of our European morality." But Nietzsche looked past the destruction and disorientation to a new dawn of possibility for those strong enough to bear the weight of a world without God. "Indeed, we philosophers and 'free spirits' feel, when we hear the news that 'the old god is dead,' as if a new dawn shone on us; our heart overflows with gratitude, amazement, premonitions, expectation. At long last the horizon appears free to us again, even if it should not be bright."[3]

Nietzsche understood that humans naturally long for order. We seek unity. We seek to grasp meaning in the world about us or to impose meaning if native meaning cannot be found. In the absence of God, there exists, to be sure, proximate meaning—e.g., this tastes good or she loves me—but ultimate meaning is far more illusive. When the possibility of ultimate meaning is gone (or at best doubtful), individuals will experience a kind of disorientation as they attempt to ground the meaning of their existence in something stable. Worship of the natural world in pagan societies is replaced in ours by the worship of the future (progressivism), worship of science (scientism), worship of pleasure (hedonism), or even the worship of self (narcissism). These various attempts to fill the void of God's nonexistence have this in common: they are pseudoreligious attempts to provide an orientation for the manifold particulars of reality cut loose from the anchor of God's existence. They substitute human will for God's will. But where the idea of God is equal to the task of meaningfully orienting the particulars of existence into a coherent universal whole, these pseudoreligions are not.

Nevertheless, they do, in fact, attempt to colonize that territory once occupied by God. They attempt to establish an empire on illegitimate grounds. Secularism creates the conceptual and metaphysical space that gives birth to and nurtures these impulses. But, because they are essentially incapable of accomplishing what we demand of them, we constantly insist that they enlarge their territories in the hope that eventually they will succeed. Secularism tends to breed contempt for multiplicity and a longing for the whole. It breeds restlessness in search of unity. These secularized, restless—and consequently ungrateful—hearts are insatiably hungry for the God who has been denied. In their restlessness, they embrace surrogates that promise to satisfy but do not. At least not yet. And so the expansion continues.

If humans are, in fact, creatures created by God, then the scale proper to humans is one that acknowledges human dependence on God. It recognizes human limitation. It acknowledges human fallibility, contingency, and need. When humans acknowledge fundamental limits, we are better positioned to see the world correctly. When we recognize our dependencies, we are, ironically, better equipped to live well. When we deny or ignore these, we naturally attempt to demonstrate our adequacies. We naturally seek to find a venue by which we can truly realize the autonomy we claim as our right. We naturally seek to swallow the world only to find ourselves choking on reality.

PROGRESSIVISM

While the rise of new science—and the technology that accompanied it—provided empirical evidence that humans were progressing, the progressive is concerned only secondarily with technology. Rather, the focus of interest and optimism lies squarely in the moral arena. Human beings, it is believed, can improve and will improve indefinitely. Such a faith in human progress prompted Immanuel Kant to write a treatise with the hopeful title "Perpetual Peace," in which he lays out a program to achieve just that. Moral failure, both public and private, could, he thought, eventually be overcome, and a world without war could be inaugurated. A generation after Kant, John Stuart Mill wrote hopefully of the world that could be achieved by human effort. Through advances in science and medicine, disease would be conquered. Through more equitable distribution of food, hunger could be ended. Through an educational program that trained all people to respect the rights of others, happiness could reign on this hitherto planet of misery and pain. Progressivism is an expansive doctrine of human will. In an act of faith coupled with works, humans can mold not only the world about them but the world within. That is to say, human nature can be reshaped.

Progress is an open-ended affair. The upward trajectory on which the human race has embarked is full of promise and possibility. Like leaven, the spirit of progress works through the entire structure of a society promising to make all things better, to make all people happy, to bring about a world of peace, security, and contentment that has until now been merely the stuff of dreams. The price of progress is change. The old is, by definition, unprogressive, at best a mere stepping-stone to the glorious future toward which we strive. But in light of the promised future, the price of change is a small one. Who, after all, wants to be thought of as against progress? As backward and unmodern? These indictments are difficult to overcome in a world where progress is the orthodoxy and where denying it is to reveal oneself as a heretic or, even worse, a pessimist.

Progressivism was born in an age when traditional religious beliefs were being challenged. After all, the idea of original sin puts a serious damper on the idea of perfection through human effort. To be sure, orthodox Christianity itself has some notion of progress, but it is only by virtue of redemption and is ultimately realized outside of time. Progressivism does not totally reject that trajectory, but it does recast the temporal horizon. In the Christian tradition, perfection is achieved in eternity. In the progressive model, perfection can be achieved—or at least approached—in time. Whereas the former depends on an act of God and is suffused with divine grace, the latter relies on human effort suffused with optimism. Whereas Christian theology appreciates humans as limited creatures, progressives see humans as autonomous actors in need merely of the opportunity to refashion the world. Individuals and society as a whole provide the canvas upon which the improvements can be wrought. Progressivism, it turns out, is little more than a Christian heresy championing terrestrial salvation—indeed there is no other—achieved by works rather than grace. Eden can be regained and God will be out of the picture or at least inconspicuous.

How can humans aspire to attain the lofty goal of future perfection? This is the challenge of progressivism. The idea of a perfect God, a residue lingering from an earlier time, sets the bar impossibly high. Yet strive we do. And in striving to achieve this longed-for perfection, the barriers erected by the old doctrines of original sin and the need for divine grace are set aside. The promised possibility, the wages of our efforts, expands to encompass all reality. The limits entailed by our creatureliness are jettisoned as the promise of overcoming those old strictures is grasped. We quickly lose sight of what is properly human when we are infected by faith in progress.

All this is not to deny that conditions can improve. That the slave trade was ended in the west is a notable improvement not only for the lives of slaves but also for the lives of slave-owners whose souls were corrupted by participating in that institution. But while individuals and societies can improve, they can also, as the twentieth century so indelibly demonstrated, deteriorate. So-called progress is not necessarily permanent. Human vices are forever present, and each generation must guard carefully the tender flame of civilization. As Aleksandr Solzhenitsyn reminded us, "The line separating good and evil passes through . . . every human heart."[4] Progressivism tells us that the line can be erased. When we succumb to that notion, we are closer to the danger than at any other time, for it is then that hubris blinds us to reality and tempts us with the old promise "you shall be as gods." But gods are neither creatures nor obliged to be grateful. Humility is not a virtue of deity.

Perhaps it is not surprising that when we set our hearts and minds on progress, we begin to think of sweeping solutions to persistent problems. The scale of the solution must match the scale of the problems, and because so many of our problems extend beyond local or even national borders, the logic of expansion appears justified and even demanded. Because progressivism is animated by the confidence that humans are essentially good, there is a diminished fear of unitary power vested in one body or institution. The centralization of political and economic power is seen as the best means of advancing the progressive cause rather than as the origin of a dangerous entity capable of great mischief. The state becomes the vehicle for progressive aspirations rather than a less grandiose protector of individual rights or national security. The state becomes an agent of positive (and sweeping) good rather than an agent tasked with preventing, or at least limiting, evil.

Because the modern state is rooted in the will of the people, it is seen as far less dangerous than states of yore ruled by monarchs. The people, as individual voters, will vote according to their interests, and their interests will, it is believed, ultimately coincide, for they are all seeking peace, security, and happiness. Small associational units, the family, local congregations, guilds, and the like—what Burke called the "little platoons"—appear terribly ineffective and inconsequential in the program of progress. In fact, these various associations may actually undermine the unity for which the progressive mind yearns. When mediating institutions are undermined, the individual becomes the primary entity. But bereft of the various little platoons that give one a sense of belonging, the individual finds him- or herself isolated and alone. Individuals long for security and community, but the traditional means of participating in these have been compromised. All that is left is the state. And the state is all too willing to fill the roles that were once filled by nonstate institutions. The state becomes our community, protector, and the source of meaning in our desiccated lives. The void is filled by a state whose power must necessarily increase to accomplish that which we demand. In this way, the centralized state increases exponentially in an age of individualism.

Economic centralization has occurred alongside government expansion. An economy the size of ours today requires a huge governmental apparatus to keep it functioning. Global markets and international corporations cannot exist apart from centralized political power of a scale to match that of the economy. Furthermore, the illusion that our enormous economy happened as a result of individual market choices is just that: an illusion. The central government adores centralization of every kind, and our government has been a key player in the creation of our corporate economy. The level playing field between small proprietors and huge corporate entities is another illusion. If the field were level, would corporations continue to contribute significant amounts of money to candidates of both major political parties? Do financially astute individuals pay significant amounts of money for nothing in return? The answer is obvious. Scale gives some economic entities access not simply to economic power (which in market terms makes sense) but to political power, which clearly shows one way that economic giantism complements political giantism.

SCIENTISM

Modern science has been a boon. We who are fortunate enough to live in the age of the X-ray, Novocain, and penicillin have avoided many of the miseries and premature deaths suffered by our ancestors. Advances in our understanding of physics, weather, and agriculture have all served to improve the lives of millions. We live in a time when scientific breakthroughs seem to come daily. It is little wonder that these advances would induce us to think optimistically about the future and the possibility for human progress.

But, as with most stories, there is a dark side that must not be ignored. The scientific method is marvelously suited to exploring the physical world. Yet, when Newton wrote that the physical universe is like a machine with regular movements that can be predicted, he was only partially correct. Although many aspects of the physical world are machinelike in their regularity, we deform nature by attempting to reduce it merely to a machine. The dis-analogies are as significant as the analogies. A machine is a self-contained artifact built by an intelligent being to accomplish a particular outcome. The universe may have been created by God for some particular purpose, but that purpose is beyond the ken of human insight, and so at best we must relegate that to mystery.

Those early modern scientists and philosophers who spoke of the physical world as a machine generally maintained that humans possess nonphysical souls. This, of course, saved human beings from the determinism to which machines are doomed. A nonphysical soul preserves a realm of freedom in a world otherwise subjected to the laws of physics and chemistry. Obviously, if the existence of the soul was ever denied, freedom would be the first casualty. In the late eighteenth century, the skeptic David Hume did much to shake belief in the soul, miracles, and the very existence of God. If something cannot be known empirically, he argued, then it is not an object of knowledge. It is impossible to call such a thing a fact. In the field of ethics, he articulated the so-called fact-value distinction. Facts, in this account, are external to the knower and observable by anyone.

Values, in contrast, are private and subjective, like preferring chocolate to vanilla ice cream. While it is possible to say with confidence that this particular animal is furry, barks, and wags its tail, and to tell a person she is wrong if she disagrees, it is not possible to argue with someone about whether she prefers chocolate to vanilla ice cream. If I say, "I feel happy," it is equally impossible for someone else to tell me, "No, you don't." My feelings are subjective states, just like my preference for chocolate is a subjective preference. Values, according to Hume, are another category of subjective preferences, so when I say "lying is wrong" I am saying something akin to "I feel lying is wrong" and not something like "this is a dog." The former is purely subjective and is therefore immune from critique; the latter is objective and can be either verified or disproven.

When the soul is denied and the fact-value distinction affirmed, humans are seen as merely temporal creatures with no connection to eternity. Any notions of moral truth must be rooted not in conscience or in divine writ or even in human reason but in private feelings and in publically observable benefits. In this scheme, murder, for instance, is not intrinsically wrong. We can condemn it only because it is not beneficial to society. But while murder in general may not be beneficial to society, it is still possible that this particular murder might be, and so there is no way to argue that murder, per se, is wrong. Ultimately, we see here the rise of public opinion as the arbiter by which all is decided. Public opinion is merely the aggregate of individual desires at a particular moment in time. The law of God or natural law is replaced by the principle of majoritarianism, and as we all know, the majority can be fickle. The stability of law is replaced by the instability of opinion, and the realm of objective truth gives way to the empire of subjective opinion.

The success of modern science gave birth to the technological age. That we have gained new insights into the natural world is obvious. These new insights were put to work with the goal of easing man's estate, as Francis Bacon put it. The model of the machine, as an analog for the physical world, had already taken root in the imagination, so it should not surprise us that a multitude of machines emerged in this new effort to apply science to improving the human condition. While basic tools are applied by humans at a pace equal to the human wielding them, the machine is capable of increasing the speed of production to a pace that outstrips human capacities. The industrial revolution gave birth to machines on a scale that had never before been contemplated.

The very structure of families underwent a change as the machine came increasingly to dominate economic life. Rather than working together on a family farm or a home-based enterprise, fathers took jobs in factories. This removed them from the day-to-day lives of their families. Because the factory system was no respecters of persons, women could take their places beside the men, and even children at times found themselves laboring at the machines. These new economic forces severely strained the little platoon of the family by promising a wage to workers but reducing their control over their economic lives. In short, the Industrial Revolution was a two-edged sword. It freed many from the drudgery of farming and home industries only to introduce a new kind of drudgery in which human scale was forfeited in the name of economic efficiency. Today wages are much higher than they were during the early, lurching days of the Industrial Revolution, but were the attendant loss of human scale and the centralization accompanying that loss unambiguous goods?

That our world is characterized, in large part, by the technologies we use is obvious. The personal computer has changed business. The Internet has changed dating relationships. The automobile has changed the way we think about distance. The airplane has changed the way wars are conducted, and the microwave has changed the way we eat. But we have also learned how to make mustard gas, and the piles of corpses in the trenches along the Marne testify to the new kind of warfare unleashed by our creativity. So too the devastation of Hiroshima showed the world at large that killing on a scale never before contemplated was now possible. For the first time in human history, the very real possibility of destroying the entire human population of the planet was in our grasp. The scale of our destructive powers made necessary an increase in those political and military forces tasked with preventing Armageddon. Political bureaucracies—themselves a kind of technology—made it possible to control people to a degree that absolute kings had never imagined.

The centralization of power to prevent catastrophe was not limited to the threat of weapons of mass destruction. The environment came under increasing strain as pollutants from various industries, pesticides, and trash made the prospect of a future without clean air or water a very real possibility. Toxic rain respects no borders. Global warming is not limited to a particular region. The economic turmoil of 2008–9 called forth dramatic actions at the national and international levels. County and state governments are simply ill equipped, as a matter of scale, to do much about these concerns. Even national governments seem less than adequate to deal with issues that are truly global. The scale of our challenges seems to point toward increasing centralization. Any appeal to human scale is silenced by the incessant demand for adequate solutions to the ills besetting us.

MATERIALISM

Quite apart from these practical manifestations of our technological enthusiasm is a malady made all the more insidious by virtue of its invisibility. I am talking about the subtle but determinative way our view of the world has changed. When the soul is denied, or at least practically ignored, and when technology unleashes the possibility of widespread wealth, it is tempting to conceive of reality in merely material terms. This temptation is difficult to resist, and when combined with the momentum provided by secularism, it is no surprise that materialism should emerge. This is not to say that all people today are materialists. Far from it. Many still believe in the soul and in God, but even then, it is possible to bracket these beliefs and to live in practical terms as if only the material world existed. The fact-value distinction works a convenient palliative allowing those with a residual religious inclination to hold those beliefs privately while living in practical terms as a materialist.

Materialism results in another sort of aggrandizement. When we come to see the world only in material terms, we fall victim to the cult of quantity. Quality, as a meaningful category, is reduced to the merely subjective, and quantity rules the day. How do you know something is better? If it is bigger. If some is good, then more is clearly better. And even more is better still. Our modern obsession with quantity is evident all around us. Consider, for instance, the relative value placed on the study of poetry versus the study of business. The all-too-frequent question to the first endeavor is some version of "what's it good for?" More precisely, this means, what is the economic payoff? If the aspiring student of poetry were to reply, "It's good for my soul," chances are he or she would be met with a blank stare or perhaps a contemptuous snort, indicating the relative value placed on soulish benefits in a world of practical, if not thorough going, materialism.

The triumph of quantity over quality has given rise to a preference for "hard data" that has lent prestige to the social sciences and relegated the humanities to the periphery suited to those who cannot master the skills of quantification. In the process, the social sciences, in attempting to mimic the approaches of their big brothers in the hard sciences, have gotten increasingly adept at making confident declarations about hitherto obvious facts now bolstered by the authority of numbers.

Eventually, philosophical materialism led to a materialism of a more mundane sort. In a world obsessed with quantity, where the needs of the soul are denied, the accumulation of material goods becomes the primary means of measuring success. This is the materialism of the consumer. That all living things are consumers is a truism. That humans have always consumed a disproportionate amount of natural resources is probably true and not surprising or intrinsically disturbing. But the age of the consumer represents consumption on a new scale. To be sure, there have always been individuals who, by virtue of their positions, consumed far more than they needed. But with the benefits of the industrial age, a time in which vast quantities of goods can be produced and more people than ever before have disposable resources, the sheer volume of consumption is breathtaking.

The economy depends on this consumption, for the standard of a successful economy is not the health or happiness of the people but the growth of the economy itself. Perpetual growth, we are told, is good. Stasis is bad. Decline, or what is called "negative growth," is terrifying. We work to have disposable income so we can purchase goods to consume, and in doing so, we contribute in our small way to sustaining economic growth. Consumption becomes a patriotic duty. If the consumables satisfied or lasted, we would cease buying and the economy would suffer. The advent of so-called planned obsolescence, along with relentless advertizing, ensures a steady stream of consumers in need of an updated model. The triumph of quantity over quality ensures that products will not last and so must be replaced. Humans have always consumed to live. What is new is that many now live to consume.

The modern corporation is the perfect entity to oversee this vast orgy of consumption. The corporation is considered a legal person and therefore enjoys many of the rights and protections granted to individuals by the U.S. Constitution. But the corporation is not a person. Unlike a person, the corporation is, in theory, eternal. In a world of consumption, in which humans can engage in lives devoted to acquiring massive piles of stuff, threescore and ten is still a pretty good rule of thumb. Some might eek out a few more years, but death occurs regardless of how much one has accumulated or lost. The concrete and definite cycle of the human life provides a certain scale to human existence and lends an element of seriousness to moral issues. A corporation, however, enjoys the legal benefits of personhood and never dies a natural death. In a world from which the eternal God has been banished, the eternal corporation reigns. Aided by the power of the government, the corporation, whose liability is legally limited, can enjoy a perpetual life providing goods for consumers intoxicated by the heady fumes of acquisition.

A life given to consumption is, of course, a life given to pleasure, or at least the promise of pleasure, for it is not altogether clear that a consumer's life is pleasant as much as potentially pleasant. A life given to the pursuit of pleasure is a life of hedonism. It is a life characterized by the practical denial of eternity, of noble acts, of the dignity and goodness of personal sacrifice. Hedonism, in other words, distracts us from the very things that were once prized above all else. When our lives are given primarily to acquisition and consumption, we lose sight of the true meaning of our humanity. Lost is the profound sense of our creatureliness through which we are daily reminded of our dependence. Lost is a sense of gratitude to God, to the natural world, and to generations past. And while the eternal corporation may receive our regular acknowledgment in the form of our tithes and offerings, it is possible to imagine that we are beholden to no one. Truly, the hedonistic consumer is the quintessential example of the autonomous individual. Such consumers sate their desires with all dispatch, and the credit card and online shopping steadily reduce the time between desire and consummation. But the objects of consumption are not simply material goods, for in a world where all reality is seen through the lens of materialism, people as well as things become items to consume.

If pleasure is the chief object of the hedonist's pursuit, security becomes the necessary condition making all else possible. If this world is all that is, and if pleasure in this world is our chief object, then a life cut short is the greatest tragedy. It becomes difficult to imagine a situation in which sacrificing one's own life would be warranted, for noble causes have been subsumed under the hedonistic tide. In such a setting, insecurity is an evil to be eliminated at all costs. Rather than cherishing liberty and tolerating some degree of insecurity to make liberty possible, individuals will tend to become what Bertrand de Jouvenel called "securitarians."[5] Securitarians seek to render the world innocuous so that the pursuit of pleasure will be unimpeded. Securitarians want to eliminate or at least significantly reduce the risk that characterizes human existence. The ideal situation for this group would be a world in which one could reap profits without risk of loss, a world in which disease and illness could be eliminated and lives would be long and death painless. While the dream of eliminating death is still only a dream, we can imagine—and often accomplish—deferring it, and we can ignore the thought of death while we work tirelessly to put it off. A perfect world for the securitarian would be a world without risk, a world in which all uncertainties are removed, a world from which mystery has been banished.

But, alas, the world is a dangerous and mysterious place. It always has been. If we know where to look, we will encounter mystery on every side. There are questions that will never be answered. Disease will strike. Children will die. Cities will be ravaged by pestilence; farmers by drought. To attempt to limit these maladies is natural. To seek to eliminate them at the cost of our freedom, at the cost of our humanity, is a fool's errand that will reduce us to quaking minions longing only to continue our lives of consumption so long as we are not bothered. Hedonism, and the securitarianism that accompanies it, ultimately represents a profound loss of courage and a profound opportunity for the centralization of power.

In an age of religious belief, the uncertainties of time were rendered bearable by the hope that eternity would offer not only solace but answers. Temporal existence was understood as part of the human condition but not the sum total. The uncertainties encountered in time were held to be under the ultimate guidance of an omnipotent and benevolent deity. Security existed in the bosom of faith. In an age of materialistic hedonism, security in God is replaced by the demand for secular security. What better instrument to usher in this new age than the arm of political power? The benevolent hand of God is replaced by the power of the state. Faith in God is replaced by faith in political power.

The longing for security is not, to be sure, an unnatural desire. The idea that human existence can be rendered secure is nothing more than a longing for Eden. But this new Eden, where uncertainties are no more and where all desires are sated without delay, is one from which God is conspicuously absent. And the absence is deeply felt. The pleasures of Eden must be guarded lest they be stolen away by the winds of uncertainty. The vacuum of a godless paradise must be compensated for. Up from the verdant plains of Eden rises a new tower of Babel: a tower that will unify humanity around a common endeavor; a tower that will touch the heavens and prove ourselves equal to the God who has absconded; a tower built by political power working hand in hand with economic might; a tower whose scale dwarfs the humans who clamored for it even as it draws them into its vortex. We now have the ideal image of this brave new world of the materialistic hedonist: the Garden of Eden with the Tower of Babel in its midst. Hedonistic plenty with secular security to boot. Big, it turns out, is better, for only the massive can pretend to render the human condition safe from the vicissitudes of life.

This new Tower of Babel takes many shapes. Medical technology that promises eventually to extend life indefinitely—or at least make possible long, active lives free from pain—is but a dream, but the dream is imaginable in these heady days of technological marvels. Globalization is another obvious example, one whose advent, we are assured, is as inevitable as the goods that it will bring. The prophets of globalization paint optimistic pictures of the peace and prosperity to which globalism will give birth. As trade becomes possible throughout the world, differences will fade in the light of the common interest in commerce. Individuals will be empowered as new markets emerge. Wealth will increase, and poverty, with all its attendant ills, will decrease and eventually disappear.

The same impulse is behind many attempts to bring democratic reforms to nondemocratic regimes. Worldwide democracy, we are told, will usher in an era of peace and prosperity for all. While there are, of course, pragmatists championing both globalization and democratization, who argue that working toward these ends will serve to improve, to some degree, national security or economic well-being, there are also the idealistic champions whose rhetoric betokens far less modest aspirations. These are the utopian dreams of our day. What makes them so seductive is the secular context within which they are advanced. What makes them so powerful is the technological apparatus that makes them possible. Like God, their scale is universal.

SCALE MATTERS

In a world increasingly obsessed with favoring the big at the expense of the small, it is essential that we reorient our minds to consider issues of scale. This problem is especially acute in the United States. We Americans have, right from the start, been induced by geography to think in terms of the oversized. Tocqueville noted that the sheer quantity of available land in America helped shape the minds of those who settled our shores. America was a place with a limitless frontier. Young men could go west to find their fortune. They could acquire great tracts of land; they could hit the mother lode and become fabulously rich; they could remake themselves out of the raw material of that unsettled land where the horizon stretched beyond imagination and possibility was everywhere.

In a sense, all Americans are Texans, only the Texans are simply more noisy about their claims. We love words like "awesome" and "amazing." We favor Big Macs and Whoppers, pickup trucks with "the biggest payload," and sports cars with "more horsepower than any in its class." We want the fastest Internet, the clearest television, and the highest fidelity sound. We favor mega-churches, buffets, Costco, and if the number of plastic surgeries in recent years is any indication, we favor big breasts. Truly, America is a land of superlatives. Of course, this obsession with size is not limited to America, but Americans do lead the way, for good or ill.

It is essential that we realize that bigger is not necessarily better. There is a proper scale to particular artifacts as well as institutions, and to exceed that scale is to compromise the integrity of whatever has grown beyond its natural limits. A piece of furniture, a committee, or an institution can all suffer hard and perhaps fatal consequences when a certain size is exceeded. A table ceases to be an effective table when it no longer conforms to human scale. A committee that exceeds a certain size generally fails to function well. Institutions that exceed an optimal size become less efficient, far more difficult to manage, and often change their very nature merely to survive the burden of size.

While we are accustomed, by virtue of a culture that fairly worships bigness, to think in terms of quantity, we give precious little thought to propriety of scale. Our natural inclination is to think that bigger is probably better. But as we have seen, this is not a truth rooted in reality. Instead, it is a predilection exacerbated by certain dispositions that emerge in the modern world. If we are to understand these dispositions, we must learn to see the world differently. We must consciously train ourselves to think in terms of appropriate scale. As soon as we begin asking questions of this sort, we will discover a world of possibilities before us. We will be able to ask whether or not the biggest version of a thing is necessarily the best version. We will begin asking questions related to the purposes for which things exist. Most would readily acknowledge that the purpose of a thing is not to be the biggest. The purpose of a chair is not to be the biggest chair. Rather its purpose is to provide comfortable seating for a human being. The purpose of a school is not to be the biggest. Rather, its purpose is to accomplish, in the best fashion possible, the education of students. The purpose of an economy or a nation is not to be the biggest but to provide the best conditions within which humans can flourish. The same principle applies to a burger, a shopping mall, a church, or a stadium.

These questions of scale apply to all areas of our lives. The fact that we so often neglect to ask questions related to scale is one indication of our blindness.

Fortunately, this blindness is not necessarily a permanent condition. It can be remedied, and the best remedy is simply to raise the question. If we are to deal adequately with problems in the political or economic spheres, we cannot neglect questions of scale. If we are to deal wisely with environmental challenges, we must think about matters of scale. So too when we engage questions about education, agriculture, or architecture. In all of these, we will fail to address a central issue if we fail to address matters of human scale.

A denial of our creatureliness leads to a denial of the various ways we are indebted and gives rise to the autonomous individual. Autonomous individuals are marked by ingratitude, for their faces are turned unstintingly toward the blinding light of progress, and they cannot recognize either limits or debts. Such people live on borrowed capital just as a nation, blinded by consumption, lives on money borrowed from future generations. The ungrateful person (and the ungrateful society) is characterized by hubris, which seeks to dominate reality by a sheer act of will. But such a will to power necessarily entails expansion as the uncertainties of reality press in from every side. The ungrateful person or society cannot get the question of scale right because the human question is so badly answered.

In contrast, the grateful person (and society) recognizes dependencies on every level. Such a person is characterized by humility, which gives birth not to the urge to dominate but to the desire to preserve that which has been passed down, that which has been tended and cultivated, that which has and will produce good fruit. In short, grateful people are stewards. They understand that they are part of a chain, a succession of responsibility. They grasp that their stewardship is not solitary but bound to a long line of stewards, stretching back in time. Indeed, grateful people understand themselves as members of a community of stewards, and among this membership are the living, the dead, and the yet to be born. Such people can rest in the mystery of existence, the goodness of community, and propriety of a scale suited to human beings.

4

Place: The Allure of Home

"Naturally," Nikolai said, "you were born here, so everything
should seem very special to you."
"But, Papasha, it doesn't make any difference where a man is born."
"Well . . ."
"No, it really doesn't make any difference."

Ivan Turgenev, *Fathers and Sons*

All of them call it home, but they never stay.

Marilynn Robinson, *Home*

The notion of home naturally emerges from the three concepts we have explored thus far. When we acknowledge our creatureliness, we acknowledge the fact that we are embodied. We occupy space. We live and breathe and have our being in the context of a particular place in time. We can express gratitude for the places we inhabit, for they provide the raw material upon which our lives are written. Each place has a unique history embodied in the land, the people, the human artifacts, and the stories. Without a connection to these, individuals are nomads, strangers in a strange land, with no hope of becoming native to some place. To be native requires a scale suited to the extent of our capacities. The scale cannot exceed the limits of our knowledge or perhaps even the limits of our love, for our knowledge, much less our love, cannot extend indefinitely. Therefore, a place, when it is a home, is naturally of a scale suited to the limits of our creatureliness and the capacity of our gratitude.

Yet with all that, the concept of home is elusive and perhaps no more so than today. In her book *The Need for Roots*, French writer Simone Weil notes that, "To be rooted is perhaps the most important and least recognized need of the human soul. It is one of the hardest to define. A human being has roots by virtue of his real, active, and natural participation in the life of a community which preserves in living shape certain particular treasures of the past and certain particular expectations for the future."[1] If this is the case, then a society characterized in large part by its mobility, a society that seems to take a sort of satisfaction in its own deracination, would be ill equipped to provide one of the central human needs. According to Weil, modern rootlessness is not merely geographical or even cultural but spiritual as well. Writing of mid-twentieth-century France, but sounding as if she were writing for twenty-first-century Americans, she describes "a culture very strongly directed towards and influenced by technical science, very strongly tinged with pragmatism, extremely broken up by specialization, entirely deprived both of contact with this world and, at the same time, of any window opening to the world beyond."[2] This suggests that humans have a need for physical or geographical roots in a particular place embodying particular traditions, habits, and practices. But equally, humans require roots in a transcendent world, a world of spirit and moral truth. In short, the uprootedness of many today is both spiritual as well as geographic.

The idea of home is deeply embedded in our cultural heritage. Homer's *The Odyssey*, one of the core texts of the Western tradition, recounts the wanderings of Odysseus, who, in the aftermath of the Trojan War, spent ten long years struggling to return home. *The Odyssey* works as a piece of literature because Odysseus has a home. He is the ruler of Ithaka, and that land provides the orientation that makes Odysseus's quest to return meaningful. Ithaka is a particular place. It includes the land Odysseus owns, his vineyards, and the cattle that graze on the hillside. It is the place where his father and mother live, where loyal servants tend his flocks and work the soil. It is the abode of his friends and the place where his wife and son anxiously await his return. The richly rendered descriptions of home and homeland invoke a sense of longing that pervades the poem and gives the return of Odysseus its poignancy. Without Ithaka there is no story, for without a home Odysseus is merely a wanderer bereft of direction or longing.

The idea of the promised land, a land flowing with milk and honey, is a prominent symbolic representation of home that lies deep in the consciousness of cultures influenced by the Bible. The Hebrew children suffered in Egypt under the whip of slavery for four hundred years. God called Moses to deliver them out of bondage and lead them to a new land, one promised to their forefathers. This land of promise was a land of plenty, but it also represented freedom. It was a place the children of Abraham could call their own, a place where they could build homes and pass them on to their children. The promise of a home where they could live in freedom motivated the Hebrews to leave Egypt and, although the dream dimmed during forty years of wandering in the desert, it never died. When Joshua led the people across the Jordan, they celebrated the realization of the promise long hoped for and finally attained.

The idea of a promised land, of course, was not limited to the ancient Hebrews. The Pilgrims in America saw themselves as reenacting the Hebrew exodus from the land of oppression as they fled the Old World to seek a new land across the sea. They sought a place where they could settle and worship as they chose, a place they could call their own.

Christian theology, however, made the concept of home more complex for the Pilgrims than it was for either Homer or the Hebrews. Augustine, in his *City of God*, suggests that Christians are pilgrims sojourning through this world on their way to the celestial city, their real home. Does this Augustinian conception of a heavenly home undercut the possibility of an earthly home? Must religious believers, Christians in particular, shun affection for earthly places as they await a glorious future in another world? While that is certainly one way of reading this Augustinian dilemma, it is by no means the only way.

Augustine undermines the utopian impulse that is a perennial human temptation, one that characterizes much of classical political thought. By speaking in terms of two cities, the City of God and the Earthly City, Augustine places the hope of perfection outside of time. Perfection is put off until heaven, which exists in eternity and is achieved not by works but by divine grace. The politics of perfection is replaced by a realism that acknowledges the frailty of human will, the fact that power may be abused, and the transient nature of political structures. In this context, utopian aspirations are replaced by more modest expectations. The purpose of political power is to ensure order. Peace, not perfection, is the goal. Thus, by removing the expectation that a physical home in this world could be perfect or perfectible, the Augustinian view makes it possible to love our imperfect and temporary homes in this world without demanding perfection of them. We can love them despite their imperfections and incompleteness. When understood in these terms, Christianity can defuse the utopian impulse and ratify the goodness of an earthly home.

Augustine shows how it is possible for a person to be content even when the promised land is not immediately available. This principle appears even before the Christian era. Consider the example of the Babylonian captivity of the Jewish people. Because of their failure to obey the commands of God, Israel was conquered by the Babylonians. The temple was destroyed, and the people were taken into captivity. Through the prophets, it was foretold that the people would not return to their land for seventy years, a lifetime for most. God commanded the captives to settle down for the long term rather than continue lamenting their sad fate: Make a home in Babylon. Marry. Raise children. Build houses. Plant vineyards. Harvest. In short, they were to make a life and prepare for a future in that imperfect place where God had put them. Augustine's two cities yield the same practical results.

Today we live in a world where mobility is the coin of the realm and the idea of being settled in one place appears terrifying to some and impossible for others. Commitment to a particular place is a significant challenge in the modern world, and there are a variety of factors contributing to this restlessness. We do well, then, to consider some of the dynamics that have facilitated this change.

TECHNOLOGY

With our technologies we have sought to overcome both space and time. In the process we have created an illusion that it is possible to exist apart from these limitations or at least nearly unhindered by them. With automobiles and the Interstate Highway System, we can travel hundreds of miles in a day. With air travel, we can go from coast to coast in a few hours. This spatial contraction has facilitated the restless motion that characterizes much of our lives. It has served to expand our imaginative scope so that relocating across the state or across the county is now a fairly simple process. Although in an earlier, less mobile age, moving across a continent was possible, it required a sort of determination and commitment that not everyone could, or was willing to, muster. People tended to look for employment, not to mention a spouse, in the vicinity of their homes and moved away only reluctantly. Today, individuals extend their job searches to include the entire nation and in some cases the whole world. Under such strains, the idea of stable communities, where a majority of members enjoy a temporal continuity from generation to generation, becomes a dim memory of an earlier time.

Communication technology has revolutionized our lives as well. In recent years, we have witnessed a dramatic shift in the way our bodies are used for communication. We have e-mail, text messaging, Facebook, blogs, and Twitter. These modes of communication have made it increasingly possible for face-to-face human interaction to give way to communication mediated by a screen. Flesh and blood bodies, so long assumed integral for the deepest and most meaningful kind of communication, have gradually been replaced by IM, texts, and tweets.

Face-to-face communication, of course, occurs when two embodied souls encounter one another in the same spatial proximity. But as we become increasingly comfortable with electronic communication technologies, as our lives become increasingly oriented around them and shaped by them, it is now the case that much of our communication is mediated by a screen, and someday in the not too distant future, it is conceivable that most of our communication will take place in this manner. The primacy of communication sans bodies has important consequences for how we understand our essential creatureliness as well as the scale proper to human beings. When our lives proceed on terms that cause us to neglect the fact of our embodiment, we can easily be tempted to forget the goodness of our physical, embodied condition. We can imagine ourselves untethered to a physical world of limits and constraints. But is such an imaginative enterprise a good thing? To the extent that such a life is impossible, this enterprise is an illusion. To the extent that we are enticed by the illusion, our commitments to particular places, inhabited by particular bodies, will be eroded.

I am not necessarily arguing against these various technologies or suggesting that they need to be eliminated, as if that were possible. I am suggesting, though, that we need to be aware of the ways our technologies shape our view of reality and that we must act intentionally to use—and if necessary, have the wisdom to limit—technologies so they enhance human flourishing instead of detracting from it. If human flourishing requires acknowledging the goodness of bodily existence in a particular place, then a good technology is one that helps us to live better in the places we inhabit. A harmful one will cause us to neglect those same places and even act as if they do not exist.

DENIGRATION OF TRADITION AND THE RISE OF INDIVIDUALISM

One aspect of the modern mind is a deep suspicion of tradition. In today's vernacular, to call something traditional is to invoke a sense of age, to be sure, but it also suggests a condition of brittleness, of resistance to change and the failure to keep up with the times. To be stuck in the rut of tradition is seen as a failure to be creative, a loss of nerve, and perhaps worst of all, the inability to "think outside the box."

Yet, tradition plays an indispensable role in human experience, for within various traditions resides the collective wisdom of many generations. Through tradition (religious, moral, scientific, etc.), human minds participate in an ongoing project of discovery. The modern romantic image of the solitary individual boldly pushing beyond the perceived limits of understanding disregards the centuries of tradition that makes new discovery possible. As T. S. Eliot points out in his essay "Tradition and the Individual Talent," meaningful innovation always presupposes the prior existence of and participation in an authoritative tradition.[3] This is the case even when the tradition itself is subjected to scrutiny by those within it. Thus, any attempt to circumvent or deny the role of tradition is necessarily harmful to a proper understanding of the process of discovery as well as to our knowledge of reality itself.

It might be useful at this point to distinguish between two ways of understanding tradition, both either implicitly or explicitly denigrated by many modern thinkers. The first we can call "tradition as a repository." Edmund Burke, for example, held this view. Tradition, in this sense, is a storehouse that individuals may tap to access the accrued wisdom of human history. In a famous passage Burke writes, "We are afraid to put men to live and trade each on his own private stock of reason; because we suspect that this stock in each man is small, and that the individuals would do better to avail themselves of the general bank and capital of nations, and of ages."[4] Tradition, in this sense, resembles what G. K. Chesterton termed "the democracy of the dead."[5]

The second conception of tradition might be termed "tradition as an epistemological necessity." That is, tradition per se is not something a person simply chooses to embrace or reject. Humans do not enjoy a privileged vantage point from which to acquire purely objective and universal knowledge. The tradition we inhabit provides us with the initial conceptual framework by which we comprehend the world.[6] Tradition in the Burkean sense can be ignored or set aside, although, according to Burke, such neglect will exact a terrible social and political cost. The content embedded in tradition is what Burke emphasized. In contrast, one cannot coherently deny the epistemological role of tradition. To do so would, at the most basic level, require that we refrain from speaking at all, for language itself is a product of tradition. A proper understanding of tradition will acknowledge both conceptions.

If acknowledging the necessary role of tradition in both of its meanings is essential to produce a coherent account of human understanding, as well as to create a buffer against social and political chaos, then to deny any role for tradition is simultaneously to create an incoherent account of knowledge as well as to increase the possibility of serious trouble. Thus, appreciating the dual function of tradition is essential to human thriving, and we deny this truth at our individual and collective peril.

It is important to point out, though, that not all traditions are good. Some are downright vile. But seeking to eliminate bad traditions is quite different from attempting to ignore or denigrate all tradition regardless of content. The former should be the task of all conscientious individuals. The latter is a fool's errand rooted in a kind of hubris that denies any need to access resources beyond one's individual capacity.

Because traditions embody the habits, practices, and beliefs of particular communities, and because communities are rooted in a particular geographic locale, to ignore or denigrate one's own tradition is to ignore or denigrate the history of one's people and place. Attending properly to the future of a community is possible only if the past is both understood and respected. Thus, to ignore or denigrate the traditions of a local community is simultaneously to neglect its future. It is to undermine the foundations of a place and thereby make it less suitable for habitation.

It is not surprising that disregarding the role played by tradition necessarily leads to an excessive emphasis on the individual. Each person is believed capable of ascertaining truth unassisted either by individuals who possess authority or by the collected authority of tradition. This autonomous individual will be reluctant to commit to any particular place, for commitment entails a restriction of alternatives, and open alternatives are precisely what the autonomous individual most cherishes. At the same time, the notion of natural or even transcendent obligations necessarily constrains autonomous action, and constraint is despised by one who recognizes no binding authority, save individual will. Thus, radical individualism reduces the likelihood that a person will commit to any particular place or submit to any transcendent authority. If these are necessary components for any robust account of community, radical individualism, quite obviously, is inadequate.

On a practical level, local problems are best addressed by the wisdom of those intimately familiar with and committed to the long-term prospects of a particular place. Such wisdom comes only through a reverence for the history of a particular place, a reverence born of knowledge, understanding, study, and ultimately, love. On the other hand, communities linked by nothing other than the desire for pleasure or security will tend toward cosmopolitan universalism, and cosmopolitan universalism is inimical to local communities, for it seeks to homogenize and regularize that which is by nature particular and idiosyncratic.

SKEPTICISM

The rise of modern secularism has given birth to an altered way of seeing ourselves and the world we inhabit. The decline in religious belief and the corresponding demise of the two cities of Augustine opened the door for the return of the politics of perfection. But, of course, no place is perfect. The result is an essential restlessness, in which people constantly seek that which can never be found. This restlessness represents the ideal of progress combined with practical futility. It makes settling in one place difficult, for a better place is always just over the horizon, just out of reach but tantalizingly close. Here's the irony: in the Augustinian scheme, the promise of a heavenly home made an earthly home possible, but with the denial of the heavenly home, an earthly home became illusive.

The very way humans conceived of the world changed in the wake of the Enlightenment and the secular impulse accompanying it. The medieval mind was, of course, shaped by its view of reality. All creation was connected in a great chain of being that extended from the highest creatures, the angels, down to the lowest, most insignificant atom. Humans, created "a little lower than the angels,"[7] had a distinct place in the order of creation. All things were arranged in a hierarchical fashion with the infinite and eternal God presiding over all. This vertical chain unified all reality under the authority of God, but it also provided a means by which all classes of things could be properly categorized as distinct from all other classes of entities. Thus, both unity and diversity were captured in this conception of reality. The hierarchical ordering provided a clear place for human beings in the order of being. Humans belong to the creation, and because they are the highest of the embodied creatures, they are also, according to this vision of reality, tasked with ruling the rest of the physical creation. Thus, humans had a clear place in the order of reality, and they had a clear responsibility that accompanied their privileged position.

With the collapse of the medieval world, the great chain of being slowly crumbled as well. The geocentric cosmology, which was so easy to reconcile with the great chain of being, was, in the wake of Copernicus, replaced with a heliocentric conception of the solar system. With the earth no longer at the physical center of reality, it became much more difficult to assert that humans were at the center of anything. The invention of the telescope brought into view a stunning array of stars and galaxies that overpowered the imagination with the vast extent of space. Earth, it seemed, was merely an insignificant planet orbiting an insignificant star on the fringes of an infinite space. The elegant hierarchical order represented by the great chain of being was replaced by a growing skepticism about the significance of human existence.

The links in the chain were sundered. The order of reality was lost to the imagination and the hierarchical arrangement was replaced by a flattened conception of reality. No longer did all parts of creation have their neatly assigned places in the created order. In the process, humans lost sight of their clearly delineated privileges as well as their responsibilities. Set adrift on the tides of a seemingly limitless universe, the sense of place that existed in the medieval world was exchanged for alienation and uncertainty. The longing for a place, understandably, remained intact, for the comfort afforded by the great chain of being was enormous. Yet the modern person, bereft of that ordered view of the world, finds himself seeking the kind of place that the earlier vision of the world provided. Modern restlessness is, at least in part, the product of a world in which the chain joining all things has been severed and each person is striving to find his own place without the structure of a hierarchically ordered creation. The disorientation was severe, the sense of loss real, and the resulting search frantic.

Skepticism about transcendent reality leads invariably to philosophical materialism, and philosophical materialism in our age has opened the door to the more general materialism of consumerism. After all, if we are merely pleasure-seeking creatures who cease to exist with the demise of our physical bodies, then our chief concern will be the enhancement of our personal pleasure, and to be sure, personal pleasure is greatly enhanced, if only temporarily, by the things money can secure. When members of a society make material gain their central concern, that society will embrace an ethic of mobility, for each person will be quite willing to relocate in pursuit of affluence. Thus, we see "communities" of transient individuals each committed primarily to the acquisition of material gain and the betterment of their immediate family members. Home tends to become merely a launching place for economic and hedonistic endeavors, and individuals tend to lose any abiding concern for the long-term future of the local community.

In such a setting, any notion of community membership, which evokes ideas of commitment and loving concern over a lifetime, is replaced by the much narrower concerns for personal affluence and individual pleasure. But skepticism not only undermines commitment to a geographic place, it also eliminates any idea of a heavenly home, which can serve to moderate and even redirect the sort of consumerist passions engendered by modern society. Thus, it seems that the same set of beliefs that create geographic homelessness also create a spiritual homelessness as well. Too many modern people find themselves without a place either in this world or the next.

A PLACE IN THE WORLD

Going hand in hand with the pathology of consumerism is the tendency toward centralization. Centralization of consciousness, of culture, and of political and economic power all serve to undermine local communities. As people orient themselves toward the centralized authority, their focus of attention and care is directed away from their local communities. Indeed, in an age of centralization, the local is equated with the provincial, the small, and the backward. In contrast, embracing the cosmopolitan is seen as a means to escape the strictures of the rustic and the static. To be a citizen of an empire is surely more glorious than being a citizen of a local community. Yet the very notion of a national community is stretching the idea of community beyond recognizable limits. There is no American community. There can never be. However, there can be many local communities within the nation.

A healthy local community comprises particular people inhabiting a particular place and sharing local customs, activities, and stories. In short, community members participate in a complex web of relations that are flavored by the particular history, geography, and culture of that place. When we describe a local community in those terms, it becomes clear how a massive national community is simply an impossible ideal. Even more fanciful is the notion of a world community. To be sure, because we share a common nature and many common needs and desires, we can empathize with and render aid to humans from radically different communities. But the cosmopolitan ideal that one can be a "citizen of the world" is only imaginable if we strip down the rich notion of community to mean something like "the brotherhood of man." The idea of universal brotherhood is appealing, and as far as it goes, it is true, but abstract brotherhood is not the same as living in a local community with men and women of flesh and blood. Local communities include, along with the images of pleasant hominess, the rude woman at the market, the town drunk, and the idiosyncratic recluse who lives at the end of the lane. Ivan Karamazov, in Fyodor Dostoevsky's *The Brothers Karamazov*, gets at this distinction when he declares that he loves humanity but hates human beings. Oddly enough, it may be easier to love the world than to love our neighbor. Ultimately, when love for a particular place and the people inhabiting that place is lost, community is lost as well. Centralization shifts the focus of our love away from the local and toward the abstract and universal. In the process, love itself becomes an abstraction.

The loss of commitment to a particular place results in the restless mobility that characterizes so much of American life. And even when particular individuals stay put in one place, the very possibility of easy mobility makes it possible for people to inhabit the world of the potential future rather than the concrete present: "I must keep my options open" means, in practice, refraining from committing to any particular place. Of course, potential communities are far more desirable than actual ones. We can always imagine a place better than our present one. Holding out for the perfect situation is, in some ways, easier than getting involved in the conflicts and irritants that inevitably exist in reality. But although the temptation to stay at arm's length, to inhabit a place with ironic detachment, is alluring, the implications for a robust and healthy local community are grave. Indeed, if a critical mass of such people occupy a certain place, they are merely a collection of individuals rather than a community. They are mere residents and not stewards. In such a situation, local stories and traditions that are kept alive only in the telling and the practice are lost.

But why is this necessarily bad? There are plenty of traditions that we are well to be rid of; there are plenty of stories not worth retelling. But when local communities are lost, stories and traditions, both good and bad are lost, and while we need not lament the loss of the bad, losing the good stories and traditions is a tragedy. These are the very things that provide context and meaning to our social lives. They provide us with guidelines for acting together. They are the source of manners and customs that make life in a community possible. With the loss of common traditions and shared stories, we lose the cues that help us navigate a particular local world.

The loss of intact communities creates a context in which the notions of the noble and the shameful are lost. Noble ideals have throughout the centuries motivated great deeds. Individuals have risen above the ordinary when confronted with the possibility of acting in a way that will be recognized as noble. But the very idea of a noble act presupposes a social context in which the noble can be recognized and praised. If a common moral life, which is transmitted through traditions and stories, is lost, so too is the possibility of a noble act—or at least one that will be recognized. In the same way, the possibility of shame is lost as well. Shame or the threat of shame, though it can be abused, does play an important social role. If a person belongs to a local community and is committed to it, then the possibility of shame will dissuade him or her from certain acts deemed shameful by the community. With the fragmentation of communities, is it any wonder that noble acts seem rare and fear of shame loses its power to motivate?

A loss of local community makes anonymity more possible, and anonymity is not good for individuals or for a society. Anonymity makes accountability difficult. And again, while the sort of accountability that a local community facilitates can be abused—as when small town gossip infringes on the privacy of neighbors—a loss of any accountability, except perhaps to the police, is a disaster to a community. Local communities enforce local standards through censure and shame but also by the repetition of stories that teach community standards to child and newcomer alike.

Finally, local communities are of a scale that complements human beings. A nationalized, centralized system is not. In local communities, individuals can easily gain access to those in power to petition them, congratulate them, cuss them, or offer advice. Representatives know their constituents and are accountable to them in a way that is impossible when constituencies are numerous beyond knowing. Today when one attempts to engage or oppose a federal bureau, the very magnitude of the bureaucracy is daunting. When one is repeatedly put on hold or transferred from one department to another, the sense of helplessness is palpable. Who hasn't labored over the arcane and seemingly endless regulations of the Internal Revenue Service only to finally—and with no little fear and trembling—sign the forms and slip them in the mail hoping that your best guesses were right? Who hasn't felt impotent at the Kafkaesque fortress of bureaus and agencies erected by our national government? The individual is easily disoriented by the sheer mass of the modern centralized state. By virtue of its size and extent, the state comes to replace the local community in our imagination as it promises to meet our every need.

In the end, where commitment is feared and deracination is seen as a virtue, living contentedly in one place is a countercultural act. It is an act born of gratitude, for it recognizes the subtle and simple gifts native to a place, many of which are visible only to those who love the place and are committed to its future. Grateful creatures, living together through time, will necessarily be mindful, perhaps only intuitively, of the kind of scale that is necessary to both enjoy the gifts inherent in a place and care for those gifts in a way that preserves them. Contentment is the offspring of humility, for humility seeks not to dominate or exploit but to steward good things well. The practical result is lives constituted by propriety, in which the human world of artifacts and relationships complements the geography, flora, and fauna of the natural world. Lives constituted by propriety are lives well lived in the context of a particular place, lives in which harmony, not dissonance, is evident in the wisdom and affection that characterize the actions of individuals.

Of course, living well in a place is not idyllic, for the world is an imperfect place filled with imperfect people. Even when we strive for harmony with others and with the natural world, we will often fail. Ignorance, conflicts of will, differing notions of how to attain good ends—all of these will intrude into human relations. It is, though, the difficult times that test one's commitment.

Much has been written about community in recent years, and the decline of community is a theme taken up today by many, both on the right and the left. The solitary bowler, a memorable image from Robert Putman's book *Bowling Alone*, gives voice to the intuition that despite the many advantages of the modern world, something has been lost. The situation is made more complex by the fact that the word "community" has been so overused as to approach meaninglessness.

There is, indeed, something in the word "community" that touches on a deep and abiding human need. Consider the way real-estate developers advertise their wares. They regularly employ words that invoke a sense of belonging, security, peace, and happiness, a place to enjoy neighbors often in the context of a Disney-fied version of nature: "Falling Waters: A Real Community" or "Come Home to Rolling Acres" or "Experience the Good Life: Spring Meadows." Rarely do such developments actually contain a waterfall (except for the artificial falls tumbling over the jumble of rocks at the gated entrance) or a meadow, much less the wildlife that such words evoke. But the fact that these words are successfully employed to market homes indicates an important fact: humans long for a community to which they can belong.

Wendell Berry understands the intimate connection between rootedness and a properly framed human life. Unlike those who use the term "community" rather loosely to refer to anything from a collection of houses situated in the same suburban development to the grossly abstract notion of a global community, Berry argues that a meaningful community must include the ideas of rootedness and human scale. "By community, I mean the commonwealth and common interests, commonly understood, of people living together in a place and wishing to continue to do so. To put it another way, community is a locally understood interdependence of local people, local culture, local economy, and local nature."[8] Berry identifies the corrosion of flourishing communities as the result of an excessive individualism that places rights ahead of responsibilities and economic gain ahead of meaningful and durable relationships—relationships with neighbors, with local customs and practices, and with the land itself. As he puts it, "If the word community is to mean or amount to anything, it must refer to a place (in its natural integrity) and its people. It must refer to a placed people. . . . The modern industrial urban centers are 'pluralistic' because they are full of refugees from destroyed communities, destroyed community economies, disintegrated local cultures, and ruined local ecosystems."[9] Ultimately, according to Berry, "a plurality of communities would require not egalitarianism and tolerance but knowledge, an understanding of the necessity of local differences, and respect. Respect, I think, always implies imagination—the ability to see one another, across our inevitable differences, as living souls."[10] For Berry, community requires commitment to a particular place and the people, culture, economy, and ecology of that place. At the same time this localism ultimately requires that people recognize other persons, whether members of one's community or not, as living souls, biological creatures but much more: creatures who exist as members of both a physical world and the world of spirit, creatures capable of labor, of love, and ultimately of worship.

Berry's teacher, the novelist and essayist, Wallace Stegner, wrote extensively about the American West and the kinds of men and women who settled it. He describes two distinct personality types: boomers and stickers. Boomers are always on the lookout for the fast buck, for the next big thing. They sit loosely, always ready to light out for the latest gold rush or land rush that promises wealth, excitement, and success. Boomers are transients who never commit to a place, for they are convinced that there is always some other place that is superior, one that will finally satisfy the restless longing that constantly agitates their minds. In a real sense, a boomer can be a boomer even if he or she never gets the gumption to move, for failing to commit to a place and see oneself as a part of the ongoing story of a place characterizes the mind of the boomer.

Stickers, in contrast, stick. To be sure, the American West—and America as a whole for that matter—was settled by people who left their homes and went out seeking a new place. Some were motivated by a desire for land; some sought religious freedom; some were on the run from the law. Nevertheless, from among this variegated band, many chose to settle down, build homes, raise kids and crops, start businesses, and plan for the future. In imagining themselves in their places for the long haul, they learned to think in longer terms than the boomers. Rather than attempt to extract quick profits, stickers think of passing on a legacy of care to their children and grandchildren. According to Stegner, a recognizable indigenous culture emerged in the West, and this was "the product not of the boomers but of the stickers, not of those who pillage and run but of those who settle, and love the life they have made and the place they have made it in."[11]

In 1895, Booker T. Washington gave what came to be known as the Atlanta compromise speech before the Cotton States and International Exposition in Atlanta. Washington expressed his hope that through hard work and honest living, former slaves would be accommodated into the tapestry of Southern culture. They could, he argued, make a place for themselves and live lives of satisfaction and propriety if they only committed to the places they inhabited. Washington made his point with a story:

> A ship lost at sea for many days suddenly sighted a friendly vessel. From the mast of the unfortunate vessel was seen a signal: "Water, water. We die of thirst." The answer from the friendly vessel at once came back: "Cast down your bucket where you are." A second time, the signal, "Water, send us water!" went up from the distressed vessel. And was answered: "Cast down your bucket where you are." A third and fourth signal for water was answered: "Cast down your bucket where you are." The captain of the distressed vessel, at last heeding the injunction, cast down his bucket and it came up full of fresh, sparkling water from the mouth of the Amazon River.[12]

Many of us have left our homes. Some never had one. For most, returning home is not a viable or even a desirable option. Nevertheless, we can heed Washington's admonition and cast our bucket down where we are. We can commit to making our places our homes. While it may appear that brackish water is swirling all around, we may be surprised to find hidden springs, available only in the wake of a commitment, that nourish us in that place. Commitment then takes the form of membership, and membership in turn becomes joint ownership in a living tradition embodied in a community that transcends any one person even as all its members, living and dead, sustain it by their fidelity and loving care.

PART II.
THE CONSEQUENCES

5

Politics: The Art of Freedom

Habits form in freedom that may one day become fatal
to that freedom.

Alexis de Tocqueville, *Democracy in America*

Many Americans seem to be obsessed with national politics. Presidential campaigns that last more than two years, and the media frenzy that reaches a fevered pitch in the final weeks, serve to encourage (or reflect) this obsession. We find ourselves inundated with daily public opinion polls, talking heads (that often shout), and campaign ads exaggerating both the virtues and vices of the candidates. Many people find themselves caught up in the excitement. They read the papers, watch cable television, surf the Internet, and listen to talk radio. And while the intensity might diminish somewhat in the wake of a presidential election, there is always another campaign, another issue, another scandal that demands our attention. An obsession with politics must surely color the way one sees the world at large. If a person spends significant numbers of hours each day consuming political news, that person will tend, not surprisingly, to see the world in political terms.

At the same time, judged by voting behavior and civic awareness studies, there is another part of our society that is completely detached from politics. They have little or no knowledge of our political system and seem not to care. Studies have shown that this is increasingly the case even among college graduates. Many who pay little attention to politics are, nevertheless, dependent in some way or another on government assistance. Members of the so-called permanent underclass tend to be simultaneously detached from politics and public policy even as they participate in the system by virtue of their needs. Thus, at least some portion of both the politically apathetic and the politically obsessed, for different reasons, breathe life into the political system. Because the focus of energy and interest is directed toward national politics, these very different groups of people have in common something quite striking: they both facilitate the centralization of our attention and thereby aid in the centralization of political power.

Many citizens would insist that politics is somehow important. But just how important is politics? And why? Given the concepts we explored in the first half of this book, how should we approach politics? Can notions such as our creatureliness, gratitude, scale, and place contribute to a more healthy approach to politics than what we see today? How, for example, could a renewed sense of gratitude, or the lack thereof, affect our understanding of politics? Might we engage the political sphere differently if we consistently recognized ourselves as creatures? Might a habit of putting questions of scale to political problems change the way we act? Could a renewed commitment to a particular place alter the way we see the world of politics? The answer to these questions, I will suggest, is an emphatic "yes." Before we apply these concepts to our political situation, though, it is necessary to lay some groundwork.

In 1831, a twenty-five-year-old Frenchman, unhappy with the political situation in his country, managed to receive the permission of his country to visit America and report on its penal system. Nevertheless, Alexis de Tocqueville had a much larger project in mind: to understand the very essence of democracy as it existed in America. The report on democracy (he also reported on the penal system) that resulted from this nine-month field trip in America is his justly celebrated *Democracy in America*, by all accounts one of the best books ever written on democracy and surely one of the finest books ever written on America. His book is both descriptive and prescriptive: he describes democracy as he found it in the United States, yet he goes beyond the particulars of the American system to make general observations about the nature of democracy itself. Tocqueville was convinced that the democratic movement was an irresistible fact of history, but he also recognized that the very strengths of democracy could, if not held in check, undermine the liberty that democracy seeks to champion. Thus, the great efforts he makes in describing democracy serve as a framework by which he explores ways to mitigate the potential dangers inherent in it. What follows is a description of the democratic mind that is informed by Tocqueville's account, but not confined to it. We do well to listen carefully to Tocqueville, for he is as relevant in the twenty-first century as he was in the nineteenth.

RESTLESS AMBITION

Americans, Tocqueville observed, are a restless people. Of course, America is a country of immigrants, people who have left their homelands to seek their freedom or fortunes in a strange place. Yet, even immigrants can settle, make a home, and commit themselves to forging a life in their new places. While this is no doubt exactly what many immigrants to America did, there has always been a powerful opposing current. Americans, Tocqueville observed, tend to favor movement, and this movement is accompanied by a sort of anxiety. This incessant motion was not limited to a few intrepid adventurers. Tocqueville, perhaps with some exaggeration, describes an entire society on the move and obsessed with obtaining wealth and doing it as quickly as possible. While he was ultimately less than sanguine about the habits of mind and heart that this restless energy created, Tocqueville recognized the attraction. Americans were clearly prosperous, and this prosperity seemed to be tied closely with the restless motion that characterized American life.

American westward expansion certainly underscored Tocqueville's point. This steady movement toward the west was possible because of the unique geography of America. In Europe, the notion of a frontier had faded. People tended to remain settled because there was no place for them to go. Americans, on the other hand, found themselves on the edge of a vast and empty continent (the Native Americans—immigrants themselves—were usually left out of consideration), the limits of which were difficult to imagine. These two elements—a desire for economic prosperity and apparently limitless land—helped to ensure that a large percentage of the population kept on the move, pushing continually into lands that were waiting to be claimed and put to profitable use.

On one level, American restlessness seems to be the product of a desire for prosperity. Such a claim leads only to a more fundamental question: what kind of a people willingly and even anxiously abandon their homes in pursuit of affluence? Again, such an exchange is certainly not an unusual choice for humans to make, but Tocqueville was struck by the sheer number of Americans he saw embracing the promise of profit over the pleasures and security of home. This movement, perhaps, would have been far less remarkable had the immigrants been starving or oppressed. But while there were, to be sure, many poor people seeking fortunes in the west, the impulse was not limited to those in desperate straits. The scope of this restlessness is significant, for it indicates a way of thinking and acting in the world that was shared by many Americans of a variety of backgrounds and social conditions. What antecedents could conspire to create such a pervasive impulse? Tocqueville finds the answer in the changing social conditions that were sweeping the Western world in his day: in short, equality.

Tocqueville saw himself on the brink of a new historic epoch in which traditional aristocratic social forms were dissolving and equality of conditions prevailed. Where the Old World was held together by rigid social conventions that prevented—or at least greatly impaired—both social and geographic movement, equality of conditions destroyed the social structures of the aristocratic world. People were no longer inexorably constrained by the social conditions into which they were born.

This change, Tocqueville argues, represents nothing less than a democratic revolution, a revolution that has been building for centuries. Inventions such as firearms, the printing press, and postal services all served to make power and information available to all, breaking the monopoly previously held by the aristocratic classes. The Crusades and the English wars divided lands previously held by only a few. The Protestant Reformation advanced the idea that all men are equal before God and thus undermined the hierarchical institution of the Catholic Church. Ultimately, this movement toward equality was, in Tocqueville's assessment, an act of God. Thus, to resist the spread of democracy and the equality that necessarily accompanies it was to pit oneself against providence itself.

While the spread of equality (at least in the West) appeared to be fated, Tocqueville was not fatalistic. He argues that democracy can manifest itself in one of two ways. The first is democratic freedom. The second is a form of government in which equality is present but the citizens are debased and isolated, members of a vast, paternalistic state. Tocqueville calls this democratic tyranny. Because the democratic revolution will clear the way for one of these two conditions, Tocqueville recognizes the need for social and political leaders to "educate democracy." *Democracy in America* is a handbook for leaders as well as concerned citizens. It points out the various pitfalls in the road to democratic freedom and explains how equality tends naturally toward democratic tyranny. Tocqueville, however, believes democratic tyranny can be resisted, but not without both effort and commitment informed by a clear understanding of the new situation facing the West. He writes his book to help provide the necessary understanding.

To grasp how the movement toward equality produces the anxious restlessness Tocqueville witnessed in the American people, it is necessary to consider several intermediate steps. As we will see, equality tends to isolate individuals both from the natural constraints of social position as well as from the traditions handed down from the past. But isolation, and the individualism that necessarily accompanies it, tends to induce skepticism, and skepticism leads to philosophical materialism. A society of materialists will tend to view pleasure as the highest good. People released from the bonds of social expectation and committed to the pursuit of pleasure as their chief end will readily leave their homes in pursuit of that for which they most long. And because human longings are never adequately satisfied by material wealth, these rootless skeptics will be filled with an anxiety that is a direct result of their material success and spiritual failure. A society of such individuals will develop habits that are not easily shaken. Tocqueville believes that much of the material success of Americans is the result of this restlessness combined with an empty continent full of promise.

We do well to ask, though, what becomes of the habitual motion when the frontiers are gone. The apparently limitless land to the west made possible a movement that could, at least in theory, produce settlers, people who sought land on which to forge a life characterized by permanence and commitment. But with the frontiers gone, the impulse remains. Thus, today we continue to move but have no obvious place to go. Because settling on an unoccupied piece of land is no longer a viable option, the democratic person too often pursues affluence apart from any commitment to a particular place. Such a pursuit represents a placeless existence in service of an abstract idea.

EQUALITY AND INDIVIDUALISM

Many of the most important events of the last millennium have conspired to move society toward equality. Theologically, in the sixteenth century the Protestant Reformation served to break down the hierarchical structure of the church. No longer were priests needed to serve as mediators between God and man. Individuals could now approach the divine quite apart from any ecclesiastical structure. Rather than a hierarchy that induced individuals to see themselves as parts of a larger whole, and in which the very hierarchy tutored minds toward community as well as toward the verticality of transcendence, the world in the wake of the Protestant Reformation was dramatically flattened. Each individual stood naked and alone before God and from that posture was responsible for working out his own individual salvation with fear and trembling. In the most radical versions of Protestantism—rejected even by most Protestants—the church faded into the background, and the individual emerged as a priest without hierarchy, a priest with a congregation of onc.

Philosophically, this same flattening occurred in the seventeenth century. This is most vividly evidenced in the antischolastic reaction of figures such as René Descartes and Francis Bacon. They led the charge in attempting to sever philosophy and natural science from dependence on the traditions and strictures of the past. Both believed that it was possible, and indeed desirable, for individuals to come to absolutely certain conclusions independent of any authority. As a result, the role of history as an invaluable resource necessary for properly understanding the world was diminished. In an attempt to throw off the shackles of medieval philosophy—a synthesis of Aristotlelian and Christian thought—both Bacon and Descartes sought to begin anew, unencumbered by the burden of the past. The individual was seen as sufficient in himself; thus, the authority of both experts and tradition was undermined. In this orgy of epistemological egalitarianism, the community was no longer seen as essential. If each man is sufficient in himself, then the community becomes purely optional. If individuals are no longer understood to be parts of a community in a fundamental sense—a sense that makes possible a fully human life—then individuals are clearly free to wander in search of a community that suits them or perhaps eschew community all together.

Accompanying this theological and philosophical flattening was a collapse of hierarchical social structures. Like the hierarchical structure of the Catholic Church, the aristocratic arrangement of society bound individuals together in a vertically ordered community. As a result, people were constantly reminded, by the very structure of society, that they were parts of a larger whole. They were integral members of a particular social class. They were socially rooted. Because social mobility was virtually unthinkable, the aspiration to move and change one's status was rarely strong. One understood one's place, both geographically—because generations on the same piece of land produce intimacy with that place—and socially—for one was mindful of one's ancestors, contemporaries, and descendents. The individual, in such a society, was rooted to a place both spatially and temporally. This social arrangement served to tutor the minds of its members in a manner that constantly reminded them that a line of authority existed, and people were expected to understand their place in that line and the obligations and privileges accompanying it. Such a social order, while clearly fraught with perils and potential abuses, did nevertheless suggest an ordering of reality that was best reflected in traditional theism.

With the dissolution of the aristocracy and both the philosophical egalitarianism of Bacon and Descartes and the theological egalitarianism of Protestantism, individuals could now envision themselves as separate from all other individuals, equally capable of being whatever they set their minds to be. No longer constrained by dependence on the past (either philosophically or socially), individuals could now view themselves and their ideas as equal with all others. This egalitarian individualism created the context out of which modern democracies grew. But to the extent that equality forces people to rely only on their own resources, they are induced (or perhaps seduced) to imagine that their own ideas and resources are sufficient. As Tocqueville puts it, "Aristocracy links everybody, from peasant to king, in one long chain. Democracy breaks the chain and frees each link."[1] With the breakdown of the ties that previously bound individuals to one another, people tended to forget about the communities to which they belonged. They became absorbed only with their own narrow interests and concerns.

Tocqueville calls this condition individualism. In a world characterized by individualism, people tend not to concern themselves with their community. Instead, they focus on the narrow circle of their own immediate interests, and in so doing, their isolation is constantly reinforced by their circumstances. Thus, equality tends to breed individualism, and individualism tends to blind people to the importance of place, to the people, history, and customs of a particular locale. As focus is turned inward to the self, the community tends to fade into the background and personal pleasure and material success takes center stage.

EQUALITY AND SKEPTICISM

Individualism, though, is not the only consequence of equality. A heightened sense of freedom also accompanies the breakdown of hierarchies, for when the constraints that these structures provided were removed, individuals found themselves not only isolated but free to act. Limited only by imagination, individuals could now fancy themselves free to create worlds of their own choosing. Unconstrained by social conditions, they could pursue wealth, land, power, success, and fame. Because all people were now (at least in theory) on an equal footing, each could justly imagine himself achieving successes that in an aristocratic world, no one would dare to have dreamed. Tocqueville argues that this newfound spirit of freedom was tempered in the American context by the countervailing spirit of religion, specifically, Christianity. Thus, while the spirit of freedom tended to cast everything into disarray and tempt individuals to question virtually all that was conventionally accepted as true, the spirit of religion set limits on the extent of the questioning.

We can here see the interplay between the spirit of freedom and the spirit of religion. The spirit of freedom seeks to throw open all questions that have, in an aristocratic age, been deemed settled. But this frenzy of questioning pulls up short at the gates of religion and goes no further. The spirit of religion stands guard, if you will, flaming sword in hand, and although the spirit of freedom has produced a riot, the spirit of religion ensures that the rioting occurs only within certain parameters. Confined to the mundane world, the questioning is often harmless (and at times even beneficial). Tocqueville is convinced that the spirit of religion harnesses the energies produced by the spirit of freedom and channels them to benign ends. One must wonder, though, what would become of the spirit of freedom if the spirit of religion put down her sword. Or was disarmed. Ultimately, Tocqueville is not sanguine about the long-term prospects of the spirit of religion. Equality, it seems, tends to produce skeptics, and of course skeptics have no fear of angels with flaming swords, for the skeptic denies not only the effectiveness of the sword but the reality of the angel.

In the America Tocqueville visited, Christianity was widely accepted as true, even if the affirmation was unreflective for many. Because the Christian religion includes a substantial number of moral teachings, those moral principles were adopted by Americans in the same unreflective manner. They were accepted as truth, and people habitually arranged their lives in accordance with the truth of those moral principles. Thus, even though many were not wholly committed to all the doctrines of the churches, a critical mass of people was committed, and even those who were not tended to live according to the general moral principles rooted in the Christian faith.

As we have seen, though, equality tends to break down the very things that once linked people together. As individuals come to perceive themselves increasingly as isolated theologically, philosophically, and socially, they will of a necessity come to believe that their own mental faculties are sufficient in themselves.

They will tend to be dismissive of traditions and authorities that require an element of submission and trust. Such people will fancy that they can think thoughts never before thought and blaze new and unique ways for themselves. They will become suspicious of beliefs that have not been thoroughly vetted by their private rational faculties. At the same time, though, it is clearly not possible for each individual to refuse to believe anything based on authority. If individuals in an age of equality tend to doubt those beliefs that have not been subjected to the test of reason, and if it is impossible for any one individual to apply reason to every question, then it follows that the individual will necessarily be forced to trust in the authority of the mass of humankind. Thus emerges the reign of public opinion, and in our own day this is most evident in the ubiquitous public opinion poll, that scientific-sounding substitute for thought.

This reliance on the self and public opinion, ungrounded in any firm religious commitments, will tend to produce a certain kind of person. Individuals in such a climate will gravitate toward skepticism. That is, they will be suspicious of the claims made by religions that postulate a reality beyond the visible. But this philosophical materialism will eventually give rise to an attitude about life that ignores the possibility of transcendent meaning and focuses exclusively on the pleasures of this world. Thus, skepticism tends to produce materialism, and materialism tends to reduce the concerns of the individual to satisfying the desires of a purely mundane sort. That is, materialism of the philosophical sort tends to produce the materialism of the consumer. But if humans actually possess a spiritual element that is not fully satisfied by a life of acquisition and pleasure, then the skeptical consumer will live a restless existence, seeking to acquire more and varied possessions and experiences. Such a life will, in most cases, require a wholehearted effort to acquire the money necessary to secure the desired possessions and experiences. Thus, the skeptical consumer will tend to be obsessive and energetic about work.

But this new democratic person, equal, isolated, skeptical, and driven, will reduce the range of his or her concerns to those of physical pleasure and affluence. Thus, it would seem that the most powerful emotion of the democratic age is the passion for well-being. This passion will tend to strip away all political passions save a love of peace and a sense of security. On the one hand, in a world where a love of peace is the only political value, conflict will be avoided at all costs. When this sentiment matures, there will be no possibility of noble political causes for which an individual might willingly sacrifice, for noble causes are the stuff of ideals that extend far beyond the goals of peace and personal affluence. On the other hand, a demand for security can manifest itself in an avalanche of regulations intended to achieve perfect safety as well as military ventures abroad. The demand for both peace and a militarily achieved security will not conflict as long as the fighting takes place far away. In the America Tocqueville visited, the desire for wealth and the things wealth can secure were coupled with an apparently infinite source of natural resources just waiting to be exploited. Ambition met opportunity and the anxious American busily set off to make a fortune.

The promise of unlimited wealth served to produce a restlessness among the American people, but because the focus of their restless pursuit was physical pleasure, the soul too often went untended. However, when the soul is untended, it is not muted. When the pursuit of wealth and pleasure invariably fail to satisfy the longings of the soul, those longings will still be felt, although not comprehended. Materialists, who deny the existence of the soul, will nevertheless still possess a soul. Because they deny a part of reality, they will not be able to identify, much less remedy, the source of their longing. They will translate these soulful longings into the only idiom they know and assume the anxiety will cease when enough wealth and pleasure are secured. But the harder they labor, the less attention their souls receive. The anxiety intensifies, and the frantic movement continues. Thus, this restless movement is the product of a desire for wealth and pleasure, but when wealth and pleasure are pursued exclusively, the soul is ignored and the ignored soul produces a restless anxiety in the individual that spurs more restless motion that in turn distracts from the soul. The cycle is vicious.

The irony, of course, is that one must be still if one is to attend to the needs of the soul. One must not only be open to the possibility of a transcendent realm but must also be quiet enough to hear the intimations of the infinite within creation. One must be willing to pay close attention not only to the external world but also to the inner world of spirit. Alas, this is no easy feat in a society consumed with consuming and characterized by ingratitude and misdirected longings. Inattention to serious concerns is the natural state of individuals whose lives revolve around the pursuit of pleasure. In a world where voluntary inattention ossifies into habitual inattention, the needs of the soul will first be ignored, but eventually they will not be heard, at least not in such a way that they can be identified for what they actually are.

EQUALITY, UNIFORMITY, AND CENTRALIZATION

There is another problem brought about by the rise of equality: perfect equality can never be attained. In ages when equality is the highest social ideal, differences will offend. The irony is that as conditions approach equality, differences will offend more readily. When equality is the goal, uniformity becomes a necessity, but the desire for uniformity runs into the hard rock of reality, for in many ways, humans are not equal. In fact, the only uniform truth that seems naturally to emerge from an examination of various human beings is that people are wildly different. This, as might be imagined, will cause serious problems for those infected with the love of equality. First, if differences are thoroughly endemic to the human race, then attempts to effect absolute uniformity will be frustrated. This is not to say that many differences cannot be eliminated. As we have seen, theological, philosophical, and social changes have all served to bring individuals more nearly to a state of perfect equality. But if some differences are rooted in nature, then those very differences will be impossible fully to eradicate, and this will create a heightened sensitivity to any difference whatsoever. When an insatiable desire encounters a situation that precludes the satisfaction of that desire, the emotional toll will be high, and vast energy will be expended to alleviate the incongruity.

We see here two sources of dissatisfaction brought about by the historic movement toward equality. First, skepticism undermines any belief in a transcendent realm, and with that incredulity comes a shift in focus from the transcendent to the immanent, from the immaterial to the material. This shift gives rise to a hedonistic consumerism in which the needs of the soul are routinely ignored. Because those needs do not cease, people who deny the reality of the soul continue to long for something that their philosophy simply cannot countenance. The second source of dissatisfaction is rooted in the sheer impossibility of perfectly achieving equality. If equality is the social ideal to which an individual or a society is committed, the individual and society will suffer a continual sense of failure. The first source of dissatisfaction breeds, as we saw, a restless ambition to achieve financial success that leads to personal pleasure and peace. A desire for peace leads to a desire for a centralized authority capable of securing that peace. This ultimately induces individuals to seek political centralization, for the only imaginable hope of achieving equality is through a centralized state capable of securing equality of conditions for all members of society.

Thus, equality leads to a desire for uniformity, and uniformity requires centralization. The scope of centralization, of course, is limited by practicalities. Geographical distances as well as cultural and national boundaries have traditionally provided limits to centralizing impulses. But as technology makes these barriers less formidable; as the globalization of the marketplace makes people increasingly aware of each other; and as Western culture, especially in the form of entertainment, is exported to a world hungry for American pop culture, the potential scope of centralization will increase. As cultural barriers are broken, the possibility of uniformity increases, and this uniformity has led to a homogenization of culture with pop culture as one of the main ingredients. This sort of cosmopolitanism is one in which local differences are not appreciated but despised or at least denigrated as the benighted practices of unenlightened people. Thus, economic and cultural homogenization make political centralization across traditional boundaries increasingly possible.

This is not to suggest that all people directly favor centralization. But if equality is the highest social ideal and if centralization is perceived to be the most effective means of achieving equality, then centralization will be embraced as the best means to a cherished end. At the same time, the state will be all too willing to take up the very same cause, for by embracing uniformity and the centralization it requires, the state gains power. For different reasons, then, both individuals and the state will cherish uniformity: the first out of love of equality, the second out of love of power.

Of course, Americans today still have a passionate love for equality, but to a significant degree, they have lost any suspicion of power per se. Conservatives once decried the centralization of political power even as they embraced unfettered economic power; liberals once decried the centralization of economic power even as they appealed to the state to help limit it. Both seem blind to the danger of consolidated power itself. According to Tocqueville, "democratic peoples often hate those in whose hands the central power is vested, but they always love that power itself."[2]

Even though democratic people tend to love the power of the state, they are not necessarily inclined toward the complete centralization of the state. One impetus for centralization, however, is the isolation that equality tends to produce. When individuals are isolated, they are weak and quite powerless against the whole. If they seek to remain in their isolation and at the same time achieve the political ends they desire, they must enlist the power of the state in service of their private goals. Thus, although centralization is not embraced as a general principle, citizens, perhaps unwittingly, help to increase the power of the state, for they invariably favor state power when their special interests are at issue. In light of this dynamic, Tocqueville argues that it is merely a matter of time before a democratic society finds itself ruled by a centralized government.

War is perhaps the most effective means of centralizing power. History bears this out, and it is intuitively easy to grasp. War, or the threat thereof, forces the state to mobilize its resources to meet the enemy. The efficient mobilization of resources is best realized when the central command is strengthened. There cannot be competing centers of power when a war is being waged. The twentieth century saw more war than peace, and even in those few moments when the dogs of war were not tearing each other to bits, a cold war and an arms race provided a compelling justification for granting increased powers to the federal government. Furthermore, the prevalent language of war in political discussions has done much to facilitate the centralization of power, not to mention the centralization of thought. In the past forty years we have waged wars on poverty, drugs, and illiteracy, and of course, we have the culture wars. The rhetoric of war, and the attendant language of crises, is a powerful means of political persuasion and empowerment. After all, if those in power can convince voters that a crisis—one that threatens their way of life—is at hand, the machinery of state power can be invoked to avoid catastrophe. Thus, while sometimes necessary, war is the tyrant's best friend.

Although the fall of the Soviet Union in 1989 provided a brief respite from the fear of communist expansion, 9/11 inaugurated a new age: a war on terror. This war, according to Vice President Dick Cheney, could last for a century. Shortly after the attacks, President George W. Bush suggested that the goal of his administration was to rid the world of evildoers. Such rhetoric should have made every right-thinking American shudder. A war against evil is an endless war, and an endless war is ideally suited to the consolidation of power, even if the men and women presiding over it do not intend that inauspicious outcome.

In addition to a love of power, there is another reason the state will prefer centralization: uniformity is easier to manage. Local particularities make governing difficult. They require that officials be familiar with local customs and practices, and such familiarity is undesired for two reasons. First, it takes time and effort to learn about local communities. Governing well requires willingness to vary laws, or at least vary the interpretation of particular laws, to accommodate local differences. But the larger and more centralized a state becomes, the more difficult it will be to govern while respecting local variations. Thus, the centralized state will invariably favor uniformity, for "uniformity saves it the trouble of inquiring into infinite details, which would be necessary if the rules were made to suit men instead of subjecting all men indiscriminately to the same rule."[3] The problem here is one of propriety. To the extent that people are unequal, local communities will be unequal as well. If local communities are different from one another, a central authority imposing a uniform rule across the board will inevitably fail to govern in a way that is best for local communities taken individually. Second, familiarity with local customs and practices is undesired because the cosmopolitan ideal has been accepted as true. Cosmopolitans will have a natural aversion to the local, for they see the entire nation—if not the entire world—as their community, and they have been trained to believe that anything less than the whole is an undesirable provincialism.

This cosmopolitan ideal is reinforced by the educational structure. Tocqueville notes that in most Western countries, education has been taken over by the state. Of course, because the state tends to be passionately attached to the idea of uniformity, a state educational establishment will present uniformity as an important virtue. The state's interests are clear. If the citizens cherish uniformity, they will tolerate and even embrace centralization. Thus, to the extent that the state seeks to expand and consolidate its power, it will seek to inculcate its citizens with a love of uniformity. This is not a difficult task, for democratic citizens already have a love of equality, and the connection to uniformity is not a difficult one to make. On the subject of state education, Tocqueville predicts that the state will increasingly insert itself into the education of children as "it takes the responsibility for forming the feelings and shaping the ideas of each generation. Uniformity prevails in schoolwork as in everything else; diversity, as well as freedom, is daily vanishing."[4] It is difficult not to recognize the relevance of Tocqueville's words today. From Head Start programs to No Child Left Behind, the federal government—in the name of educational success—has insinuated itself into all aspects of the educational process.

When Tocqueville laments the loss of diversity produced by an affection for uniformity, one might be tempted to suggest that he is wrong. After all, diversity has in recent years become almost a fetish in our educational system. Tocqueville, however, would look askance on what passes for diversity in our time. Diversity for Tocqueville is not the accidental variations of ethnic origin or gender or sexual orientation. He laments the diminishment of authentic diversity, diversity that is the product of free and creative minds rooted in local communities with all their respective strengths and idiosyncrasies. To the extent that state educational systems seek to inculcate a uniform cosmopolitanism, the diversity of locality will be eroded. It is no stretch to imagine that Tocqueville might be an enthusiastic supporter of private education as well as the more recent surge in homeschooling.

Ultimately, the cosmopolitan ideal destroys the possibility of place, for when home is everywhere, home is nowhere. Uniformity destroys the local and particular and replaces it with a bland veneer of commonality devoid of any unique attributes that make it lovely. The natural human affection for a particular place is transposed into an ideal of universality that simply cannot sustain a free people. At the same time, as we have seen, skepticism undermines the possibility of belief in the transcendent. But humans are fundamentally religious, and when the possibility of a transcendent God is denied, something will fill the void. The centralized state does just that. It aspires to "unity," "ubiquity," and "omnipotence." Democratic citizens will come to "think of the government as a sole, simple, providential, and creative force."[5]

It is difficult to miss the godlike attributes Tocqueville uses to describe this political power. Whereas in an age of religious belief, God was vested with attributes of unity, simplicity, omnipresence, and omnipotence, these very attributes have, in a skeptical age, been transferred to the state. Thus, although transcendence has been rejected, religion remains, and the state naturally assumes the role once played by God.

Tocqueville argues that individuals in a democratic age will tend to be isolated and weak, and such people will be poorly equipped to resist the centralization of power. As we have seen, equality tends to produce that very centralization that these weak, isolated people find irresistible. Motivated only by a concern for security, citizens will be naturally disposed to cede power to the state if only it will keep them safe and provide for their needs. In such a state the people might continue with the basic outward trappings of self-government but such outward elements are illusory. Tocqueville imagines a situation in which "citizens" occasionally rouse themselves from their complacency only long enough to elect new masters. If an individual happens to object to the notion of a strong, centralized authority, he or she is too weak and isolated to halt the juggernaut. The result is a state that brooks no limits on the extent of its own power.

The effects of equality, however, will produce a sovereign altogether different from the classical tyrant who rules by fear and threat of force. The despotism of this new age will be "more widespread and milder; it would degrade men rather than torment them [for] the same equality which makes despotism easy tempers it." This kinder, gentler despotism will include not "tyrants, but rather school masters." Tocqueville imagines an "immense, protective power" superintending the lives of a docile citizenry. Although the state "is absolute, thoughtful of detail, orderly, provident, and gentle," it also provides "security, foresees and supplies their necessities, facilitates their pleasures, manages their principle concerns, directs their industry, makes rules for their testaments, and divides their inheritances." This vast bureaucratic state "covers the whole of social life with a network of petty, complicated rules" that "softens, bends, and guides" individual wills. The state does not destroy; rather, it "hinders, restrains, enervates, stifles, and stultifies so much that in the end each nation is no more than a flock of timid and hardworking animals with the government as its shepherd."[6]

Again, the godlike attributes of the state should not be ignored. Neither should the citizens' infantile dispositions. In a curious sort of symmetry, when God is rejected, humans are degraded and freedom is lost.

Neil Postman, in his brilliant book, *Amusing Ourselves to Death: Public Discourse in the Age of Show Business*, reminds his readers of two books, written in the early part of the twentieth century, that depict futuristic dystopian worlds from which freedom had vanished. George Orwell's *1984* describes a harsh world where force, power, and fear keep citizens in check. Aldous Huxley's *Brave New World* describes a society in which citizens are so bent on pursuing personal pleasure that they have lost the taste for any sort of meaningful liberty. According to Postman, citizens in *1984* "are controlled by inflicting pain. In *Brave New World*, they are controlled by inflicting pleasure. . . . Orwell feared that what we hate would ruin us. Huxley feared that what we love will ruin us."[7] Postman believed that history had proved Huxley's vision more accurate than Orwell's. Certainly with the fall of the Soviet Union, the specter of totalitarianism seems to have receded, and with the advent of economic globalization, we can now at least imagine the possibility of a peaceful world of consumers united in their pursuit of appetitive desire (assuming we can get the Islamists to stop their jihad and start shopping at Walmart).

A reader familiar with Huxley's *Brave New World* will be struck by the uncanny parallels with Tocqueville's "orderly, gentle, and peaceful slavery." In Huxley's book, the Resident World Controller for Western Europe, Mustapha Mond, explains the benefits of the brave new world: "You can't make tragedies without social instability. The world's stable now. People are happy; they get what they want, and they never want what they can't get. They're well off; they're safe . . . they're so conditioned that they practically can't help behaving as they ought to behave." He continues, "There isn't any need for civilized man to bear anything that's seriously unpleasant. And as for doing things—Ford forbid that he should get the idea into his head. It would upset the whole social order if men started doing things on their own."[8] This sentiment echoes a point Tocqueville made a century before Huxley: "A despot will lightly forgive his subjects for not loving him, provided they do not love one another. He does not ask them to help him guide the state; it is enough if they do not claim to manage it themselves."[9]

I am not suggesting that we are living in the equivalent of Huxley's brave new world. Neither was Postman. The question is one of trajectory. Does the world we have fashioned tend in the direction Tocqueville suggested? Surely we must admit that any social and political structure has both strengths as well as weaknesses. Is a democratic society susceptible to the kind of individualism and isolation that Tocqueville describes? If so, do those factors create a dynamic that fosters political centralization? It is difficult to deny that our political structures are far more centralized than originally envisioned by the framers of the Constitution or witnessed by Tocqueville. Does the centralization of our political system run counter to the idea of human scale? Does an affection for giantism cause us to forget local traditions and stories and to replace them with those manufactured in far off places? Does our restless mobility erode the strength of local communities? When we neglect religious forms that remind us of our creatureliness and embrace the religion of hedonism, will we long be able to resist the temptations of consumerism? If God, local communities, and even families are ignored or fragmented by the caustic elements in our society, will our gratitude have an outlet? I ask these questions merely to raise the possibility that Tocqueville was correct. Perhaps when the maladies of individualism, isolation, frantic mobility, secularism, and consumerism reach maturity, the social and political scene will, in many respects, appear as he predicted.

At this point, it might be tempting to despair. After all, if Tocqueville was right in the 1830s, we are today much farther down the path he described. Surely the opportunities to debase ourselves and our society are even more prevalent now. We have more disposable income. We can gratify our impulses more surely and immediately than ever. Political and economic centralization have occurred to a degree that would stun the Founders. Yet, human freedom is real. The choices people make over time can change the trajectory of a society. Tocqueville rejected the fatalism of historic determinism and so should we. To despair is to retreat into the hovel of cowardice, but to ignore the peril is to be blinded by hubris. To work diligently in the hope that human actions can effect change, however modest, is the noble lot of human beings. Wise and sustained effort is necessary. Impatiently demanding immediate change is as naive as believing that a permanent solution is available. In the realm of politics there are no permanent fixes. Human nature is unchanging, and a permanent fix would require a change in human nature.

But even though human nature is a constant, the vicissitudes of history play upon our particular social, cultural, and political moment in a unique way. While general patterns in history are distinguishable, the particulars of each moment are sui generis and require the prudence of leaders and citizens alike. In sum, humans are free and their choices matter. We can work together to build political structures that enhance human flourishing rather than stifle it. The economist F. A. Hayek put the matter nicely:

> We shall not rebuild civilization on the large scale. It is no accident that on the whole there was more beauty and decency to be found in the life of the small peoples, and that among the large ones there was more happiness and content in proportion as they had avoided the deadly blight of centralization. Least of all shall we preserve democracy or foster its growth if all the power and most of the important decisions rest with an organization far too big for the common man to survey or comprehend. Nowhere has democracy ever worked well without a great measure of local self-government, providing a school of political training for the people at large as much as for their future leaders.[10]

This is a long-term project, but unless we take serious and sustained steps in the direction of decentralization and human scale, the slow march toward centralization will continue apace.

FEDERALISM AND SUBSIDIARITY

If the descent toward political centralization and the individual enervation that accompanies it is to be resisted, resources native to our society must be marshaled in the effort. One of the most potent structural principles present in our constitution is federalism.

Tocqueville greatly admired the federal structure of the U.S. government. He observed that Americans of 1831 were only vaguely concerned with the national government, for it was distant geographically and politically. As a result, it did not directly impinge on the citizens' daily lives. The individual states, in contrast, were the focus of most political activity. The power of the states "is supported by memories, customs, local prejudices, and provincial and family selfishness; in a word, it is supported by all those things which make the instinct of patriotism so powerful in the hearts of men."[11]

The principle of federalism facilitated the relative independence of the individual states. Within the states, local communities enjoyed a degree of self-government that required a combination of both individual liberty and personal responsibility. Tocqueville was duly impressed, for he understood the connection between strong local communities and robust political freedom. Local communities are energetic and vibrant only when they are free to act in accordance with the habits and customs that have organically emerged from a history of living together. Thus, the strength of the local community depends on the extent to which it can resist homogenization and centralization. This is no easy task. The full force of the historic movement toward equality presses incessantly against the local community: the isolation that prevents local action; the skepticism that undercuts the sacred nature of particular places and ideas; the uniformity that seeks to eradicate differences; and the centralization that undermines and ultimately destroys local authorities. All of these powerful influences are admitted as friends because they are the offspring of the beloved ideal of equality. As a result, equality is pursued with the ardor of the lover pursuing the beloved, and in the process the local community is first ignored and then finally, when the beloved shows herself difficult to secure, sacrificed.

Federalism is a structural principle that creates space for the emergence of robust, energetic, and unique local communities that are necessary for the health of a free people. That is the positive argument. On the negative side, the Founders feared concentrated power, for consolidated power can cause far more mischief than power widely dispersed. Thus, federalism enhances human flourishing while helping to prevent oppression. In our day, the principle of federalism has been significantly weakened. The Tenth Amendment sounds almost quaint when read against the backdrop of our nationalized system: "The powers not delegated to the United States by the Constitution, nor prohibited by it to the States, are reserved to the States respectively, or to the people." If a balance of power between the national government and the particular states existed at the Founding, that precarious equilibrium has been upset. The causes are manifold and include an assortment of crises—the Civil War, the Great Depression, and two world wars to name a few—that invariably favored the centralization of power. Perhaps maintaining such a delicate balance was an impossible ideal in the first place. The individual states, it seems, were simply not capable, over the long haul, of resisting the power wielded by the national government. Balances of power are tricky, and once the momentum went decisively toward the national government (perhaps this was right from the beginning), the states were on the losing side.

Federalism creates layers of power as a way of preventing the consolidation of power in any one place. Consider, for example, the election of senators. Originally, senators were chosen by state legislatures. This was the federalist principle at work, for such an arrangement gave power directly to the states. The constituency of the senators was the state legislatures and not the people directly. To our modern sensibilities, this arrangement somehow seems wrong. Shouldn't the people be served directly? Shouldn't the people choose those who will represent them in Washington, D.C.? Such questions reveal the change. Senators were not originally intended to represent the people. They represented states as a whole. The House of Representatives was to be the body directly connected to the individual citizens. This kind of layering of authority was intended to strengthen the hands of the states. In 1913, the Seventeenth Amendment changed this. Senators were now to be elected directly by the people. This seemingly insignificant change was a serious blow to federalism, for it weakened the states as political entities. Today the federal structure of our system is much weaker than intended by the framers of our constitution.

With the centralization of power—and thus the centralization of political interest—the states are less likely to serve as effective keepers of the particular political and social customs and practices that they once did. Aside from a few southern states (and this is diminishing), there is little in the way of state pride that serves to bolster a sense of place. Of course, many people are loyal to state university football teams, but this is hardly a commitment to a state, especially given that a good number of players on such teams have been recruited from around the nation. This is not difficult to understand. When a population is on the move as much as the American population is, when we are saturated with news and entertainment that is not particular to a local community but a product of a "national culture," people will not grow attached to any one particular state, let alone one particular community. Commitments come to rest at two places: the narrow limits of self-interest in the service of prosperity and the centralized government that has consumed all the rest. Tocqueville's pervasive regulatory state neatly fills the void between the two that was once occupied by robust and variegated associations.

It should be no surprise, then, that those troubled by the expansion of federal power have sought avenues by which to weaken the federal government and at the same time strengthen the states. It is a well-worn political axiom that whoever controls the purse strings controls the power. In this light, some have suggested rethinking the tax code and, more radically, rescinding the Sixteenth Amendment, which made a federal income tax possible. Others have suggested the possibility of nullification whereby a state could simply refuse to enforce a federal law on the grounds that the law represents an encroachment into state authority that is not authorized by the Constitution. At the very least, such an action would force a serious discussion of federalism and the balance of power between the states and the federal government. That is a discussion worth having.

At this point, it might be helpful to turn to the concept of subsidiarity, for it offers something of a philosophical complement to federalism. The term "subsidiarity" (*subsidiarius*) was first used by Pope Pius XI in his encyclical *Quadradesimo Anno* (1931), but the concept is much older. Pius XI focused his attention on the problem of individualism. Sounding a Tocquevillian note, he argued that individualism arises with the destruction or attenuation of "that rich social life which was once highly developed through associations of various kinds." In such a circumstance "there remain virtually only individuals and the State." While this situation is surely harmful to individuals, Pius thought that the state is harmed as well, for "with a structure of social governance lost, and with the taking over of all the burdens which the wrecked associations once bore, the State has been overwhelmed and crushed by almost infinite tasks and duties."[12] Pius argued that a healthy society consists of "a graduated order" of secondary associations in accordance with the "principle of subsidiarity."[13] He framed the principle in moral (and ultimately metaphysical) terms:

Just as it is gravely wrong to take from individuals what they can accomplish by their own initiative and industry and give it to the community, so also it is an injustice and at the same time a grave evil and disturbance of right order to assign to a greater and higher association what lesser and subordinate organizations can do. For every social activity ought of its very nature to furnish help to the members of the body social and never destroy and absorb it.[14]

The state, then, has functions particular to it, such as defense. Additionally, it properly acts as a facilitator ensuring that the various secondary associations enjoy the freedom to operate according to their internal principles. Practically speaking, the principle of subsidiarity, if applied, would result in a flowering of secondary associations, each free to pursue its own ends limited by the stipulation that the ends sought do not run counter to the common good.

The principle of subsidiarity, as described in Catholic social thought, begins with a robust metaphysic, complete with an account of the common good rooted in a human nature oriented toward certain natural and supernatural ends. Such an account may provide an aura of intellectual satisfaction to a person inclined to accept that complex intellectual framework, but if such commitment is a necessary condition for accepting the practical principle of subsidiarity, then one should not be surprised if the principle is not widely embraced by a society characterized, as is ours, by religious pluralism as well as metaphysical skepticism, or at least metaphysical minimalism.

On one level, common sense alone points to the reasonableness of the principle of subsidiarity. Good parents, for instance, recognize the wisdom of letting their children do things for themselves. We would find it odd if the parents of a teenager regularly made his bed, tied his shoes, and combed his hair. In the same way, something would seem amiss if a city were required by law to get the approval of Washington before resurfacing a playground or building a road or erecting a monument. So too something would appear wrong if a local government attempted to dictate the daily menus of families within its jurisdiction. Or if a state government attempted to dictate the rules of chess to a chess club.

The principle of subsidiarity can be justified simply in terms of efficiency. It would be inefficient for the national government to intervene in all the business of a local government or a family. But, while the metaphysical position lays out firm principles that admit of a degree of autonomy for local jurisdictions, families, labor unions, etc., the principle of efficiency is fluid. As bureaucratic techniques improve, as surveillance capabilities become more refined, as means of communication become further developed, the encroachment of the central government into hitherto autonomous spheres becomes, in theory, increasingly efficient. If this is the case, then while efficiency might serve as a temporary means of justifying the principle of subsidiarity, it is not necessarily a permanent buffer against interference.

If some metaphysical account of human nature and human society is necessary for sustaining the independence of various spheres of authority, then it would appear that the issue of religion is back on the table. If the principle of federalism is complemented by the principle of subsidiarity, and if subsidiarity, in its robust sense, is rooted in a particular account of human nature and society that is, in turn, rooted in certain religious commitments, then, as distasteful as it might be for some, the problem of centralization appears to be linked to questions of religion. At the very least, it seems we must come to terms with our creatureliness and all that it entails.

As we have seen, Tocqueville argued that freedom and religious belief are, at least in the American context, inextricably joined. A common religious belief does in fact provide a common moral framework according to which a local community can organize its life together. A religion provides stories that serve as a common language of discourse and expectation. Religious traditions that emerge from those stories and develop in the context of a particular community can provide the cohesion a community requires. Feasts and fasts, sacraments and liturgy, creeds and confessions—these are the ligaments that can tie the members of a local community together. But, of course, religion represents a serious obstacle to one seeking to facilitate the centralization of power, for it competes with the state for the citizen's deepest loyalties. For this very reason, Jean-Jacques Rousseau argued for a "civil religion" that would bind citizens together with a religion rooted in the state. In this light, it is not surprising that the communist and fascist experiments of the twentieth century were accompanied by the attempted eradication of traditional religions and the creation of a cult of the state.

Tocqueville believed that religious faith served to draw a person out of the narrow confines of individualism. Individualism blinds a person to the fact that he or she is part of a complex network of duties and responsibilities rooted in debts of gratitude. It induces one to forget the past and neglect the future. Religious belief induces thought about the future, perhaps even about eternity. It serves to extend the horizons of one's concerns. It teaches duties to others and to God. It reminds one of the responsibilities that come from being human. For Tocqueville, religious belief was a necessary condition for the long-term success of democratic freedom and a powerful antidote to democratic servitude.

The revitalization of religious belief may be a necessary long-term solution to the problem of centralization, for belief in God precludes, in theory as well as in practice, the state assuming that role. When religious faith wanes, the vacuum is readily filled by the state. Ultimately, a thoroughgoing secularism may not be capable of sustaining a free republic. Legislative acts and judicial rulings that assume secularism as the default position unwittingly open the door to the leviathan. At the same time, officially sanctioned sectarianism is not plausible or desirable in a pluralistic society. The challenge, then, is to encourage religious belief without establishing a state church, privileging a particular viewpoint, or discriminating against unbelievers. This is one of the long-term challenges besetting the modern liberal state.

When we are tempted to take our freedom for granted, we are in serious danger, for freedom is only sustainable when carefully preserved and wisely guarded. When it is treated merely as an item to be consumed or as a right to be demanded, freedom is in jeopardy. For this reason, Tocqueville argues that the "art of freedom" must be cultivated through associational life. The habits and virtues developed through participation in voluntary associations provide a bulwark against the despotism that threatens any democratic society.

Ironically, though, freedom can foster the social and mental habits that undermine freedom itself. As we have already seen, individualism erodes the habit of association so vital to freedom. It can induce skepticism about transcendent reality. Furthermore, freedom can cultivate ingratitude. The affluence we enjoy is, in large part, a product of our freedom. Yet affluence can actually distract us from a proper sense of gratitude. In ages of marginal or even scanty provisions, it is perhaps easier to think in terms of gratitude, for nothing is taken for granted. In times of plenty, people might easily come to think that the world simply owes them the good things they possess, as if the entire sweep of history has been for the sole purpose of making them happy.

Affluence and the headlong pursuit thereof can induce in us the belief that consuming is our proper end and that freedom is the natural state of human affairs. Neither is true. A life given over to mere consumption is not befitting creatures capable of noble acts, and freedom is a tender plant that requires jealous guarding against its natural foes. If we are not attentive, the heady wine of freedom can induce us to forget or neglect the debts of gratitude that we owe. Then, like spoiled children, we demand the benefits of freedom while ignoring the fact that these fruits are the product of generations of struggle, sacrifice, and hard work. The debt goes unpaid, and the capital is recklessly spent. Ingratitude is marked by hubris, which denies the debt, and this always leads to inattention, irresponsibility, and abuse. In political terms, the hubris of ingratitude is a caustic acid that reduces all in its wake to the fetid condition of servitude, for a spoiled child needs nothing so much as a master.

If gratitude is the mother of stewardship, ingratitude strips away the ground necessary for an adequate account of stewardship and leaves behind nothing but the narrow concern for the self. Forgotten is our collective debt to God, the natural world, a particular place, and the past, all of which are necessary for an adequate understanding of our responsibilities. When duties are neglected, all that remains is the pursuit of pleasure or power. Neither pursuit sustains freedom. In fact, as these become the focus of our individual and corporate lives, freedom is correspondingly diminished. Freedom, to be durable, must exist within the context of responsibilities that limit the extent of freedom while heightening its meaning by orienting it according to ideals of self-sacrifice, love of community, and care for others.

If freedom produces conditions that induce ingratitude, and ingratitude represents a threat to freedom, then it seems we have reached the ironic position where we extol the virtues of freedom while discovering that the very thing we champion is a danger to itself. What can be done? Clearly, we must intentionally attempt to cultivate the disposition of gratitude. This will give birth to acts of stewardship, which are necessary to sustain an orderly and mature freedom. Freedom unconstrained by stewardship and not rooted in gratitude will invariably descend into license, and license will eventually lose itself in lawlessness. In such an atmosphere, the despot is nurtured even as freedom suffocates and slowly fades.

6

Economics: Private Property and the Virtues of Freedom

The great majority of economists is still pursuing the absurd idea of making their "science" as scientific and precise as physics, as if there were no qualitative difference between mindless atoms and men made in the image of God.

E. F. Schumacher

In 1944, two very different but related books were published. The first was F. A. Hayek's *The Road to Serfdom*. In a world that seemed to be succumbing to the socialist ideal, in which planned economies represented a glorious future, and where the turmoil of the market would be replaced by the peace of a directed economy, Hayek's was a lonely voice warning that a command economy would necessarily entail the loss of freedom generally. The eventual collapse of the Soviet Union and the apparent victory of market capitalism appeared to vindicate Hayek's views. The second book, however, painted a very different picture. Karl Polanyi's *The Great Transformation* argued that a self-regulating market, not socialism, was a utopian fantasy. Polanyi, an economic historian, attempted to show that a market economy required a market society in which all things were reducible to market terms. Whereas land and labor in premodern England (and by extension Christendom in general) were not directly subject to markets, in a market society, those things that once provided a cushion against market forces were themselves folded into the market. Where Hayek worried that socialism would jeopardize freedom, Polanyi worried that market forces themselves would erode the social and cultural contexts that made freedom possible.

The worldwide economic trials that began in the autumn of 2008 provide a good opportunity to consider some of the basic questions raised by Hayek and Polanyi. There are, of course, those who argue that our troubles were the result of government meddling in the market and that recovery would best be achieved if the government stayed its hand and allowed the forces of the market to correct the effects of governmental mischief. On the other hand, there are those (and these seemed to be in the majority) who argue that unregulated market forces led to abuses that made necessary increased regulatory oversight as well as significant federal intervention into financial markets and certain business sectors.

Today we find ourselves facing the same questions Hayek and Polanyi grappled with in 1944: are unfettered markets good, or are they harmful? As it turns out, the answer is somewhat complicated, but several general statements can be advanced up front: (1) private property is essential for freedom; (2) free markets are an essential corollary of private property; (3) but free markets will undermine themselves unless they are firmly grounded in values that transcend the market.

In the fall of 2008, Americans were confronted with frightening news. The financial world was, the experts warned, teetering on the brink of disaster. Politicians from both parties grimly intoned that what was at stake was "our American way of life" and without massive intervention the country, and perhaps the world, was heading toward an "economic apocalypse." These events seem to have caught many off guard. Despite the regular warnings from cranks, doomsayers, and other pessimists, few Americans, if actions are a reliable measure, actually believed that they would be staring into the abyss of economic disaster. The price tag necessary to steer the economy away from the precipice was breathtaking, and even with such an infusion of money into the markets, no one was sure that the wild careen would be abated.

We might do well to begin with a question that many people raised in the aftermath of the crash: Are some companies too big to fail? Or, more precisely, are some corporations so big that their failure would devastate the economy? Billions of dollars were spent to shore up some corporations that were considered so crucial to the economy that public money should be spent to resuscitate them. But this simply raises more questions: Is it a fundamental problem when a corporation becomes so big that its failure would threaten the entire national economy? Could it be that scale and economic security are related? Can institutions become so large that their potential harm outweighs their actual good? If yes, then are there measures that could help ensure that economic power is decentralized and therefore less dangerous?

To answer these questions it might be helpful to turn to an early twentieth-century essay on economics, Hilaire Belloc's neglected classic *The Servile State*. According to Belloc, capitalism is fundamentally unstable and is therefore a transitory condition. It is important, though, to pay careful attention to his definition of capitalism: "A society in which the ownership of the means of production is confined to a body of free citizens not large enough to make up properly a general character of that society, while the rest are dispossessed of the means of production and therefore proletarian, we call capitalist."[1] In Belloc's mind, there are only two resolutions to the instability of capitalism. The first is socialism, and the second is what he called "the distributist state" or "the proprietary state," in which private property, specifically the means of production, is broadly distributed throughout the populace.

Why did Belloc think capitalism was unstable? Capitalism, as he defined it, tends toward centralization of economic power, but when economic power is centralized, it requires a strong political structure to manage it. Herein we see the often ignored connection between economics and politics: centralized economic power goes hand in hand with centralized political power. Belloc's friend and fellow distributist G. K. Chesterton argued that capitalism was dying, and the evidence was that the capitalists appealed "for the intervention of Government like Socialists."[2] In light of the cry for a government bailout in 2008–9, it is difficult not to see Chesterton's point. Hayek argued that consolidation of economic power in the form of monopolies would invariably lead toward socialism. "A state which allows such enormous aggregations of power to grow up cannot afford to let this power rest entirely in private control." The blame, according to Hayek, does not fall exclusively upon the capitalist class. Instead, "the fatal development was that they have succeeded in enlisting the support of an ever increasing number of other groups and, with their help, in obtaining the support of the state."[3]

Polanyi argued that "laissez-faire itself was enforced by the state."[4] The formation of a market system required a significant government involvement. "The road to the free market was opened and kept open by an enormous increase in continuous, centrally organized and controlled interventionism." This, of course, seems counterintuitive, but Polanyi's point is that the market system that grew up in the nineteenth century was not a spontaneous product. It was planned. "Thus even those who wished most ardently to free the state from all unnecessary duties, and those whose philosophy demanded the restriction of state activities, could not but entrust the self-same state with the new powers, organs, and instruments required for the establishment of laissez-faire."[5] Of course, strictly speaking, interventionism is the opposite of laissez-faire, but its establishment, according to Polanyi, is an elusive dream, the pursuit of which justifies temporary intervention. "For as long as that system is not established, economic liberals must and will unhesitatingly call for the intervention of the state in order to establish it, and once established, in order to maintain it."[6] Seen in this light it appears that economic centralization and political centralization feed off one another. Far from being antagonistic, they are natural allies. The massive regulatory state emerged with the explosive growth of market capitalism. If this is true, we might do well to consider more specifically some of the sources of economic centralization.

THE LIMITS OF EFFICIENCY

According to Harvard economist Stephen A. Marglin, modern economics is hamstrung by a false conception of reality. It has, according to Marglin, become an ideology, a self-contained worldview with its own set of values as well as a particular epistemology and ontology. In short, modern economics is not simply a means by which exchanges can be described or even a set of tools that ensure optimal efficiency of market transactions. Instead, the ideology of economics is a way of seeing the world. According to Marglin, economics "takes very much to heart the famous dictum of the nineteenth-century physicist Lord Kelvin that we know only what we can measure."[7] Such an ideology forces reality into a preconceived structure and subsequently deigns to rule this truncated world with all the authority of science. The modern discipline of economics is, among other things, imperialistic in its aims and destructive in its consequences. This claim would not have surprised Lord Edward Copleston, provost of Oxford's Oriel College, who in the early nineteenth century balked at the establishment of a chair of political economy because that discipline is "so prone to usurp the rest."[8]

The ideology of economics is plainly seen by the elevation of efficiency to the highest value. Consider the following example: Lawrence Summers, director of the White House's National Economic Council under President Obama, was previously chief economist of the World Bank. While in that position he sent an internal memo to a colleague arguing that the World Bank should encourage poor countries to sell space for Western pollution. "A given amount of health-impairing pollution should be done in the country with the lowest cost, which will be the country with the lowest wages. I think the economic logic behind dumping a load of toxic waste in the lowest-wage country is impeccable and we should face up to that." *The Economist* got hold of the memo and, while acknowledging that the language was "crass," went on to admit that "on the economics his points are hard to answer."[9] If "economic logic" leads to the obvious conclusion that it is good for developing countries to voluntarily assume the toxic waste of developed countries, perhaps there is something wrong with economic logic. Could it be that it is blind to important facets of reality? Summers's conclusion is thinkable, though, if we conceive of the individual as the only legitimate player or the nation as the only community that matters.

If individuals are the primary unit of analysis and if individuals are concerned only with maximizing their own interests, then surely a business owner can see the economic logic of acquiring toxic waste for a profit. At the same time, a nation can agree to sell pollution rights because the nation per se will profit. Perhaps, though, some goods cannot be calculated in economic terms. Perhaps there are future consequences that, while they can be intuited, cannot be clearly factored into a rational calculus. If so, the narrow idolatry of efficiency contributes to economic centralization if centralization is efficient or perceived to be efficient. Even if centralization can be shown to be efficient in the short term, the long-term costs are easily ignored because they cannot be assessed with the kind of accuracy or confidence that would make them susceptible to the efficiency calculus. But to ignore all that cannot be rationally calculated is to ignore elements of reality, for while intuition, tradition, and custom are slippery concepts and difficult to nail down, they are still nevertheless important forms of knowledge. Even hardheaded economists employ these kinds of knowledge to live in the world. They only ignore them when constructing economic models by which to ostensibly explain the world. This affection for efficiency has trickled down into the society as a whole. Or it might be better to say that the modern affinity for quantification has shaped the field of economics, and it has, at the same time, shaped the mind of society at large. In other words, the cult of efficiency paved the way for the cult of the colossal.

Efficiency finds itself allied with security to the detriment of goods that are simply invisible to the efficiency calculus. Consider something as simple as fire insurance. Today, I can pay a premium of, say, three hundred dollars per year, and if my barn burns down, the insurance company will pay me the replacement value of the structure. This simple transaction is far more efficient than a complex system of mutual help that culminates in neighbors converging on my property for a barn raising. If efficiency is the only value, the insurance wins hands down. But is anything lost? Is the mutual dependence of the members of a community worth anything? Is the ongoing sense of neighborly responsibility and mutual need something that fosters a kind of community that is richer and deeper than a community in which each family is insured by the insurance corporation?[10] The answer is obvious to anyone whose vision has not been blinkered by an undue commitment to the idea of efficiency.

But the very kind of community that can, to some degree, sustain itself apart from dependence on insurance companies has been eroded by many of the forces that we have previously discussed. When a market economy is combined with individualism, it will appear quite different than when it exists in the context of robust and healthy communities. According to Robert Nisbet, "Capitalism is either a system of social and moral allegiances, resting securely in institutions and voluntary associations, or it is a sand heap of disconnected particles of humanity. If it is, or is allowed to become, the latter, there is nothing that can prevent the rise of centralized, omni-competent political power. Lacking a sense of participation in economic society, men will seek it, as Hilaire Belloc told us, in the Servile State."[11]

The unattached nomad plays a key role in the idealized world of efficiency-driven economic theory. Consider, for example, the concept of a free market in labor described by Frank Knight:

> Every member of the society is to act as an individual only, in entire independence of all other persons. To complete his independence he must be free from social wants, prejudices, preferences, or repulsions, or any values which are not completely manifested in market dealing. Exchange of finished goods is the only form of relation between individuals, or at least there is no other form which influences economic conduct. And in exchanges between individuals, no interest of persons not party to the exchange are to be concerned, either for good or ill.[12]

While Knight's description is admittedly idealized, Ludwig von Mises makes the same point, which, he argues, holds true in "the real world." If workers "did not act as trade unionists, but reduced their demands and changed their locations and occupations according to the requirements of the labour market, they could eventually find work."[13] Indeed, that might be true, but it is the economist's constricted view of reality that makes it impossible for him to acknowledge that something good might be lost in this world of nomadic wage seekers.

THE AMERICAN WAY OF LIFE

The breakdown of community and the rise of individualism leads to the centralization of political as well as economic power. Consider the changing face of the typical family. Setting aside for a moment the breakdown of the nuclear family, we have seen in the last century a striking breakdown in what we might term the three-generation family.

Because the pursuit of economic opportunities has engendered mobility, many families are willing to move across town, across the state, or across the nation to avail themselves of opportunity. As a result, children are separated from their aging parents and grandchildren know their grandparents primarily through telephone calls and an occasional visit. In such a situation, the nursing home is the logical end for the elderly who have long since ceased being a vital and integral part of a family. Once they become empty nesters, they are encouraged by society to retire and perhaps relocate to sunnier climes. But the separation only makes them increasingly dependent upon government programs. So too the nuclear family separated from extended family by geography, not to mention affection, finds itself relying on the safety net of government programs rather than family or friends. Thus, it is not simply the elderly whose orientation is turned toward Washington. When the complex web of community—of which extended family ties are a part—is attenuated, the cold breath of insecurity chills everyone, and the obvious savior is that ubiquitous power called social service. The leviathan slouches to the fore as the source of our security. The economist Wilhelm Röpke puts the matter succinctly: "The modern welfare state is, without any doubt, an answer to the disintegration of genuine communities . . . of which the most indispensible, primary, and natural is the family."[14]

This being the case, it is curious that many on the right have made a fetish out of the nuclear family. Perhaps it is understandable since any traditional notion of the family has lost significant ground in recent decades, but given the preceding analysis, it seems clear that nuclear families alone often do not provide the kind of security, economic and otherwise, for which people long. The recovery of the three-generational family would be a step in the direction of economic security for several reasons. The elderly can contribute to the household economy and thereby add wealth. For example, the elderly can help care for children. Furthermore, children can learn much about what it means to be an adult, a caretaker, and a family member by living with their grandparents and then caring for them and even in watching them decline and die. In three-generation homes, the elderly have a concrete place, and therefore the need for retirement centers and nursing homes is diminished, as is reliance on Medicare and other government programs to pay the monthly bills. Finally, three-generation homes are less mobile. They tend to stay put. This affects the larger community, for a critical mass of families committed to a particular community will create the kind of security that makes the security offered by the anonymous corporation and government program less appealing.

With all that, it seems clear that in many quarters families are changing. Perhaps the most striking change is simply the reduction in the size of the average family. Plenty has been written recently about the precipitously declining birthrates in Western nations. These rates have, in many nations, dipped well below replacement levels, which means that in the not-too-distant future, the number of individuals demanding social services will skyrocket as the workforce simultaneously declines. The economic consequences of this unprecedented dynamic are grim.

Clearly Thomas Malthus did not anticipate this. But on the surface it does make sense that as we gradually ceased being a nation of farmers, the size of families would decrease. On the farm, there is always of need for workers, and a large family filled that need. It is far more difficult to imagine a large family living comfortably in an apartment in Manhattan. On the farm, children are an economic asset. In the city, they are economic liabilities. Their worth must be measured merely in terms of subjective satisfaction, which though not to be denigrated, is impossible to quantify.

If we embrace without qualification the ideal of efficiency, the prospect of a large family becomes highly suspect. The very way one looks at wealth and property is affected. Joseph Schumpeter, who argued that capitalism would fail—not because of its weaknesses but because of its strengths—thought the shift would significantly impact families. According to him, the stunning material success of capitalism would lead people to think increasingly in terms of material goods. But once a person begins to assess options only in terms of economic utility, children become a dubious choice. "Why," the progressive and successful capitalist might ask, "should we stunt our ambitions and impoverish our lives in order to be insulted and looked down upon in our old age?"[15]

Furthermore, the decline in the idea of the family leads one to relate differently to time. According to Schumpeter, "With the decline of the driving power supplied by the family motive, the businessman's time-horizon shrinks, roughly to his life expectation. . . . He drifts into an anti-saving frame of mind and accepts with an increasing readiness anti-saving *theories* that are indicative of a short-run *philosophy*." In other words, "he loses the capitalist ethics that enjoins working for the future irrespective of whether or not one is going to harvest the crop oneself."[16] One is reminded here of John Maynard Keynes's glib remark that "in the long run we're all dead." True, but such a view does not serve to engender responsibility, sacrifice, thrift, or any of the other dispositions upon which vibrant communities depend. The desire to pass a legacy to one's children fosters certain virtues that benefit the community at large.

The kind of human being described by Schumpeter is one whose life is given to the pursuit of pleasure. The hedonist, in a world of markets, is a consumer whose life is preoccupied with consuming and acquiring. The appetite for material satisfaction, though, is notoriously fickle, and satisfying it generally results in a treadmill existence in which complete satiation is always just beyond one's grasp. Appetites, in fact, grow even as they are temporarily sated, and a society of consumerists will be driven to grow its economy indefinitely.

While economic growth is measured in the abstract by figures such as gross domestic product (GDP), it is spoken of more intimately in terms of that most innocuous of phrases "standard of living." In 1992, during his first presidential campaign, Bill Clinton's campaign advisers constantly reminded themselves, "It's the economy, stupid." Recession seemed to be in the offing, and people were worried. In one of the debates, Clinton made a striking statement: "I got into this race because I did not want my child to grow up to be part of the first generation of Americans to do worse than her parents."[17] This claim was intended as evidence that something was seriously amiss. But is it reasonable to assume that our standard of living can continue to increase indefinitely? Furthermore, why should it? Is it possible to conceive of a standard of living that is satisfying? Would we know enough to say "enough"? Given the consumerist's expansive desires, the answer to these questions seems to be no. More recently, the economic crisis of 2008 elicited plenty of handwringing and head wagging, while billions of dollars were committed to protect our "American way of life." That such a reason was offered without justification indicates that our way of life is an axiom that must be assumed but never questioned. But is it too much to consider, if only for a moment, that perhaps our way of life is precisely the problem? Of course, a way of life is a complex thing, but insofar as the "American way of life" consists of living beyond our means, it is unsustainable. To the extent that consumer credit is at an all-time high and personal savings is at an all-time low, the "American way of life" is irresponsible. And to the extent that we imagine that growth can be perpetual, we are living in a fantasy world that is every bit as utopian as the dream world inhabited by the communists.

In his book *Small Is Beautiful: Economics as if People Mattered*, economist E. F. Schumacher argued that the idea of perpetual growth is an error lying at the heart of modern economic thought. The idea of growth is attractive because it is quantifiable, but focusing exclusively on quantity neglects the idea of quality, which would seem at least equally important. For example, the economist can measure the gross national product (GNP) and determine that it has grown, say, 3 percent. But if one were to ask whether the growth was good or bad, the economist would dismiss the question as nonsense. According to Schumacher, "He would lose all his certainties if he even entertained such a question: growth of GNP must be a good thing, irrespective of what has grown and who, if anyone, has benefitted. The idea that there could be pathological growth, unhealthy growth, disruptive or destructive growth, is to him a perverse idea which must not be allowed to surface."[18] In other words, the vast majority of economists seem to assume, as an article of faith, that growth is necessarily and always good. Yet we could, of course, stimulate growth by legalizing prostitution, narcotics, and child pornography. We could stimulate growth by encouraging divorce so that two households were required where one once sufficed. Is that the kind of growth most people want? If the answer is no, then we are forced to consider the quality of growth and not simply the quantity, a task that requires studied moral judgment and not merely steadily increasing numbers.

Schumacher did see a glimmer of hope: "A small minority of economists is at present beginning to question how much further 'growth' will be possible, since *infinite growth in a finite environment is an obvious impossibility* [italics added]."[19] Given obvious problems such as pollution and the depletion of natural resources, it seems that economic models based on the possibility of infinite growth need to be reconsidered. But this, according to Schumacher, does not mean that we simply need to stop all growth. Even those economists who agree that infinite growth is not possible, "cannot get away from the purely quantitative growth concept. Instead of insisting on *the primacy of qualitative distinctions* [italics in the original], they simply substitute non-growth for growth, that is to say, one emptiness for another."[20]

We need, then, to wean ourselves from the habit of favoring quantitative facts over qualitative ones. Instead, we must learn to subordinate the quantitative to the qualitative. We must first attempt to grasp what is good for human beings—for human creatures—before we can determine whether or not some forms of growth are good. Of course, making that judgment requires hard work and much thought, and it is susceptible to error in ways that simple quantities are not. Nevertheless, it is an enterprise that must be undertaken.

ECONOMICS AND VIRTUE

Let us turn now to the issue of virtue, for a central component of my argument is that the success of a market economy requires certain moral virtues. When these are attenuated, perverted, or absent, the market becomes a powerful means by which individuals are debased. In other words, the free market flourishes only in the presences of certain premarket virtues.

In a sense it might seem a truism, perhaps even an oddity, that I would insist that market capitalism requires virtue. After all, don't all human interactions require certain virtues if they are to be successful over the long term? The framers of the U.S. Constitution, for example, insisted that the system of government they designed would succeed only when joined to a virtuous populace. This is not to say that the framers were naive about human nature. They did not imagine that all citizens would be virtuous all the time. But they did believe that freedom is tenuous and can thrive only in a social and cultural context in which the virtues are honored and their opposites scorned.

In the same way, the freedom that a market economy enjoins also depends on a certain kind of person. If a critical mass of participants in a market economy possesses the virtues of honesty, self-control, personal responsibility, and a willingness to sacrifice for others, then that economy can encourage and facilitate the enjoyment of freedom. If, however, a critical mass of participants deal in half-truths, shun responsibility, pursue immediate gratification, and refuse to sacrifice for others, then the market system will be a means by which the participants debase themselves, others, and society at large. In short, the market depends on virtues that are not necessarily cultivated by the market. In a world characterized by consumerism, these virtues are undermined by the version of the market that emerges.

Economists, though, too often deny or ignore this line of argument. Consider an early example. Bernard Mandeville was born in 1670. He gained fame, and notoriety, with the publication of an allegory titled, *The Fable of the Bees; Or, Private Vices, Publick Benefits*. As the title indicates, Mandeville argued that if everyone pursues private vices, the public will benefit:

> Vast Numbers throng'd the fruitful Hive;
> Yet those vast Numbers made 'em thrive;
> Millions endeavoring to supply
> Each other's Lust and Vanity. . . .
> Thus every part was full of Vice,
> Yet the whole Mass a Paradise.[21]

Those things that have been traditionally associated with vice are the very forces, according to Mandeville, that are most useful to society. In this light, it is not hard to imagine what an infusion of traditional virtues would do to profits. In Mandeville's view, traditional virtues would stagnate the economy and reduce the population from a vibrant hive to an indolent few. Furthermore, the hive, once the pride of its inhabitants and the envy of the world, would with the infusion of virtue, be despised by other nations and become increasingly susceptible to foreign threats.

Some have suggested that Mandeville was writing satire. Perhaps. What is certain is that John Maynard Keynes, the giant of twentieth-century economics, was no satirist. He struck a note startlingly in concert with Mandeville in a 1930 essay titled "Economic Possibilities for Our Grandchildren." Writing in the darkest days of the Great Depression, Keynes expressed his undying faith in progress. He chided the economic pessimists for focusing on short-term misery at the expense of the long-term prospects on the distant horizon. Given the tremendous surge in prosperity witnessed in the nineteenth century, Keynes argued that there was every reason to expect that over the long haul growth would continue. Keynes imagined a time in the not-too-distant future when the problem of scarcity would be solved. All people would have enough to meet their needs for life and well-being. Yet, Keynes worried about a new challenge that would beset humanity once the problem of scarcity was resolved: boredom.

Creating a satisfying life in a world of plenty is, according to Keynes, the glorious challenge humans will one day confront. "Thus for the first time since his creation man will be faced with his real, his permanent problem—how to use his freedom from pressing economic cares, how to occupy the leisure, which science and compound interest will have won for him, to live wisely and agreeably and well."[22] In this future time of peace and plenty,

> we shall be able to rid ourselves of many of the pseudo-moral principles which have hag-ridden us for two hundred years, by which we have exalted some of the most distasteful of human qualities into the position of the highest virtues. We shall be able to afford to dare to assess the money-motive at its true value. The love of money as a possession—as distinguished from the love of money as a means to the enjoyments and realities of life—will be recognized for what it is, a somewhat disgusting morbidity, one of those semi-criminal, semi-pathological propensities which one hands over with a shudder to the specialists in mental disease.[23]

The implication here is striking. At present, we do not have the luxury of ridding ourselves from "disgusting morbidity" and "semi-pathological" aspects of our collective character that, in a time of reflection, would constitute mental illness. Keynes looked forward to the day when humans would be free "to return to some of the most sure and certain principles of religion and traditional virtue," but until the problem of scarcity is overcome, we must tarry a while in the land of putative insanity. "For at least another hundred years we must pretend to ourselves and to every one that fair is foul and foul is fair; for foul is useful and fair is not. Avarice and usury and precaution *must be our gods* for a little longer still [italics added]. For only they can lead us out of the tunnel of economic necessity into daylight."[24] Like Mandeville, Keynes asserted that economic prosperity depends on greed, on the love of money, on the passion to acquire. On the backs of these vices, a world of prosperity can emerge; but if we prematurely turn from these vices, scarcity will reassert itself. Instead of acting in accord with traditional notions of virtue and sacrificing our material good for our children, even as we teach them to treasure those things that transcend the material world, according to Keynes, we must sacrifice our souls in the dim hope that our grandchildren will have the luxury of being virtuous.

Clearly something has run amiss. If market capitalism is based necessarily on the cultivation of private vices, then the system must be rejected out of hand as that which corrupts both individuals and society. But perhaps, before taking the drastic step of jettisoning the notion of market capitalism altogether, we should attempt to find an alternative account of the market that would allow us to embrace its power while creating the space to cultivate virtue. Before pursuing this course, let us consider two specific examples—advertising and the corporation—that demonstrate how the pursuit of virtue seems to run counter to some basic elements of our economy.

CHALLENGES TO VIRTUE

Ours is an age of advertising. In its benign form, advertising is a means by which sellers can alert buyers to their product. Advertising has, though, become something far more troubling. We are constantly assaulted with images and pitches geared with scientific precision to convince us that we are not as happy as we could be if we would only purchase this gizmo or that doodad. Advertising is ubiquitous. Television, radio, magazines, newspapers, Internet sites, streets and highways, buildings, sports centers, athletes, bowl games, movies, apparel, and breakfast cereal have all become modes of persuasion. Want to be like Mike? Buy shoes like his. Want to be sexy and get the girl? Drive this car. Feel fat? Buy this diet food. Want to be happy? Buy it all. And if you can't afford it, charge it.

Any attempt to criticize advertising runs up against the twin philosophies of individualism and freedom, two ideals that, in our age, are difficult to challenge: "Hey, I have the right to say whatever I want, and advertising is speech, so I can advertize whenever, wherever, and however I want (assuming I'm not too offensive for the prudes among us). And besides, if you don't like it, don't look at it." The argument sticks unless, of course, advertising serves to corrode the public spaces upon which others necessarily look. If advertising negatively affects society as a whole, then the free speech argument begins to look something like the "it's my property so I can pollute as much as I want" argument. The problem is with what economists call externalities. If there are negative implications to advertising that extend to the public in general, then the public has a vested interest in addressing the problem. Of course, in a society saturated by advertising, the perception that it might be a problem recedes in the haze of undulating desire.

Röpke argued, "Advertising, in all of its forms and with all of its effects, one of the foremost of which is to encourage the concentration of firms, is one of the most serious problems of our time and should receive the most critical attention of those few who can still afford to speak up without fear of being crushed by the powerful interests dominating this field."[25] Röpke was concerned that advertising would gradually insinuate itself into all areas of life, so that things and relationships that once stood outside the adman's purview became subject to his craft. The result is the commercialization of all of life. "The curse of commercialization is that it results in the standards of the market spreading into regions which should remain beyond supply and demand."[26]

But why would advertising work its way through the social tapestry and thereby homogenize all things under the rubric of commercialism? The answer, according to Röpke, lies in the asymmetries that exist in market economies. Money can be made from advertising purchasable goods, but not from resisting the advertiser's shtick.

> Thousands get hard cash out of advertising, but the unsalable beauty and harmony of a country give to all a sense of well-being which cannot be measured by the market. Yet the non-marketable value, while incomparably higher than the marketable one, is bound to lose unless we come to its assistance and put on its scale enough moral weight to make up for the deficiency of mercantile weight. The market's asymmetry opens a gap which has to be closed from without, from beyond the market, and it would be sheer suicide on the part of the market economy's friends to leave to others the cheap triumph of this discovery.[27]

Röpke argued that every society requires the moral leadership of men and women of virtue who will recognize asymmetries in the market, such as advertising, and work with diligence, patience, and fortitude to balance the asymmetries with resources that transcend the market. Without the efforts of people on behalf of the good and the beautiful, commercialism will consume the very things we once held most dear, or at the very least alter our ability to see them for what they are.

Consider next the modern corporation. The very structure of the corporation all too often reduces the opportunity as well as the inclination for the exercise of virtue. I am not suggesting that virtue is intrinsically incompatible with a corporation. The two are, however, not necessarily allies, and great care must be taken to ensure that virtue is not ignored. A corporation is owned by shareholders who hire executives to run the corporation. The shareholders can be divided into the large shareholders and the small shareholders. The large shareholders call the shots. They hire and fire the top executives who answer to the shareholders. The small shareholders—often owners of mutual funds—have very little power to influence the direction of the corporation. With this dynamic in place, consider how the exercise of virtue can compete against the imperative to maximize profits. Executives will lose their jobs if they fail to maximize profits, and they will lose their jobs if they are convicted of some kinds of deception or fraud. But there is a significant gap between outright crime and moral failure, and the moral failure will likely not be punished as severely as the failure to make a profit, and it might even be overlooked in executives who consistently ring up profits. In other words, there appears to be another of Röpke's asymmetries at work in this relationship, and virtue is on the light side of the scale when weighed merely against profit.

Small shareholders might, having prudently diversified their portfolios, hold a small number of shares in a wide variety of corporations. Like all investors, these small shareholders are interested in realizing a profit through share appreciation or regular dividends. However, they are removed from the daily operations of the corporation. They may receive an annual report and have the opportunity to vote to elect executives, but the bottom line in the report is their main focus, and the information they receive is generally inadequate to inform a wise choice in the polls. The very scale and remoteness of the enterprise makes careful monitoring difficult. Of course, someone might argue that if these shareholders were really concerned about virtue, they could investigate the behavior of the corporation as well as the background of each of its officers. True. But doing this for a portfolio of investments would be extraordinarily laborious, and few are willing to make such an effort. Even if such an endeavor were conceivable, the structure of the corporation makes it far easier for all involved to focus on profits while ignoring virtue. The same dynamic is even more pronounced when corporate shares are owned as part of a mutual fund. The investors are one more step removed from the corporation, and the quantifiable bottom line of the mutual fund itself—this time abstracted from the individual stocks—is the natural focus. The moral asymmetries are obvious.

Because of the scale and remoteness associated with the modern corporation, virtue is disadvantaged. This is not to say that virtue is impossible or necessarily absent. But when abuses occur, the natural response of the public, and therefore their elected representatives, is to attempt to regulate corporations. A regulatory bureaucracy is erected to compensate for the asymmetry between profits and virtue, and regulations become a substitute for virtue. Of course, as regulations increasingly pressure corporate executives, they will naturally find themselves focusing on the bureaucratic minutia of the regulations rather than on the self-imposed moral probity that virtue requires. Regulations, then, can have the unintended effect of distracting from the cultivation and practice of virtue.

But consider what has occurred. Corporations can and do hire lawyers to lobby federal and state governments on their behalf. The voices of the corporations that can afford to retain full-time lobbyists will obviously be heard above the voices of the small farmer in Pennsylvania or the owner of the independent bank in Kansas. The result, not surprisingly, is that all too often regulations tend to favor the large concern over the small. Even those regulations that appear benign can produce onerous barriers to the small business. If in the interest of clean meat, the U.S. Department of Agriculture (USDA) and various state regulatory agencies require butchering facilities the description of which is well suited to the corporate meat producer but onerous for the small farmer, then the farmer is disadvantaged. Of course, one could say that such regulations are all in the name of public safety. But if a farmer wants to butcher a few steers in his barn and if his neighbors who trust him to be a man of virtue want to buy the meat from him, why should a government agency get in the way? In one instance we have regulations attempting to substitute for virtue and disadvantaging some, while in the other we have legitimate virtue operating between neighbors. Which alternative serves to create a healthier society? Or cleaner meat?

The regulatory bureaucracy, while ostensibly intended to protect the public from corporate abuse, works hand in hand with the very organizations they are tasked with policing. Individuals move easily between government and Wall Street. Harry Paulson and Timothy Geithner, two consecutive secretaries of the Treasury with long experience and ties to Wall Street, are obvious examples. Here we see the way that the close relationship between the corporate world and the government contributes to centralization of power, both economic and political. And it can all be accomplished under the cover of "public safety." The need for security (provided by the government) can justify the massive regulatory bureaucracy. The regulators' consciences can remain clean; after all, they are serving the public. If the corporate lobbyists have done their jobs, the regulators will provide the corporations with regulations well suited to the scale on which they operate, and as a result, the small concern will often find itself disadvantaged. Here we come to a surprising possibility. Could it be that some of our economic problems are not the result of insufficient regulations, as many argue, but instead the result of a regulatory structure that creates an unlevel playing field and thereby makes it easier for the large corporation and more difficult for the small concern?

The problem of virtue has, perhaps surprisingly, brought us back to questions of centralization and scale. Röpke clearly saw the relationship between virtue, scale, and the free market: "Market economy, price mechanism, and competition are fine, but they are not enough. They may be associated with a sound or an unsound structure of society." The maximization of profits to the exclusion of all other concerns is not enough. If we reduce our concerns only to those things visible to the lover of quantifiable reality, we will be unable to properly evaluate the health of the economy much less the society as a whole, of which the economy is a part. Röpke continues,

> Market economy is one thing in a society where atomization, mass, proletarianization, and concentration are the rule; it is quite another in a society approaching anything like the 'natural order'. . . . In such a society, wealth would be widely dispersed; people's lives would have solid foundations; genuine communities, from the family upward, would form a background of moral support for the individual; there would be counterweights to competition and the mechanical operation of prices; people would have roots and would not be adrift in life without anchor; there would be a broad belt of an independent middle class, a healthy balance between town and country, industry and agriculture.[28]

The market economy is important, but it is good only if it is nested in a cultural context that is bigger than the economy. A healthy market economy depends on cultural goods that are above and beyond the influence of supply and demand. Centralization undermines these very goods by reducing the space necessary for them to flourish. Commercialism destroys these good things by subordinating them to supply and demand. The loss of virtue makes it impossible to distinguish a healthy society from its opposite.

THE POWER OF PROPERTY

If there is a connection between virtue and scale, then perhaps it would be useful to consider more closely the issue of property, for private property is an important means by which virtue can be cultivated. But at the same time, perhaps it goes without saying that not all property is equal, and it may be that some forms of property are more conducive to the cultivation of virtue than others.

We should first distinguish property from wealth. Belloc insisted that the craftsman who owns his tools is quite different from the man who owns shares in a corporation. And although there are many who would argue that wealth in the form of corporate shares is a means to achieving economic freedom, Belloc was not as sanguine: "As a craftsman at his work he is in full control, personal and alive; as a shareholder his control is distant, indirect and largely impersonal."[29] For Belloc, economic freedom is possible only when an individual owns some means of production and is trained in its use. Such a person is self-sufficient in a way the shareholder never is, for in difficult economic times, the craftsman and farmer can provide for themselves, at least partially, whereas the shareholder, as a shareholder, is completely unequipped to do so.

Schumpeter made a similar point but on a larger scale. There are, he argued, political and social consequences associated with the loss of the idea of real private property as opposed to the wealth of the shareholder. "The capitalist process, by substituting a mere parcel of shares for the walls of and the machines in a factory, takes the life out of the idea of property." Schumpeter goes on to describe how this life is drained away:

> It loosens the grip that was once so strong—the grip in the sense of the legal right and the actual ability to do as one pleases with one's own; the grip also in the sense that the holder of the title loses the will to fight, economically, physically, politically, for "his" factory and his control over it, to die if necessary on its steps. And this evaporation of what we may term the material substance of property—its visible and touchable reality—affects not only the attitude of holders but also that of the workmen and of the public in general. Dematerialized, defunctionalized and absentee ownership does not impress and call forth moral allegiance as the vital form of property did. Eventually there will be *nobody* left who really cares to stand for it—nobody within and nobody without the precincts of the big concerns.[30]

Schumpeter believed that this was the direction that capitalism would eventually take. The institution of property would be altered, people would be content with wealth in the form of corporate shares and wages, and real property would become increasingly centralized. Ultimately, the successes of capitalism would undermine the system itself and give birth to socialism. While capitalism has by no means given way to socialism, the economic crisis of 2008–9 provides a clear example of the tendency. The national government's impulse was to regulate and control. Significant parts of the banking industry were nationalized. Corporations and business sectors that were considered "too big to fail" appealed to the federal government for help. Of course, there were strings attached in the form of increased government oversight. The lumbering courtship of big business and big government continued. Its unsightly offspring will have at least some socialist features.

Thomas Jefferson famously championed the small, independent landholder as the kind of citizen best suited to political liberty. "Cultivators of the earth are the most valuable citizens. They are the most vigorous, the most independent, the most virtuous, and they are tied to their country, and wedded to its liberty and interests by the most lasting bonds."[31] In Jefferson's words we see a striking connection between economic liberty and political liberty. Jefferson believed that owning and working one's own land served to cultivate the very kinds of virtues necessary to sustain free citizens. While we cannot all be farmers, perhaps too few of us are. At the same time, many of the virtues Jefferson extolled are encouraged by owning a small business.

Exactly what are those virtues? Röpke argued that the market economy cannot sustain itself if it is stripped from its bourgeois foundation. The term "bourgeois" has been used in a pejorative sense by Marx and his followers, but Röpke meant only that the market system is necessarily rooted in the culture and virtues of the property-holding middle class: "Independence, ownership, individual reserves, saving, the sense of responsibility, rational planning of one's own life—all that is alien, if not repulsive, to proletarianized mass society."[32] For Röpke, the proletarian society is one characterized by bored wage earners who care little about private property or saving for the future but seek to alleviate their boredom through consumption of disposable goods and popular entertainment. Let us consider the benefits of some of the bourgeois virtues Röpke described.

Self-control is indispensable. Property owners tend to cultivate the ideal of saving, and they seek to maintain a margin against unseen needs. If property is a person's main source of sustenance, then he or she will seek to build up a barrier against lean times. Property owners will be loath to live on the edge, for the edge represents suffering and loss, not only for themselves, but also for all who depend on that piece of property for life. Today a significant percentage of wage earners live from paycheck to paycheck. Of course, many will reply that this is so because conditions allow no opportunity to save. But this seems disingenuous if we consider that our standard of living is higher than ever. It appears that as soon as we earn more, we use that additional money simply to increase our consumption. Could it be that so many are living paycheck to paycheck because we have failed to acknowledge the idea of limits? Could it be that we have truly come to believe that we can have it all and that we can have it now? Or at least that we deserve to have as much as possible as soon as possible? Surely the amount of consumer debt Americans carry is indicative of an ethic of immediacy and a devil-may-care attitude about the morrow. Our private debt simply mirrors, on a much smaller scale, our public debt. The fact that we are so willing to assume trillions of dollars of national debt indicates a cavalier, and downright irresponsible, attitude toward future generations.

The ideal of saving is tied closely to the idea of responsibility. Property owners seek to protect their property by living well within their means. By so doing they create a margin between themselves and disaster. This is responsible to the present, but it is also responsible to the future, for property is something that can be passed to future generations, and we can work now to make our grandchildren's lives better. I recently met a man who had planted black walnut trees on several of his acres. "They're for my grandchildren's college education," he told me. At the same time, debt too can be passed to the future. It is an indication of our ill-formed virtue that we have accumulated a public debt beyond all imagination, and it is our shame that this is perhaps our most durable legacy to future generations. What else is this than a monumental lack of self-control?

Thrift is an old-fashioned virtue that needs to be dusted off. Many of us have parents or grandparents who lived through the Great Depression (and a few among us remember it). My grandmother raised a large family during those lean years, and the frugal habits she acquired by necessity stayed with her the rest of her life. She saved and mended and lived well within her means. She was grateful to have a margin between her income and her expenses and thought it was wise to live modestly. What would our grandmothers say to us now as we struggle to maintain our "American way of life"? Furthermore, it is not clear that our current economy could sustain itself if the idea of thrift caught on. What if people began to live lives characterized by thrift? What if people began mending their clothes, growing some of their own food, sharing tools with neighbors, and attempting to purchase as little as possible? The growth economy would suffer a serious shock. But doesn't this lead us to a troubling conclusion? The virtue of thrift (that is, attempting to favor saving and preserving over wasting) may be at odds with an economy whose sole measure of health is growth. If our present economy depends on the absence of virtue, as Keynes suggested, then perhaps we need to take a serious look at the assumptions underlying our economic system.

In a society of small property owners in which saving, responsibility to the future, and thrift characterize the citizens, and in which (as Jefferson saw it) government is the background facilitator and protector of freedom rather than the source of largess, citizens would accept risk with due caution. But risk can never be eliminated from life. The very fact of risk would compel people to cultivate virtues such as generosity and neighborliness. If a person fell on hard times, his neighbors would come to his aid. Wendell Berry tells of a time when a friend, an Amish man, was asked what community meant to him. "He said that when he and his son were plowing in the spring he could look around him and see seventeen teams at work on the neighboring farm. He knew those teams and the men driving them, and he knew that if he were hurt or sick, those men and those teams would be at work on his farm."[33] Of course, the ideal of community, or neighborliness, is not utopian. Neighbors will have disputes and bitter differences can arise. But when the members of a community realize that they, as a group, are the first and best buffer against disaster, they will tend to set aside differences when needs arise. The barn will be raised, and even though Mrs. Clark doesn't particularly like Mrs. Miller, they both will show up bearing food for the workers. And although Mr. Jones has a legitimate grievance against Mr. Smith, Smith's barn burned and Jones will show up to help raise a new one, for he knows that next year he could be in the same situation as Smith is now. The reciprocity is born of necessity, and although it does not require love, it does foster mutuality, responsibility, and the willingness to sacrifice for others.

The self-sufficient property owner extolled by Jefferson will have a profound appreciation of natural limits, and an appreciation of limits is a form of humility. Farmers can sow and cultivate, but the harvest is ultimately beyond their ability to guarantee. They recognize their dependence on gifts they can anticipate but not command. They may even become attuned to the working of grace in the world as the Divine Giver sends the gentle rains and the fair harvest moon.

In a proletarianized world, populated by pleasure-seeking wage earners, the touch of divine grace may be less easily felt. Surely the humility of the yeoman farmer is less readily acquired. When government largess is the primary means of addressing economic crises, it may even be that humility disappears. After all, the abstract wealth wielded by the government creates the impression of infinitude, and because I am a citizen I have a right to my fair share of the limitless pie. Demanding one's share from the public trough is a far cry from gratefully accepting a gift from neighbors or from God. The false perception of infinitude—rooted in fiat money and therefore fiat thinking—created by government largess of breathtaking scale, cultivates precisely the opposite of humility.

The virtues that private property serves to cultivate are necessary for the long-term health of a market economy and the long-term health of a free society. Private property is good because it is one of the best means of developing the virtues necessary for freedom. This is precisely the reason that the centralization of property is undesirable: it collects property into a few hands and reduces the rest of the citizenry to propertyless wage earners. Here we can see an argument for why it is, indeed, a loss when a big-box store is built on the edge of town and the small, family-owned concerns are forced to shut their doors. The big-box store means fewer people will be property owners and more will be mere wage earners. The obvious counterargument is that the prices are lower at the big concern and times are tight. The question, though, is whether or not there are considerations other than price. Is there a price to focusing only on price?

Consider this fictional scenario: I am a longtime resident of a neighborhood. I know my neighbors and generally like them. They look after my house when I am out of town, and I return the favor for them. We borrow from each other, and various families occasionally enjoy a meal together. When he was twelve, I started employing a neighbor boy, Johnny Carlson, to mow my yard once a week. I paid him ten dollars a week. He did a good job, and I enjoyed giving him the work. As he got older, I gave him a raise to twenty dollars a week because I knew he was saving for a car. I have recommended him to several other neighbors who have also hired him. One day a man in a green truck drove into the neighborhood. He knocked on my door and informed me that he represented a lawn-care company, and he could keep my grass cut and fertilized for fifteen dollars a week. If price is my only concern, I would take him up on his offer, since I would be saving five dollars a week. But what would happen if I switched? Or to put matters differently, by hiring Johnny and keeping him for these years, have I gained something that goes beyond price? Does the friendship matter? Does Johnny's work serve in a small way to add one more strand to the intricate web of our community? Should I feel any responsibility to Johnny?

It seems obvious in this case that there are considerations that go beyond price. Price matters, but if we narrow our concerns so that price is the only consideration, then we have fallen into a kind of reductionism that fails to see the whole. If price is our only consideration, we are thinking strictly in terms of quantity and not in terms of quality. If price is our only concern, then opportunities for the cultivation of virtue will diminish as private property is consolidated. If price is our only consideration, then the thin strands that weave together a healthy community are picked apart one by one. Indeed, price matters, but it is a fool's errand to live as if it is the only matter.

The price of the centralization of property is, ultimately, freedom. This is not difficult to understand. Citizens without property, that is, citizens who work for a wage, are often one pink slip from disaster, especially in difficult economic times. Such people will have security at the forefront of their minds and for good reason. In a democracy, in which the people possess the franchise, this propertyless class will express its deepest concerns at the ballot box. That is to say, citizens who do not possess property are neither economically free nor relatively self-sufficient in the way described by Jefferson, Belloc, and Röpke. At the same time, they are politically free insofar as they have the vote. Because they realize their own insecurity, they will not surprisingly vote for the candidate who promises to provide the greatest security. The desire for security is understandable. The willingness to exchange freedom for security is made possible, and more likely, by the fact that these citizens have all too often lacked the opportunity to develop the virtues necessary for maintaining freedom. These are the virtues that private property helps to cultivate.

In this light, is it any wonder that presidential candidates fall over each other making promises to create programs that appear to increase economic security? The candidate who is considered most genuinely able to deliver the goods will win. This is one important reason why the welfare state has proved so difficult to reverse. It creates propertyless dependents. Such people, naturally, want security without pain.

It is no wonder, then, that what were once the traditional positions of Democrats and Republicans have resolved into a ludicrous and ultimately unsustainable position. The Democrats were typically characterized by a philosophy of tax and spend. Yes, they advocated increased social services (to provide security to the propertyless), but they were willing to raise taxes to pay for the programs. The Republicans, in contrast, traditionally went in for a reduction of taxes and a corresponding reduction of services. We have reached an untenable situation in which both the Democrats and the Republicans have won. Yes, the public expects more services, and both Democratic and Republican candidates seem to agree (if they differ it is only by degree), but the public also believes that taxes (at least those that affect me) should be reduced. Increased spending and decreased revenue leads to skyrocketing debt, and that is what we have: a welfare state drowning in red ink. Propertyless citizens will use their political freedom to achieve security, and the price will be economic sanity and a steady increase of government scope and power. Property is essential to freedom. Without it, there may be social security, but even that will prove less than secure.

It becomes clear that without a culture that values and protects private property, freedom is merely chimerical. A culture of property can be cultivated in a variety of ways. Most simply, individuals can seek to make choices that strengthen local ownership. Supporting local food producers is a modest but important step. Patronizing locally owned stores and restaurants is a way of using personal spending choices to encourage local ownership.

In terms of policy, the first principle ought to be this: do no harm. A careful survey of the regulatory bureaucracy should be made. Regulations that favor big concerns ought to be identified and their elimination made a priority. This can be accomplished simply in the name of fairness. Resistance will surely come from the lobbyists representing the big concerns, but public opinion would, if people were made aware, be on the side of fairness, which, in this case, is simply a matter of justice. It is unjust that the big concerns help write regulations when the small concerns do not have an equal voice in the process.

Second, the tax system should be evaluated, and tax structures that favor the big over the small should be eliminated. Again, this is a matter of justice. A small businessman or a family farmer will spend an inordinate amount of time preparing tax returns. Alternatively, a tax professional will need to be hired. Consider for a moment the vast waste of productive energy that is consumed in filing taxes. Couldn't that time and energy be put to better use? The complexity of the tax code itself is a burden to all, but it creates a disproportionate burden for the small business that must dedicate a larger percentage of resources to comply with arcane laws. A simplified tax code would be a sound goal. Dispensing with the income tax and adopting a national sales tax would be a more effective, simple, and fair way to generate revenue.

Third, the tax code should make it easy to pass property from one generation to the next. This creates a motive to save and an important means by which one can acquire property. Parents should be encouraged to work and save with the knowledge that the fruits of their efforts will not be snatched away by the tax man. A death tax, at least on property less than several million dollars, should not exist.

Fourth, if the benefits of widely distributed property are to be realized, it may be that the government will need to take a more active role. The tax structure and regulatory structure could be used, if only on the margins, to actually favor the small over the large and thereby encourage the broad ownership of property. Such a policy would require a substantial cultural shift, and it would be fraught with potential risks. Nevertheless, if there are political and social reasons to encourage the broad ownership of property, if liberty and property are in fact intimately connected, it is worth considering how ownership can be encouraged. A tax and regulatory structure intended to favor a broader distribution of property would require a vision of a propertied state that has not clearly existed for some time, yet such a vision can be recovered. The long-term success of our republic might depend on the way we as a society view and possess property.

Ultimately, these changes require that we develop a culture of private property. As a society we must come to appreciate property not simply as a means to do as we want, but as a means of developing the virtues necessary for political freedom. Private property is a canvas on which our individual personalities can be freely expressed. It teaches us how to be free and then provides us with the means to practice that freedom. Without private property political freedom will become increasingly attenuated, and when it is exchanged for security, many won't even notice the loss. The taste for freedom is a prerequisite for its duration, and private property cultivates that taste.

With only a little reflection, it should be clear how creatureliness, gratitude, human scale, and place fit into this discussion of economics. When we recognize our creatureliness, we admit of limitation. We admit of needs that transcend the material world and that are more important than material things. A proper understanding of human nature will give us some sense of the weaknesses to which we are all susceptible and thereby establish a defense against them. We will realize that a life given to consumption and the pursuit of pleasure is a life fit for beasts but not human beings. In short, when we admit our creatureliness, we begin to insulate ourselves against the hubris that so easily corrupts human efforts. When we are aware of our creatureliness, we can, as we participate in the economic sphere, experience gratitude for what we have. Gratitude begets satisfaction, and satisfaction is a strong barrier against greed, avarice, and consumerism. An economy of gratitude is an economy of responsibility. A proper appreciation for human scale will make us sensitive to the ways property can become consolidated and thereby ill fit for humans. This appreciation will induce us to support small property owners and perhaps even strive to become one.

When we come to see our lives as part of a story the end of which we will not live to see, we grasp our responsibility to live well, to give our children an inheritance rather than a burden. We can give them love, stories, security, and yes, property. Or we can give them a world of strife, lies, fear, and debt. Our knowledge of human nature makes us realize that the first option will never be perfect, but it is surely superior to the latter.

Ultimately, we can commit ourselves to a community. We can develop the virtue of rootedness, which is really only the practical outgrowth of satisfaction. Our modern economy does not encourage this. For many free market economists, worker mobility is crucial for economic success. Workers should be unattached. They should be willing and able to go wherever there is a surplus of jobs. In such a view, the nomadic, propertyless wage earner becomes an essential part of a thriving economy. No doubt the economic logic of such a solution is solid. No doubt this maximizes efficiency at least in the short term. But what about the long term? What about the goods that go beyond efficiency? It is ironic that the totally free worker—free from commitment to community or place—sets the stage for the rise of statism. Such a freedom is inherently defective and in the long run unsustainable.

7

The Natural World: Living in a Creation

Eating with the fullest pleasure—pleasure, that is, that does not depend on ignorance—is perhaps the profoundest enactment of our connection with the world. In this pleasure we experience and celebrate our dependence and our gratitude, for we are living from mystery, from creatures we did not make and powers we cannot comprehend.

Wendell Berry, *What Are People For?*

Economic matters, of course, do not exist in a hermetically sealed world. They permeate our lives, our homes, and our communities. This being the case, we should take care not to abstract economics away from the larger world of which it is a part. In the previous chapter, we saw some of the ways economics proves destructive if we fail to root it in virtues that stand apart from supply and demand. In this chapter, I want to begin with a few more words on economics and proceed beyond the economic sphere to the natural world. In doing so, I hope it becomes clear that these two topics are not unrelated. Indeed, we create an incomplete picture when we fail to consider them together. The same is true of politics and other seemingly discrete topics. The reason, I hope, is obvious. We are attempting to understand the world, and we create a false picture of reality if we fail to remember that ultimately all things are connected.

Wendell Berry is a writer who seeks to bridge the various aspects of human life. He has long argued that the modern industrial economy is antihuman, anticommunity, and unsustainable. He calls it a "total economy." According to Berry, a total economy consists of a view of reality that tends to reduce everything to the terms of the market. Berry employs the metaphor of the machine to describe our current economic system. When operating efficiently, a machine does its job without awareness of or concern for its surroundings. A good machine is efficient. It is amoral, unfeeling, and not attuned to nor sympathetic with the natural world. The machine exemplifies the ideal of specialization, and specialization is, according to Berry, a sickness that infects the industrial world. It infects individuals, and therefore it infects communities and institutions as well. Specialization, which is a failure to see the world as a whole, fragments tasks, competencies, individual character, and ultimately communities.

This fragmentation creates a false picture of reality, for as specialization blinds individuals to the whole, reality is reduced to the lowest common denominator, and in a world of specialized technicians, the most obvious aspect of reality is the material and quantifiable. What can be quantified can be bought and sold; thus, in the total economy everything, including people and communities, has a price, and the market superintends over all.

The willingness, even enthusiasm, to reduce the world into quantifiable elements requires a voluntary ignorance of those parts of reality that simply cannot be quantified. This represents a colossal moral failure that is not narrowly limited in its effects. The breakdown of communities, the pathologies of the untethered individual, as well as our various environmental crises are all the result, at least in part, of an economic crisis, and our economic crisis is, ultimately, a crisis of character in which we refuse to see the world as it is. But what would induce such an ill-fated war on reality?

The answer is as old as the human story: pride. The old lie "ye shall be as gods" persists, yet the consequences of believing that lie are, perhaps, more acute than ever, for they are amplified by our technological devices. This longing for control is, of course, only a dream, yet we have pursued it with abandon. The desire to dominate reality necessarily leads to a willful simplification whereby the complexities of creation are shorn away and a new, though false, world is embraced as authentic.

The habit of willful ignorance easily and naturally extends to our everyday economic encounters. This habit takes the form of proxies by which we delegate responsibility to organizations about which we know very little. According to Berry, most people in the "developed" world have given proxies to the corporations to produce and provide *all* of their food, clothing, and shelter. Moreover, they are rapidly increasing their proxies to corporations or governments to provide entertainment, education, child care, care of the sick and the elderly, and many other kinds of "service" that once were carried on informally and inexpensively by individuals or households or communities. Our major economic practice, in short, is to delegate the practice to others.[1]

When we delegate to corporations or the government our responsibility to care for our own needs, those of our children, and those of our aging parents, the by-products will all too often be sloppiness, indifference, and waste. The loss of a sense of responsibility leads invariably to a loss of ability, for without practice basic skills that were once possessed by a broad swath of citizens are lost through atrophy.

The fact that we can delegate many of our economic practices to organizations with no vested interest or long-term presence in our community indicates one way that size can hamper economic responsibility. The giantism that characterizes so much of our world facilitates anonymity, and anonymity amplifies the possibility of irresponsibility. Take, for instance, the small truck farmer versus the large corporate agribusinessman. The truck farmer sells his produce at the local farmers' market. He meets his customers, many of whom are his neighbors. He can receive immediate feedback on his produce. Customers can request changes or additions. He can respond. Because he must live with his customers, his participation in their lives extends beyond the simple market exchange. He wants them to be happy not simply so they will continue to purchase his goods but because these people are his neighbors. His life and the lives of his family are entwined with the lives of his customers. Their economic relationship is merely a part of a larger relationship that extends beyond economics. It is easy to see how the giant corporate concern differs. A customer can, of course, request that the Super Mart carry a new item. And one can influence, in a very small way, the products that are carried, for when I choose to buy one item over another, I am sending a message that, when combined with all the other customer choices, affects product selection and quality. But the personal connection is gone. Our relationship is stripped down merely to market forces.

The rise of our modern corporate economy signals a significant cultural change. According to Karl Polanyi, "the outstanding discovery of recent historical and anthropological research is that man's economy, as a rule, is submerged in his social relationships." But recent history has witnessed a profound reversal. "Instead of the economy being embedded in social relations, social relations are embedded in the economic system."[2] As Röpke also makes clear, an economy not firmly grounded in ideals and principles that go beyond supply and demand is corrosive of the very things that we hold, or at least should hold, most dear. It is corrosive of communities and of neighborly virtues that make communities thrive.

Specialists are obsessed with progress. The narrow focus alientates them from a proper understanding of the whole and, because of their singular concern for the future, they are alienated from both the present and the past. The past after all was a backward place peopled by benighted, miserable wretches. What could they have to teach us? What have we to learn from them? As Berry puts it, "The modern mind longs for the future as the medieval mind longed for Heaven."[3]

But this longing for a perfect future is really only a thinly disguised attempt to dominate reality by controlling what is to come. This attempt to control inevitably leads to consolidation, to the colossal. As Berry puts it, "We seem to have adopted a moral rule of thumb according to which anything big is better than anything small."[4] Such a centralizing vision cannot be bothered by the vicissitudes of local nuance or idiosyncrasies. Again the simplifying image of the machine imposes itself, but there is, according to Berry, an ironic twist. As the complex world is simplified and unified by specialists in pursuit of efficiency, humans come to conceive of themselves as merely consumers, or as Berry puts it, as "consumptive machines." The goal of control, it seems, cannot itself be controlled. Domination slyly asserts itself over those who would dominate. It appears that "the concept of total control may be impossible to confine within the boundaries of the specialist enterprise—that it is impossible to mechanize production without mechanizing consumption, impossible to make machines of soil, plants, and animals without making machines also of people."[5] In short, what Berry calls "technological totalitarianism" is dehumanizing. It leads to what C. S. Lewis memorably called the "abolition of man."

Technological totalitarianism leads also to the destruction of communities, for atomized individuals are ill equipped to withstand the enticements to leave home in search of those abstractions called "the future" and "a better place." Yet, this perfect place in the future is never found, and individuals content themselves with a life of abstract possibility, never settling, so never disappointed. They become, in short, the cosmopolitan consumers who fancy themselves at home anywhere. But such a notion is rendered plausible only by the emaciated concept of home upon which such people have settled and the reduced aspirations of a life given over to consumerism.

THE GREAT ECONOMY

A total economy stands in stark contrast with a healthy economy rooted primarily in a local community. Berry argues that the trouble with "the industrial economy is exactly that it is not comprehensive enough, that, moreover, it tends to destroy what it does not comprehend, and that it is *dependent* upon much that it does not comprehend."[6] Berry calls this all-encompassing system "the Great Economy." The Great Economy includes all reality. It admits of mystery. It imposes limits on human action, for this vision of creation leads one to humility, and humility is characterized by a willingness to accept that which one cannot understand. Humans exist within the Great Economy, for it "includes principles and patterns by which values or powers or necessities are parceled out and exchanged," but there is still, with all that, a need for a "little economy—a narrow circle within which things are manageable by the use of our wits."[7]

A little economy can be healthy or sick. Berry argues that the modern industrial economy is unhealthy, destructive, and unsustainable. Furthermore,

> the industrial economy does not see itself as a little economy; it sees itself as the only economy. It makes itself thus exclusive by the simple expedient of valuing only what it can use. . . . Once we acknowledge the existence of the Great Economy, however, we are astonished and frightened to see how much modern enterprise is the work of hubris, occurring outside the human boundary established by ancient tradition. The industrial economy is based on the invasion and pillage of the Great Economy.[8]

This denial of the existence of the Great Economy is precisely what makes the modern industrial economy a total economy.

The alternative to industrialism—an alternative that submits to the strictures of the Great Economy rather than denying them—is agrarianism. These are, to Berry's mind, the only real options, and the differences are profound. "I believe that this contest between industrialism and agrarianism now defines the most fundamental human difference, for it divides not just two nearly opposite concepts of agriculture and land use, but also two nearly opposite ways of understanding ourselves, our fellow creatures, and our world."[9] Whereas the model for industrialism is the machine and technological invention,

> agrarianism begins with givens: land, plants, animals, weather, hunger, and the birthright knowledge of agriculture. Industrialists are always ready to ignore, sell, or destroy the past in order to gain the entirely unprecedented wealth, comfort, and happiness supposedly to be found in the future. Agrarian farmers know that their very identity depends on their willingness to receive gratefully, use responsibly, and hand down intact an inheritance, both natural and cultural, from the past. Agrarians understand themselves as the users and caretakers of some things they did not make, and of some things that they cannot make.[10]

The agrarian is guided by gratitude. He or she recognizes the giftedness of creation and accepts the awful responsibility to steward it well. Such a recognition "calls for prudence, humility, good work, propriety of scale."[11] In the use of the land, soil, water, and nonhuman creatures, Berry argues that the final arbiter is not humankind but nature. This is not to suggest that Berry is some sort of pantheist. Instead, "the agrarian mind is, at bottom, a religious mind." The agrarian recognizes that the natural world is a gift, and gifts imply a giver. "The agrarian mind begins with the love of fields and ramifies in good farming, good cooking, good eating, and gratitude to God." By contrast, the industrial mind "begins with ingratitude, and ramifies in the destruction of farms and forests."[12] The difference here is striking.

Where the agrarian mind is essentially religious, the industrial mind is, it would seem, essentially irreligious or even antireligious. It is characterized by the will to power, the will to dominate the natural world. This mind fails to recognize that humans are an intrinsic part of the natural world, and to destroy the natural world is to jeopardize human existence itself. Such a way of thinking seems patently foolish, but one must never forget the technological optimism lying at the heart of the industrial mind. If the agrarian mind is essentially religious, the industrial mind is animated by a faith in technological innovation, which will solve the very problems brought on by the hubris of an ungrateful mind.

In practical terms, the agrarian model is characterized by a particular view of private property. According to Berry, "the central figure of agrarian thought has invariably been the small owner or small holder who maintains a significant measure of economic self-determination on a small acreage. The scale and independence of such holdings imply two things that agrarians see as desirable: intimate care in the use of land, and political democracy resting upon the indispensible foundation of economic democracy."[13] That we, as a nation, have become by and large a nation of wage earners rather than landowners signifies an important cultural shift. At the same time, Berry is not arguing that a healthy economy is only possible when everyone owns land. An agrarian society is one in which citizens are tied to the land by virtue of their commitments to a particular place, not necessarily by their ownership of a piece of land. But with that, Berry's vision does require that a critical mass of citizens own land and thereby shape the economic and cultural climate so that every citizen, owner or not, can enjoy the benefits of property.

CREATION OR ENVIRONMENT?

When we shift our focus and learn to see economic matters in the context of the Great Economy that encompasses everything, we can immediately see that the natural world is a fundamental part of the discussion. A healthy little economy is one that does not destroy the natural world of which it is a part. It is from the natural world that we acquire our sustenance, for in an ultimate way, everything that sustains us is the product of soil and sun. If we destroy the soil, we destroy ourselves. If we deplete the natural world without care, we are acting like the fool who glibly dines on his seed corn, ignoring the inevitable fact that a day of reckoning will come.

To claim that a healthy little economy is agrarian rather than industrial is not to suggest that in a healthy economy all people are farmers or that all the trappings of industry are necessarily destructive. It is, though, to argue that an agrarian mind sees the world in a fundamentally different way than the industrial mind. Where the agrarian mind sees the natural world as a creation, of which humans are a part, the industrial mind sees the natural world as a "resource," as something that is abstracted from the world of humans, as an "environment." There is, though, a world of difference between a "creation" and "the environment."

According to Berry, "'Environment' means that which surrounds or encircles us; it means a world separate from ourselves, outside us." This conception is born of an attempt to simplify a relationship that is astoundingly complex. "The world that environs us, that is around us, is also within us. We are made of it; we eat, drink, and breathe it; it is bone of our bone and flesh of our flesh. It is also a Creation, a holy mystery." In some ways we can lay claim to this creation, for we must live and to live is to consume. At the same time—and this is largely forgotten by the industrial mind—we also belong to this creation, "and it makes certain rightful claims on us: that we care properly for it, that we leave it undiminished not just to our children but to all the creatures who will live in it after us. None of this intimacy and responsibility is conveyed by the word *environment*."[14]

While some cultures have managed to live in relative harmony with the natural world, the technological powers now at our disposal make this imperative in our day. In the West, the troubled relationship between humans and the natural world has deep roots. According to Genesis 1:26, God, having created the first humans, gave them "dominion" over the rest of creation. The word "dominion" may, and has, invoked the idea of domination, which conjures up images of harsh oppression of the powerful over the weak. But "dominion" also carries with it the connotation of ruling. Rule, of course, speaks to the notion of justice, and just rule is not characterized by harsh oppression but by concern for the good of those ruled. This second tack seems especially fitting when we consider the context within which the mandate was spoken: a garden. Anyone with even a slight experience with gardening knows that good gardening is not the product of harsh oppression of the garden. Just rule in the context of a garden implies careful cultivation born of knowledge, experience, and love. It is only when we tear the verse from its larger context that we can be tempted to see it as justification for the harsh domination of the nonhuman world.

This adversarial posture toward the natural world has seeped deeply into the collective pores of Western society. Of course, there are and always have been those who have resisted, who have refused to see nature as the enemy: From St. Francis of Assisi to Henry David Thoreau, from the hippies of the 1960s to those today who, perhaps sporting shorter hair, object to the willful negligence of those who treat the natural world without care. Such people, though, have generally been minorities, and their voices have often been ineffectual or at least muted, for they tend to argue for restraint and limits, and such appeals face an uphill battle when confronted by the energetic forces of progress. Profit and fame are to be found in the churning cauldron of domination and power. By comparison, little is to be gained by championing restraint, by preaching contentment, by respecting limits, and living modestly. Little is to be gained, I should say, if we focus only on short-term material profits. If we but open our eyes and see that unsustainable farming practices cannot, well, be sustained, we would see the wisdom in seeking another way; if we would only grasp that building a world based on an eternal supply of cheap oil requires a faith that can, and will, literally move mountains in our frenzied search for the key to our existence, we might reconsider how we live; if we would only put to question the assumption that our corporate success depends on perpetual growth, we might see that such an assumption is not only without merit but also without possibility.

SEPARATION

It is, at the same time, important not to romanticize nature and our place in it. The curse uttered by God in Eden illustrates the adversity humans face in relating to the natural world: "Cursed is the ground for thy sake; in sorrow shalt thou eat of it all the days of thy life; Thorns also and thistles shall it bring forth to thee; and thou shalt eat the herb of the field; In the sweat of thy face shalt thou eat bread, till thou return unto the ground."[15]

Anyone who has experienced the pangs of hunger or felt the icy winds of winter has a small sense of the hardness of the natural world. Anyone who has watched an animal suffer and die or be torn apart by stronger creatures must suspect that behind the romantic's facade lies the fear of wild things lurking beyond the firelight. Indeed, our existence is, in one respect, the result of successfully constructing barriers against the forces of nature that push in on us. Drought, flood, tornado, fire, cold, heat, hunger, violence—all of these are part of the natural world. It is quite natural for humans to strive against these forces. We construct reservoirs against times of drought, dikes against floods, storm cellars and firebreaks, central heating and air-conditioning, surplus food and firearms. By these means and many more, we attempt to counter the grim forces of nature that seek to strip us of our security, our comfort, and our very lives. We naturally struggle against death, and we make efforts to ward off disease even as we struggle against illness. Pain, suffering, and death are natural if by that term we mean "an unavoidable part of human existence." But the fact that we seek to avoid these things and consider them, in some respect, evil, forces us to recognize that life is, in one way, a continuous struggle against nature.

But this is clearly inadequate. While pain, suffering, and death are natural things we seek to avoid, this is not the sum of what we mean by nature. While it is true that our lives do consist of, as Søren Kierkegaard put it, a sickness unto death, this is not the whole story. Nature, from one perspective, is "red in tooth and claw," threatening us from every side, but from another perspective, the natural word is not something from which we are estranged but that of which we are members. It is our source of sustenance, livelihood, pleasure, and beauty.

In other words, if the sum total of our relationship to nature were one of adversity, and if we were successful in our attempt to overcome nature, we would find ourselves on the losing side even as we planted the flag of victory. To conquer nature would be to destroy ourselves. We may harness its powers, tap into its resources, harvest its fruits, and consume its edibles, but the moment we fail to grasp that the natural world is essential to our existence and begin to treat it merely as a resource to be consumed and disposed of, we point the gun to our own heads.

As we have moved away from the land, as we have become more urbanized and less attuned to the natural world, it has become easier to think of ourselves as distinct from the natural world. A family farm—where people are intimately involved in sowing and harvest, in the birth, nurture, and death of animals—is a sort of nexus wherein the fundamental connection of humans to the earth is enacted. Even a humble garden serves to remind us, in the very act of tending it, that gratitude is owed, that care is necessary, and that grace often comes by simple means. When we fail to acknowledge our fundamental connection to the natural world, we create a false picture of reality, one in which we can actually imagine ourselves as autonomous creatures, unconnected to anything except by force of our individual wills. Given the human propensity to hubris, this sort of dualism is, perhaps, not surprising, but neither is it healthy. Nor can it be sustained over the long term.

There are, I think, several different directions by which we can explore this tendency toward separation. The first can be seen in the distinction between the tool and the machine. Both represent an attempt to change the environment of the person wielding them. Both can be grasped under the rubric of technology. Thus, from the start, it is important to stipulate that the problem is not technology per se. Humans have always employed technology to aid them in their various pursuits. A car is a kind of technology as is a train or a space shuttle. A hoe is no less a technology than a tractor. A quill pen and ink is a technology and so is a computer.

In writing about these matters, Lewis Mumford makes a useful distinction between the tool and the machine. The difference, Mumford writes, "lies in the degree of independence in the operation from the skill and motive power of the operator: the tool lends itself to manipulation, the machine to automatic action. . . . In general, the machine emphasizes specialization of function, whereas the tool indicates flexibility. . . . From the beginning the machine was a sort of minor organism, designed to perform a single set of functions."[16] If we accept Mumford's distinction, it becomes clear that as our lives become increasingly oriented to machines, we are increasingly separated from the world upon which the machine works.

Take, for instance, agriculture. A man operating a horse-drawn plow walks behind the plow. His feet touch the freshly turned earth. He must learn to master the art of handling the horse, which involves caring for the horse both before and after it is attached to the plow. The man must master the art of handling the plow: he must plow a straight furrow; he must not go too deep nor too shallow. He must know how to negotiate hidden boulders. Additionally, he must be competent to make repairs of the harness and plow. In short, this sort of farming requires a variety of skills, but just as important, the farmer never forgets his connection to the earth, for he is close to it, can smell its moist rankness, can speak to the horse, and must know the limits of the beast and himself.

While we must acknowledge the massive increase in productive potential, it is also true that farmers in modern tractors are more detached from the land they work. They can sit far above the field in air-conditioned comfort, listening to a talk radio program from New York City. They can program the computerized equipment to cut a furrow of a certain depth, and because their fields are so massive (a necessity to make tractors affordable and usable), they simply steer them to the end of the furrows and turn around. Of course, some simple skills are involved in operating a piece of heavy machinery, but repairing it often requires a specialized set of skills and tools that the average farmer simply does not possess. Neither do modern farmers have to attend to the capacity of their horses or even the limits of daylight, for they have horsepower courtesy of petroleum and headlights courtesy of halogen, so their machines can continue around the clock if there is someone available to turn the wheel. In such a context, farmers can conceivably plow, plant, cultivate, and harvest their crops without so much as touching the field.

If machines, as Mumford argues, lend themselves to specialization and repetitive motion, they, by virtue of these facts, require less human engagement than tools that are characterized by the absence of automation. Tools require craftsmen. Craftsmen possess skills long honed, perhaps passed down from parent to child, and carefully maintained through practice. Tools tend to connect people to their work; machines tend to separate. Tools connect people to their own bodies and the world of which they are a part; machines tend to require specialized knowledge but little in the way of physical skill. So even as machines tend to separate people from the natural world of work, they also tend to separate physical work from mental work, all the while privileging the latter and denigrating the former.

The rise of the machine corresponds significantly with the urbanization of the population. Cities, of course, are not new. But the slow abandonment of many rural communities and the steady growth of urban areas suggests a problem of balance. In a modern city, it is possible, and endlessly tempting, to live as if one is separated from the natural world. Consider, for starters, the acres of concrete and asphalt. It is possible to live an active life and yet go for days, and even weeks, without touching foot to earth. In such a context, it is easy to look upon dirt itself as undesirable. After all, conscientious shopkeepers, homeowners, and city municipalities attempt to keep the sidewalks and streets clean. Of course, one aspect of this is the disposal of trash, but in a city, dirt itself becomes associated with trash in the same way it does in a house. We sweep the dirt off the kitchen floor and off the streets. In the country, however, one does not attempt to sweep the dirt off the path or the unpaved road. It is accepted matter-of-factly as a fundamental part of the outside world. It is, if one stops long enough to consider the matter, the foundation upon which all else is built. We easily lose sight of this in a paved-over world.

A modern city is a city of lights. In fact, most cities are far more attractive at night precisely because of the concentration of light. Artificial lights emphasize specific buildings, create striking shadows, and hide the tired grime that the daylight so readily reveals. Cities are bathed in eternal light. During the day, the light is provided by the sun. At night, the artificial lights blaze. Such an arrangement does, indeed, make it possible to claim that some cities never sleep, but is that a good thing? Is anything lost when the sky is never dark? When a people never feel the awful magnitude of the night sky filled with stars, they lose one avenue by which self-knowledge is attained. When people live day after day where the most visible things are the artifacts of human invention, might it be temping to believe that human artifacts are all that matter? Might it be easier to imagine that humans can be manipulated, created, commodified, and discarded, like the various and sundry things that clutter the scene? A night sky induces one to wonder. It may even lead the mind to thoughts of human frailty and to the possibility of God. The night sky of a city reminds one only of the glorious work of human hands. Hubris lurks in the very thought.

It is not only the night that is missing in the city. Silence has been silenced. The dull roar of traffic punctuated by the scream of sirens, the squeal of brakes, and the blare of car horns provides a constant background noise. Add to this the radios, CD players, and televisions, along with iPods pumping music directly into individual brains, and one is left with a cacophony, a steady, inescapable wall of sound. This constant manufactured noise makes the more subtle sounds of the natural world far more difficult to hear. One may, to be sure, hear the flutter of pigeon's wings as they rise to avoid a pedestrian, and one may hear the barking of a dog or the wild yowling of cats fighting over trash in the alley. But these are merely a fraction of the sounds emitted on a dark night in the country, where the natural world creeps to your very doorstep with a soft snuffle, a dull hum sings through the open window, and tiny tracks appear in the mud around the pond. One must silence the human din in order to hear the sounds of the natural world. It may even be the case that silence in the presence of the natural world is a source of strength: "Be still and know that I am God" may be connected to "I will lift up mine eyes unto the hills, from whence cometh my help."[17]

Modern cities, of course, have parks. There are trees planted on sidewalks, flower boxes on windowsills, and rooftop gardens for the displaced or aspiring farmer. All this is true and not to be discounted. But one thing that is lost is any sense of wildness. City parks, if they are good ones, are well tended. They are groomed, cut, fertilized, planted, and used. In short, they are managed. They are held tightly within the purview of human will. They can create the impression that the natural world is completely subject to human hands, and this being the case, is it any wonder that parks tend to be treated like any other commodity? We "use" the park. We go there for outings and return having extracted a certain amount of plea-sure from that commodity. Even our rural national and state parks find themselves pressed into this same kind of service. The demand for access, for paved roads, for convenient services, in the heart of wild and (hopefully) untamed country is precisely the attempt to transport the artificial view of nature—born and nurtured in city parks—to the "scenic" parts of the natural world that are not surrounded by a city. It is an attempt to take the safety and predictability of a city park and com-bine it with the artificial thrill of a roller coaster. And we call it "nature." The only problem is that as soon as we control, domesticate, and commodify the wilderness, we change it. Or it might be better to say that we change the way we see it, for the bison will still gore the feckless tourist who attempts to pet it—bad for the tourist but good for the bison and wilderness in general. But when people are tempted to imagine that wild places are domesticated or that they should be, we have attempted to impose the control of the city upon the natural world.

Separation from the natural world is perhaps no better illustrated than in the way urban existence tends to change our understanding of food. Hunter-gatherer societies are never tempted to forget that food is first a living thing that must be plucked, gathered, chased, killed, peeled, gutted, cleaned, cut, and roasted before it can be eaten. Now I, for one, am thankful that the days of chasing the wooly mammoth with a spear and some hungry friends are long gone. Fortunately, humans learned that some animals could be domesticated (presumably not the wooly mammoth) and that the many benefits derived from keeping animals outweighed the trouble of doing so. These enterprising people no longer had to chase their potential dinner over hill and dale, but they, nevertheless, still had to kill and clean the animals, even as they were required to cultivate their gardens and labor in the dirt to enjoy the fruit of the land. Only a century ago, a significant percentage of Americans lived close enough to the land that they could not forget the obvious links connecting their food with dirt, dung, and death. Today many people would rather not think about the fact that the milk on their corn flakes came from the pink, dangling udder of a cow. Most would rather not think about the bloodletting that occurred to make their bacon possible. Many are even perturbed if they find significant amounts of dirt on their supermarket vegetables. Dirt? Blood? Death? Please. I'm trying to eat.

To ignore the death of the living things that we eat is to ignore the debt of gratitude that we owe those things that died to sustain us. If we allow ourselves to imagine that our food comes from the bright and sterile environs of the supermarket, we tempt ourselves to imagine that our food is the object of our own creation, another artifact like our buildings, central air-conditioning, and television. We forget our necessary connection to the soil. We forget that soil is made of decaying things that were once living. We forget that our bodies are made of the dust and are destined to return to the earth from whence they came. Humility and gratitude, both so essential to a properly conceived human life, are easily forgotten when we forget or ignore the obvious connection between food and the natural world.

Closely connected to food is waste. In a society oriented by agrarian principles, waste is returned to the earth where it can contribute to soil health. However, industrialization—and here I mean industrial thinking—finds itself confronted with the problem of waste, and the solutions are rarely satisfactory. Industrialization tends to imply concentration. It is characterized by standardization and mechanization. Take, for example, the manner in which most food animals are raised in the United States today. Concentrated animal feeding operations (CAFOs) are the generally accepted method for processing beef. CAFOs use the idea of concentration and scale to prepare an astounding number of animals for the market. But in so doing animals are necessarily treated as meat-producing machines rather than as fellow creatures to whom we owe our gratitude and care. Typically, beef cows are shipped from around the country to feedlots where thousands of head of cattle are "finished" on a diet of corn. This fattens them quickly and cheaply before their trip to the slaughterhouse. The animals are fed about twenty-five pounds a day, and they produce around nine pounds of waste during the same period. It doesn't take a math whiz to see that thousands of cows concentrated in a small area and producing nine pounds of manure a day will create more than beef. Yes, there is the smell, but there is also a mountain of crap. In 2005, a feedlot in Milford, Nebraska, found itself in deep doo-doo when its two-thousand-ton mountain spontaneously caught fire and lay smoldering on the Nebraska plain like some grotesque parody of a volcano. How to put out the fire? People were complaining about the stench, and besides, clean-air laws were obviously being violated. Call the fire department and hose it down? No. The mountain would turn to a muddy sluice that would run off into streams and possibly contaminate the groundwater.[18]

Of course, most manure mountains don't combust. Feedlots generally sell their "product" back to farmers and to companies that bag the stuff and sell it to gardeners. Farmers end up purchasing the manure or chemical fertilizers their fields require even though, if things were handled differently, they would have all the fertilizer they needed for free. This concentration in the feedlot creates incomplete or inefficient natural cycles that tempt us to forget that the food we eat requires the waste products of the animals we raise. When we neglect or ignore the necessary connection between manure and the broccoli in our salad, we separate ourselves from reality.

Does this modern separation from the natural world put us in curious tension with our own bodies? Does our separation from rot and death in our food cycle tempt us to avoid thoughts about our own aging and death? Could our modern infatuation with youth and the concomitant attempt to remain young at any cost be tied to our failure to acknowledge the reality that living requires killing and in the end leads to decrepitude and eventual death? In our fanatical attempts to keep our bodies young, do we reveal an underlying hatred of natural processes? Has our separation from the natural world served to usher in a new gnosticism by which we deny the reality of bodily existence (which includes aging and death) and act as if we will be forever young if only we exercise, eat enough prunes, and take our daily dose of vitamins? Might living closer to the land and the food we eat bring us into a more realistic and sober understanding of the fleeting nature of our lives and therefore the preciousness of each life?

I am not, with all that, advocating the wholesale (or even the retail) abandonment of the cities or machines. Farmers can be as industrial as urbanites, and city dwellers can possess agrarian minds. I am suggesting, though, that urban life is more conducive to separating human existence from the natural world than is rural life. If so, then what can be done? Obviously, things like urban gardens are a good first step. More radically, the urban homesteading movement is a hopeful sign that some are coming to realize that food production is something everyone can participate in and that, with creativity, substantial amounts of food can be produced in relatively small areas. It also seems that we must learn to appreciate the quiet and the dark and take the time to seek them out. Having wild places to visit is important because they remind us of our fragility; they shake us back into seeing the world and ourselves in a proper perspective. They remind us of the things so easily forgotten in the blare and lights of the city.

SUBURBS AND NATURE

It is not merely the cities that induce a separation from the natural world. The suburbanization of America has, in more subtle ways, accomplished the same thing. Americans have always had an ambivalent relationship with the city. In the nineteenth century, the idealization of the virtues of the yeoman farmer collided with the industrialization of urban centers. Industrialization, and the mass immigrations that accompanied it, turned many American cities into places teeming with noise, pollution, and overcrowded slums. Rather than being the locus of the best kind of human life, as Aristotle once taught, the city came to be seen as something from which to escape.

Of course, before the era of cheap and efficient transportation, moving outside the city was no easy feat and generally required cutting ties with the city. If one's job was in the city, living there was usually a necessity. With the advent of commuter rail lines and later a complex system of highways, it became possible for people to live in the country and commute into the city to work. For the wealthy, a country estate provided sanctuary from the grime and perils of the city as well as access to the pleasures of country life. A wealthy man could run a company in the city and operate a hobby farm in the country to which he returned each night via train or automobile. Such a person could, in many respects, enjoy the benefits of both the city and the country. But a country estate was beyond the means of most. Real estate developers subdivided land (often farmland) into small plots ranging anywhere from a quarter acre to several acres and marketed these as a means to enjoy the best of both the country and the city. People flocked to these housing developments, and the suburb was born. The French architect and urban planner Le Corbusier recounts an extreme version of this ideal found in a bit of Soviet propaganda promoting deurbanization: "The city will be part of the country; I shall live 30 miles from my office in one direction, under a pine tree; my secretary will live 30 miles away from it too, in the other direction, under another pine tree. We shall both have our own car."[19]

Unfortunately, rather than securing the benefits of both city and country, the modern suburb often partakes of the disadvantages of both. The mixed-use neighborhoods, ideals extolled by urban writers like Jane Jacobs and the New Urbanists, are typically ignored in favor of isolated single-use pods of homes connected to the rest of the world by feeder roads. Stores, schools, and employment of any kind are absent, generally rendered illegal by zoning laws and homeowner associations that operate under the assumption that the best neighborhoods are those uncontaminated by nonresidential buildings and uses. The automobile makes such an arrangement possible, but not without consequences. For instance, suburbs create a situation in which a car is necessary, and a person without an automobile (or a chauffeur) is estranged from the wide variety of human activities not allowed in the suburban development. In such a context, those without access to cars, namely, children and the elderly, find themselves virtual prisoners in a residential bubble devoid of many facets of human life. Even those with cars find themselves spending inordinate amounts of time encased in their steel cocoons traveling to and from work, school, shopping, and entertainment. Of course, such a lifestyle separates one from encountering the natural world that lies just beyond the confines of the house and the car.

The separation is a result of the underlying specialization—not of people but of places—for what could be more specialized than designing a town according to discrete zones designated by use? Of course, single-use areas are simple to comprehend, and they look good on paper because they are clean, unambiguous, and easy to grasp. But such an approach often fails in practice, for it does not reflect the complexity of the human creature. Fragmentation becomes a necessity, since generally one cannot live and work in a suburban neighborhood. One cannot shop or worship or recreate. One can, we are assured, live. When these vital activities are removed, however, one is left wondering what exactly constitutes living.

The predilection for specialization has infected those disciplines that traditionally concerned themselves with city design. For example, according to the authors of the New Urbanist manual, *Suburban Nation*, town planning, which "until 1930 [was] considered a humanistic discipline based upon history, aesthetics, and culture, became a technical profession based upon numbers. As a result, the American city was reduced into the simplistic categories and quantities of sprawl."[20] Sprawl represents the culmination of specialization, which, in fact, represents the rejection of traditional urban design that had for centuries recognized the conditions necessary for vibrant and healthy human existence. Thus, the ideal sought by the New Urbanists is not new at all, for by championing mixed-use walkable neighborhoods, they are merely attempting to recover a simple truth long known and only recently forgotten: cities, towns, and neighborhoods should be constructed to facilitate human flourishing and not to simplify the job of urban designers.

If we take Mumford's definition of a machine, it seems possible to argue that suburbs are machines for living. They separate activities. Like the machine they make the active integration of various skills unnecessary. Want to work? You must leave the suburb. Want to shop? Drive away. Want to go to church? Leave. While never completely successful, the suburb attempts to reduce human life to that which is left over when work, worship, commerce, education, and most entertainment are stripped away. Yet, is anything lost in such an arrangement? How does this artificial segregation of human activities undermine, or at least make more difficult, an integrated life in which various activities occur in a seamless relation to each other? How does this separation contribute to further separation of humans from the natural world?

I think we can get at some of these questions by considering the aesthetics of suburbia. Consider the ideal: single-family homes surrounded by a patch of green. Generally, homeowners associations dictate the setbacks from the curb, so the houses are uniformly characterized by a swath of green between the house and sidewalk or street. The grass must be neatly cut. No grazing livestock allowed! The lawns are kept a stunning color of green by regular doses of chemical fertilizer and weed killer. Dandelions, clover, and any other nongrasses are anathema and must perish. A good yard is part of a monoculture that extends to the highway or the field against which the suburb abuts. There are, of course, other ways to use the land, ways that can at the very least complement a yard: A large garden is an obvious alternative. What about fruit trees? What about sowing clover for the bees? What about keeping a hive? Or maybe a chicken coop? Eggs and meat raised right in the back. Of course, we are now back to blood and dung and death, those inevitable by-products of agriculture and all life in general, but this merely takes us to compost, the best means of increasing soil fertility and putting to good use the organic waste that in many homes is trucked away to the landfill.

But now reality sets in, for even if a person wanted to do these things, chances are good that the homeowners association would object or local ordinances would be violated. This simply highlights the scope of the problem and demonstrates the extent to which our culture as a whole has succumbed to the ideal of separation. Happily, some communities are relaxing rules that impede these kinds of activities, and flocks of hens and bee hives are increasingly common in urban and suburban communities.

Ultimately, we cannot have a proper understanding of ourselves when we are separated, intentionally or not, from the natural world. We cannot be good stewards when we have lost contact with that over which we exercise responsibility. Stewardship and absenteeism are incompatible.

This principle of stewardship is no better illustrated than in a person's relationship to a garden. While I was growing up, my family moved several times. In each new place my parents carved out a garden. They spent hours and great care tending the vegetables and tried, I think, to help us kids appreciate both the work and the benefits and the connection between the two. While I enjoyed (most) of the edible benefits, I despised the work and determined that I would never have a garden so I would never again have to pull weeds. Now I have children of my own, and I long to help them develop an appreciation for the work and the benefits of a garden. When we finally bought a house with land enough to plant a garden I, notwithstanding my youthful vows, eagerly prepared the soil, sowed the seeds, and cared for my small piece of the earth. But as anyone who has ever planted a garden knows, there are no guarantees. While my tomatoes, corn, and lettuce did well, my cucumbers and peppers did not even break the soil. A bit frustrated (after all, what could be so hard about making a seed grow?), I filled some cups with potting soil and carefully planted the cucumber and pepper seeds in the cups. I watered them regularly, and soon tiny sprouts appeared in the dark soil. When the plants were several inches high I transplanted them into the garden. The cucumbers flourished. The peppers did not. And while the corn grew well and put out fine ears, a worm began to eat them and then a raccoon.

What does tending a garden teach a person? First, one cannot assert oneself over a garden and control it by dominating it. Gardeners must work with the garden and cultivate it; they cannot command it. Second, the kind of guarantees that we long for are simply not available. Despite the best of intentions and the most loving care, my peppers did not produce. Life is full of disappointments as well as successes and even surprises. Absolute control and certainty are beyond human experience. There is no money-back guarantee. Third, planting a garden requires commitment. When one plants a garden, one cannot simply leave the next day. Or the next. A garden represents a promise that is fulfilled only if one perseveres. Fourth, a garden is an exercise in faith. We put a tiny seed in the dark, moist earth, water it, and then we wait. We have faith that something we cannot see or fully comprehend will occur in that dark place and new life will push out of the soil. Life from death, something from nothing—grace. Fifth, a garden represents hope for a harvest in the future. We can anticipate the texture and taste and the satisfaction of eating that which we have tended, and we work to bring that day about.

Finally, the gardener learns what it means to love a particular place in the world. It is difficult, maybe impossible, to mix one's labor with the soil and comprehend the perfect balance between work and rest, gratification and delay, vitality and exhaustion, and not experience the sheer delight in loving a place. We see, then, that in cultivating a garden we, on a small but humane scale, act as stewards of a particular place as we responsibly fulfill the God-given duty to care for the earth. In so doing, we experience ourselves not as aliens, pitted against the earth, but as loving caretakers who, in committing ourselves to the care of a particular place, find that in addition to cultivating plants, we are also cultivating the virtues of faith, hope, and love, virtues that ultimately point back to God.

Humans and the entire nonhuman world are part of a creation with all that such a term entails. The Great Economy encompasses the world as a whole. Our little economies will never approximate health unless they exist comfortably within this larger context. Yet even by thinking in these terms, we are forced to acknowledge that there is much we cannot know, much that exceeds our capacity to grasp. By acting wisely and humbly, we can learn to see ourselves as participants in the Great Economy, a reality we can touch only tangentially but one through which we can feel the hum of mystery, beauty, and truth.

8

Family: The Cradle of Gratitude

The supreme adventure is being born. There we do walk suddenly into a splendid and startling trap. There we do see something of which we have not dreamed before. Our fathers and mothers do lie in wait for us and leap out on us like brigands from a bush. Our uncle is a surprise. Our aunt is, in the beautiful common expression, a bolt from the blue. When we step into the family, by the act of being born, we do step into a world which is incalculable, into a world which has its own strange laws, into a world which could do without us, into a world that we have not made. In other words, when we step into the family, we step into a fairy tale.

G. K. Chesterton, *Brave New Family*

What is the place of the family in this account I am developing? On the one hand, there are those who insist that the so-called traditional family is merely a form of patriarchal power masquerading as domestic bliss and that we can choose better arrangements built on mutual respect and equitable distribution of power. On the other hand, there are those who see the nuclear family as the sum total of God's intention for the family. Both views, I think, overlook important elements about the family that are easy to miss in a world characterized by autonomous individuals roaming the earth seeking personal satisfaction or material gain.

Those who deny that the traditional family is in any way normative argue that people are first and foremost individuals who have needs, desires, and the capacity to choose. Furthermore, any decent society will work to ensure that individuals possess the political and economic freedom to exercise their autonomy to the fullest extent possible, limited only by the rights of other individuals. This view of human nature will give birth to new and unique family structures, each tailored to the needs and desires of those participating in it. One man, one woman, and a handful of children? Fine, albeit a bit old-fashioned. Surely someone is being oppressed and likely abused. Two men and a baby? Wonderful. Traditional roles are merely social conventions that should be overturned. Two women, three kids, and a dog? Sure. The white picket fence adds a nostalgic veneer over this novel arrangement. Three men, one woman, and children fathered by all three? How progressive. Only a judgmental prude would think to object. As long as there is love and no one is being coerced, then the family that emerges is just fine.

But are things really that simple? Can individuals call the tune and expect nature to caper forth ready to dance? Or does the structure of reality limit the ways that we arrange ourselves socially? Of course, we can choose to ignore limits and let our imaginations run unfettered, but ignoring or denying natural norms is not the same as making them disappear. One can, presumably, dance on the edge of a precipice, but sooner or later gravity is going to demonstrate some very old-fashioned truths.

What are the natural limits, the natural structures, to which the family ought to conform? Note, in passing, how the simple word "conform" causes a slight shudder. We have been taught, by word if not by deed, that conformity is evil or at least in bad taste. We should, instead, think in terms of novelty. Each person should be an original. Of course, such thinking is really the product of the autonomous individualism and the progressivism that so infects our collective self-understanding. Is conforming to something a bad thing? Only if the thing to which one conforms is a bad thing. If one seeks to conform to standards that are good and natural and healthy and sane, then conformity is clearly a good idea.

Certain standards do exist for the family. First, one function of families, perhaps the most important, is to provide a loving, healthy environment in which children can be produced and nurtured with the hope that they will one day be mature adults capable of raising families of their own. In short, families are the means by which the human race and human culture are perpetuated. On the biological level, babies are naturally made in only one way: One man, one woman, a few sparks, a few months, and along comes Junior. It's all quite simple, elegant really. Biological reproduction is as natural as eating and sleeping.

It seems, then, that from a biological view, a family necessarily begins with one man and one woman. This arrangement has been the norm for humans as cultures naturally built upon the structures imposed by biological reproduction. This, of course, does not automatically mean it is the best or that is it morally superior, but when biology and culture both point in the same general direction, surely the burden of proof is on those who propose an alternative.

There are some who will point to the single mother or the single father or the home in which two men are raising a child and say, "What about them? Aren't they normal?" First, it's admittedly odd that in a world where conforming to a standard is so denigrated, people would long to be considered normal by the rest of society. Second, the existence of families that deviate from the norm does not obviate the norm nor does it necessarily condemn those who do not conform to the norm, just as the existence of blind people does not obviate the fact that seeing is normal or imply condemnation of blind people. The existence of single mothers, for instance, does not force us to admit that single motherhood is the ideal toward which all families ought to aspire. A norm is an ideal representing the way things should be under ideal circumstances. Unfortunately, the world is not a perfect place. But to say the world is not a perfect place is to tacitly admit that a standard of rightness exists, a standard to which we can compare the world and recognize its imperfections. In terms of the family, the two-parent (male and female) model is the norm. That this standard to rooted in biology is obvious. That a majority of societies have affirmed this is not conclusive, but it does provide evidence that cannot be ignored even if one objects to the standard.

So a family based on the biological unit of a mother and father is the norm for the creation of children. It appears, then, that the nuclear family emerges as the standard, rooted in nature, representing the norm for the family. Here we need to pause. While it is undeniable that a man and a woman are the necessary elements for the begetting of children, men and women do not exist in solitude prior to their union. They themselves belong to families. When a man and woman join to form the basis of a new nuclear family, they bring with them the stories, memories, habits, customs, practices (as well as the social and genetic anomalies) of their respective families. When the two raise their children, they are surrounded by a great cloud of witnesses (and busybodies), both alive and dead, that envelopes the family they have initiated.

The nuclear family may be the norm for the simple production of children, but it has not been the norm for their upbringing. In the premodern world, in which people tended to stay put, extended families created an atmosphere of nurture, care, discipline, advice, and meaningful work, as well as stories that provided the narrative context for the lives of each individual. In the West, the intact extended family has largely given way to the transient nuclear unit that encounters extended family members only at reunions and holidays at the beach. In a mobile age, when leaving home is as easy as calling U-Haul, the nuclear family has come to be seen, by many conservatives, as the ideal. Forgotten is the richly textured world of multi-generational interaction made possible when nuclear families are embedded into the larger structure of the extended family.

The family has not escaped the individualism that pervades our society. The isolated nuclear family, existing as a lonely island on the sea of society, is not the ideal, and it can be seen as a step in the direction of fully fledged individualism in which any unchosen attachment is deemed undesirable. Of course, in particular cases, this sometimes cannot be avoided, but exceptions are concessions, and when exceptions become the norm, propriety has been lost.

LOCUS OF LIFE

Reproduction, as I said, is unavoidably the function of one man and one woman. (For now I'm setting aside technologies that may one day reduce the entire process to something that takes place in a laboratory using only human parts—egg and sperm—and an artificial womb.) Beginning with this one fact, how should we think about life?

If we assume that life itself is a good thing, then the birth of a child is the cause of celebration. It is the beginning of a completely new set of possibilities, of choices to be made, of memories to be created, of love to be shared. Life is the first gift we receive, although we were not capable of asking for or expecting such a boon. It is fitting to celebrate a birthday, but in addition to the cake, gifts, and a song, perhaps we should think of our birthday as a day of gratitude for the life we have been given out of the bounty of reality.

When we think of life in these terms, conception itself would seem to be a cause for celebration as a tiny person begins its journey through this life, the gifted-ness of which is revealed in a gentle kick felt only by the mother carrying the child in her womb, or a baby's smile or the toddler's first steps, or a child's first words when the parent's hope and love swells to the breaking point at the sound of this little creature saying "Dada."

Compare this vision of human life with the contemporary notion that all too often sees conception as a disease to be prevented via birth "control" and squelched by abortion. Something seems amiss when bodies functioning naturally cause the "disease" of conception while sidetracking that normal functioning is seen as the surest avenue for enjoying sex unfettered by anything other than the choice of partners and the location of the deed. While I am not arguing that all acts that reduce the possibility of conception are necessarily and intrinsically bad, I am suggesting that a culture that does not recognize the sheer giftedness of life is one that comes dangerously close to embracing an ideal of sterility, in which conception is the (mostly dreaded) exception.

Celebrating the conception and birth of a child is an expression of hope. It is a commitment to the future. It is an act that defies despair even in the face of turmoil, fear, and uncertainty. To bring a child into the world is to say that the world is worth preserving. It is worth the effort of raising this child, nourishing her physically and spiritually, and equipping her with the abilities to do the same when her time comes to rear children of her own. Having children is to cast one's lot with our ancestors who, in hope, often desperate hope, embraced the future believing that all was not lost.

The very act of becoming a parent has a sobering effect. What parent has held a newborn baby and not felt the burden of responsibility grow at that very moment? Becoming parents can make men and women out of people who were previously uncertain about the meaning of life or their place in the world. When we come to grasp the sheer helplessness of a baby, we can better see our own responsibilities, and we open the door to the possibility of understanding our own frailties: frailties in the past, when we were cared for by our parents, frailties in the future, when we may need care, and perhaps frailties even in the present, for no man is an island.

In light of all this, the current trend in many Western countries toward childlessness, or perhaps one or at most two children, reveals itself to be an act (or a nonact) of stupefying despair. When the birthrate of a country drops below replacement level (about 2.1 children per couple), the sad result is the death of a society. This societal death wish is, in many cases, curiously accompanied by a corresponding societal commitment to hedonism, consumerism, and diversion. Could the two be related? On the surface, this conjunction appears incongruous. If the ideal life consists merely of pleasure, no generous person would hesitate to bring a new participant into the merry world of variegated delights. The issue becomes clearer when we put it in these terms. A life dedicated to hedonistic pursuits is a life of hopelessness, for it sees no wisdom in deferring pleasure or preserving resources against future hardship or saving for the next generation. A life dedicated to hedonism is a life of perpetual possibility never consummated and therefore never attained. Endless supplies of consumer goods merely add to the illusion that happiness can be achieved via this road. Endless opportunities for diversion serve only to distract us from considering other possibilities even as they numb the hopelessness.

THE PLACED FAMILY

Today there is little expectation that the lives of parents and their adult children will remain intimately connected on a day-to-day basis. It has not always been this way. In his book *From Cottage to Work Station*, Allan C. Carlson shows that the dominant social and economic system at the time of the American founding was characterized by the following five qualities:

1. *The primacy of the family economy.* Homes were vibrant centers of activity unified by the need to make a living. All members of the family were integral parts working toward a common goal.
2. *The continued power of kinship and ethnic and religious communities.* People identified themselves with a particular ethnic or religious group as well as with their extended families. They were members of a community, and this membership had economic ramifications, for they intentionally did business with members of their respective communities.
3. *The central focus on land.* In a society that was predominantly agricultural, it is no surprise that land would be a central concern. While land is obviously needed to grow crops and cows, it also represents tangible, improvable property that can be passed on to children who, in turn, can pass it on to their own. Unlike other forms of wealth, land is not mobile, so the centrality of land helped facilitate the kind of stability that kept families connected.
4. *The abundance of children.* Because work was centered around the home, children could participate in the economy of the family. Children were seen as valuable economic assets. A family with many children could accomplish more—could produce more—than a family with few or no children.
5. *The power of intergenerational bonds.* Because the locus of the economy was the home, children, parents, and grandparents lived and worked together. There was an expectation that children would care for their parents, as the

parents had once cared for the child. Because the economy centered on the ownership of land, there was a tangible and viable form of economic livelihood that could be passed from one generation to the next. Carlson, quoting the historian James Henretta, notes that parents raised children to "succeed them" not merely to "succeed."[1]

But this, of course, merely raises the question: is the unity of the extended family a good that trumps all others? Surely not. We can all think of examples of righteous people leaving their extended families to serve the poor or God in a place not of their birth. A call from God may make all other considerations moot. It is not clear that a call from Intel should elicit the same response. My concern is that we have forgotten, or at least neglected, the humble goods that accompany proximity to extended family. All things considered, is it preferable for grown children to live near their parents? Their siblings? Is it beneficial for children to know their cousins and grandparents well and to interact with them regularly? These are good things that should not be lightly discarded.

Of course, in the preindustrial world, it was not difficult to imagine extended families remaining intact through successive generations. But even in agrarian communities, this kind of familial stability is today more illusive. As many have noted, higher education, now considered the necessary passport to success, has exerted a tremendous pressure on the family. Children are encouraged to go away to college, where the content of study almost invariably induces a cosmopolitan disposition accompanied by a love for the fast, the simple, the modern, and perhaps most of all, for the big. Places and economies of modest scale will seem hopelessly antiquated to one whose tastes have been formed by an industrialized, centralized, super-sized world. Who would want to go back? After all, progress is the basic assumption of modernity, and to resist progress, or to be merely contented with the status quo, is to be backward and, well, unmodern. The indictment sticks.

Do children, though, miss out on something important when they do not live in the presence of grandparents, even if that means watching them decline and eventually die? Are there lessons—hard lessons no doubt—to be learned that are missed when the elderly are removed from the home and news of death comes via a polite telephone call? Might a child, as well as an adult, come better to understand the full significance of life if aging and death were close at hand and, indeed, an integral part of life?

The elderly, as we all know, seem compelled to tell stories: to tell of their experiences, to recount (repeatedly) tales from the past that have impressed themselves deeply on their memories and, indeed, shaped who they became. In a nursing home, who listens to the stories? Of course, the employees will, if they have time, endure for a while stories that have no context, and ultimately no meaning, for they do not share the common past that knits a family together over time and space. That the elderly long to tell stories seems perfectly tailored to the fact that children love to listen to stories. To separate the elderly from the young is to deprive both of a gift. And it is to deprive the family of the narrative continuity that makes a family endure. But, at the same time, children raised on a steady diet of television and video games will not tolerate for long the rambling stories from Grandpa in a rocking chair. "That's boring," say the children, whose attention spans have been fragmented by the frantic pace of their electronic gadgets and whose imaginations have been seared by the fires of Hollywood.

So in the end, both lose. The elderly die with stories untold, pent up and irrevocably lost when they breathe their last. The children grow up bereft of an important conduit to the past, to *their* past, and so they develop the false illusion that the world, at least the important part of it, came into being with their own births. They lose the sense of connection to the particular stories of a living emissary from the past. They lose the possibility of loving and caring for another person who will not recover but continue to decline into greater dependence. They lose the example of a life lived completely and concluded with grace, even as the dying may be hard. They lose the example of a life of faith that endures to the end.

The sort of generational attachment to a particular place, which invariably served to forge attachments between members of a family, was once possible because the home was the center of vibrant activity. But consider how much has changed. In the typical household today, the father works away from the home, and often the mother does the same. The children are bused to various age-segregated schools. During the days, many homes are empty. They are not vibrant centers of meaningful activity but merely hotels awaiting occupants who arrive in time to eat a hastily prepared meal and then collapse into easy chairs before the stupefying and isolating television, only to repeat the cycle when the alarm jolts them into another day.

Children's lives too often consist of being transported from one organized activity to another, during which they learn to cooperate with others, to work as a team, to feel a sense of satisfaction for working hard and performing well. But they do all this with peers and not their families. Consequently, families do not learn to work together and thereby come to think of themselves as members of a family team. Neither do children learn the invaluable lesson of working and playing with people who are not their own age. In short, we often teach our children to think of themselves as members of organizations and teams that are outside of the family at the expense of cultivating a sense of membership in a vibrant and productive enterprise centered in the home. Of course, outside activities are not intrinsically bad, and in many ways they are beneficial. But when there is no meaningful activity in the home around which the family is oriented, is it any wonder that children, by their late elementary years, show precious little interest in being with their parents and a restless anxiety to hang out with their peers?

While some sort of rural agrarian lifestyle might seem like an ideal, if romantic, remedy, this is not realistic for most. And even then, the same forces threaten to fragment rural families. How then can parents inculcate an appreciation for family unity in a way that counters the forces that seem bent on driving families apart? Carlson suggests that the home school movement represents a hopeful step in once again making the home a hub of meaningful activity.[2] To be sure a home school, organized well, might help to forge a sense of family unity. The content of the curriculum might be intentionally designed to educate young people to know and love their own local communities. But quite apart from that, families can develop and foster joint activities. A family enterprise—whether a business or a hobby—serves to unite members around a common cause. When families see themselves as pursuing a common good in the context of a particular place, they will be able to imagine themselves embracing a life together. Finally, parents need to make a place to which children can return. In our world of hypermobility, we all should reflect on the price of rootlessness. For if the unity of the extended family is a good that should at least be factored into our decisions, we must consider with fresh eyes what constitutes a home and seek to set an example to our children as we practice the art of homemaking.

EASY MOBILITY AND BOREDOM

But how can we make an enduring home for our children and grandchildren when we ourselves have set such a poor example? How did it come to pass that the extended family fragmented? If we recall Tocqueville's description of Americans, we can begin to grasp part of the answer. Tocqueville was impressed by the frantic pace of American life, by the restlessness that animated the democratic soul, by the relentless pursuit of material gain. Americans are a mobile people. The restless pursuit of economic advantage has the effect of cutting the nuclear family loose from the extended family, as well as from the larger community. One element of the individualism described by Tocqueville is the atomistic nuclear family adrift in the world of commerce, driven to seek a better standard of living. Of course, this impulse is not simply irrational nor is it possible to condemn it out of hand. There are times when circumstances dictate that leaving one's place is the obvious remedy to a desperate situation. Yet, as with most choices, we do a disservice to the complexity of the human situation if we neglect to acknowledge those goods that are lost in the process. And one of the things that is lost in this world of easy mobility is the natural and regular affiliation of extended families.

This mobility, of course, characterizes the daily lives of millions of Americans and comes to represent the norm, so that even once a family settles in a place, the mobile life continues out of both habit and necessity. The habit is deeply engrained and is, at least in part, motivated by a kind of boredom that dreads quietude, for in the stillness, the emptiness of our pursuits echoes loudly in the inner reaches of our souls.

At the same time, the necessity of mobility is a product of the way we build our towns and cities, which first reflect our ideals and then subsequently shape the way we interact with the world around us. The rise of the suburb and commuter culture in the postwar decades has served to make mobility an almost unavoidable part of life.

In our era of specialization and easy mobility, generational attachments are also rendered far more fragile, and multiple generations rarely live in close proximity. Even when families seek to remain close to each other, most suburban developments cater to a specific demographic. It is therefore often difficult, if not impossible, for a couple to downsize once their children have grown without moving to another neighborhood.

In typical urban and suburban homes there is little regular work for children and teens. To be sure, there is the constant incidental upkeep that any house requires, and dishes must be washed, carpets vacuumed, and grass cut in the summer. But these sporadic jobs, many made inaccessible to children because they are done with machines, mean that there is very little steady work for children. Children, because they have been denied the satisfaction of being productive members of the family economy, become simply consumers. Parents find themselves frantically striving to fill their children's time with activities. They are driven by a fear of that most ubiquitous complaint of the modern child: "I'm bored." And they are bored, in part, because they have been deprived of meaningful work, and even apart from work, many of the activities for which they long require transportation outside the neighborhood. Thus, family members turn their concerns toward the individualized desires that require constant activity in a variety of directions. Everyone of driving age needs not only access to a car but, ideally, a car of his or her own, for without this, they are prisoners of boredom.

In his essay "The Work of Local Culture," Wendell Berry describes a sort of institution that once existed in rural Kentucky affectionately known as "sitting till bedtime." After supper when the chores (family work) were done, families would walk across the fields to visit their neighbors. They might pop corn or eat apples, but the center of the evening was the stories they told. "Sometimes they told stories about each other, about themselves, living again in their own memories and thus keeping their memories alive. Among the hearers of those stories were always the children. When bedtime came, the visitors lit their lanterns and went home."

Consider how things have changed. Although most people live in closer proximity to their neighbors than those Kentucky farmers did, they remain far more isolated, for their lives do not touch in consistently meaningful ways. Many of the descendents of those farmers "sit until bedtime watching TV, submitting every few minutes to a sales talk. The message of both the TV programs and the sales talk is that the watchers should spend whatever is necessary to be like everyone else." And what of the stories? Stories serve to bind neighbors together as they reminisce about a shared past even as they anticipate a shared future. By sharing stories, neighbors preserve a local culture, a culture particular to a community situated in a particular place. "But most of us no longer talk with each other, much less tell each other stories. We tell our stories now mostly to doctors or lawyers or psychiatrists or insurance adjustors or the police, not to our neighbors for their (and our) entertainment. The stories that now entertain us are made up for us in New York or Los Angeles or other centers of such commerce."[3] The shared stories, which for Berry are so essential to healthy communities, are possible only if the members of a community share the complex, overlapping aspects of their lives over a significant amount of time. Isolation and mobility, features so common in many neighborhoods, undermine the possibility of shared stories and therefore render a healthy community impossible.

Ultimately, isolation and disintegration of the family leads to the disintegration of local communities. This, in turn, signals the disintegration of culture, for when the local and particular are sacrificed in the name of the universal and homogeneous, the result is a featureless monoculture in which tastes are set by Madison Avenue admen and Hollywood stars. When culture is no longer predominately local in nature but national or even international, the cult of the colossal has triumphed. The integrity of the family is swallowed up by the leviathan of the welfare state, which promises to meet every need and wipe away every tear. This signals the death of freedom, for, as Berry puts it, "bigness is totalitarian; it establishes an inevitable tendency toward the *one* that will be the biggest of all. . . . The aim of bigness implies not one aim that is not socially and culturally destructive."[4] Thus, cultural homogenization results in a loss of freedom that ultimately destroys the liberty afforded by democracy, for as Tocqueville put it, "the strength of free peoples resides in the local community."[5] I will add a coda: the strength of local community resides in the family. The thrust of the modern world is away from the local and toward the universal; away from the concrete present that requires our love and care, toward an abstract and perfect future in which all concerns will be alleviated by specialists; away from intact extended families and toward attachments rooted only in consent.

The destruction of local communities leaves a cultural vacuum that is filled with a homogeneous culture that is as bland as it is broad. This homogenization leads to boredom, apathy, and a diminished sense of care or responsibility. If we hope to create a context within which human lives can be lived with dignity and joy, then we must turn our attention to preserving local culture, local customs, local beauty, local economies, and families. This, obviously, cannot be accomplished by political action at the national level; it will be realized only when individuals commit to raising healthy families in a particular place and commit to the long-term work of making a place. Only through such a process will people fully recognize and enjoy the responsibilities and pleasures of membership in a local community comprised of strong families. These good things are not the unique provenance of agrarian or rural settings. They can and have been achieved in cities and towns. The means to this end are clear. What is needed is the energy and creativity to bring it into existence and the will to sustain it.

FAMILY AND ECONOMICS

When examining the family from the perspective of economics, we can discover another set of challenges. The postwar years brought an unprecedented surge of economic wealth to the people of the United States. Europe was a shambles, and the United States was intact and poised to rebuild the world. The flurry of building and manufacturing created jobs, steadily increasing wages, and a sense that the hard days of the Depression and the war were giving way to new era of prosperity and peace. Although the ravages of two world wars had temporarily cooled the optimism of those who thought that human nature could be changed, the fires of industry ignited a new kind of progressivism, one that tacitly promised more and better for all. A new era of increasing wealth and opportunity was being born, and Americans would lead the way.

People and their politicians all began to believe that each rising generation would enjoy a standard of living better than their parents. The prospect of unlimited growth and, as a consequence, unlimited happiness was in the air. After all, America had shown itself resilient to the designs of both fascism and communism, and—despite the inconveniences of a muddled war in Southeast Asia and the oil shortages of the 1970s—when the Berlin Wall fell in 1989, the American way of life seemed vindicated. With cheap oil as the universal lubricant, the American economy motored on, perpetually growing and spreading prosperity to all.

This party of indulgence could not last, but it has endured long enough to dramatically affect the family. The illusion of perpetual economic growth requires, as one article of faith, a commitment to consuming ever greater quantities of purchased goods. Homeowners obliged. Over the course of the twentieth century, homes steadily increased in size and price. The invention of the thirty-year mortgage in the wake of the Great Depression made possible the acquisition of more house and the assumption of half a life of debt. Homeownership, then, became something closer to a rent-to-own scheme with the banks enjoying interest for three decades. In 1950, the square footage of the average house was 983. In 1970, it was 1,500 square feet, and by 2004 it had reached 2,349 square feet.[6] Costs increased dramatically as well, so that by 2008 the average price of a new home was $232,100 compared with $55,700 in 1978.[7] Ironically, during the twentieth century, the size of the average household decreased from 4.60 in 1900 to 3.38 in 1950 and a mere 2.59 in 2000.[8] The trend suggests that individuals will one day see fit to live alone in mansions. Increasingly the standard expectation is that children will have their own bedrooms, and each bedroom will have its own bathroom. After all, sharing a bedroom or even a bathroom burdens children unnecessarily and squelches both their individuality and their liberty.

Of course, expanding possibilities were not limited to the housing market. The connection between happiness and the acquisition of stuff became more of an assumption than a dubious assertion. The idea of doing without became more difficult to countenance in an age of immediate gratification and ample supplies. The virtue of thrift, necessarily cultivated during the difficult years of the Great Depression, gave way to an ethic of disposability, planned obsolescence, and waste. Why fix something if you can purchase a new one for cheap?

One of the results of this binge of buying was a corresponding decline in the perceived value of anything homemade. The pasty Styrofoam called Wonder Bread was seen as a boon to sandwich makers around the nation as "delicious" precut bread took the place of the homemade loaves brought into being by the sweat of the housewife's downtrodden brow. Homemade clothes quickly fell before the onslaught of identical, machine-produced apparel. Only those who couldn't afford store-bought clothes wore homespun items, which quickly marked the wearers as poor or at least poor consumers. The skills of bread making and sewing went the way of soap making, candling, and butchery. I am not suggesting that all specialization is necessarily bad or that the elimination of some of the grueling work our ancestors did is to be mourned. But perhaps we have gone too far in the direction of specialization so that basic skills have been forgotten and the ability to make do, to enjoy some semblance of independence, has been lost. Perhaps we have become too dependent on purchased goods. Ironically, when we lose our ability to make do, we also lose many of the means by which we can practice neighborliness, for we lack the practical skills to be of any help.

The homemaker, once a generalist who could run a complex assortment of enterprises from the home, became a cliché of boredom and loneliness. But this problem was quickly remedied because the urge to consume required one thing above all else: disposable income. And with the advent of inflated expectations and inflating currency, prices rose along with desires into the giddy reaches of consumerdom, each person asked only to keep consuming and keep working, for if either of these two elements should wane, the entire merry-go-round would slowly grind to a halt leaving citizens-turned-consumers wondering what to do with the full garage and pile of debt they had so assiduously accumulated.

The two-income family has increasingly become the norm, so that homes and neighborhoods stand vacant during the day, like well-manicured ghost towns, welcoming the inhabitants home every evening through automatic garage doors that swallow their cars like a mechanical monster. Two-income families create the need for a day care industry of vast proportions, and because not everyone can afford the same quality of day care, the government moved to subsidize child care via tax credits and programs such as Head Start. The welfare state edged into the child care business to facilitate a larger work force to support the economy that would grow forever.

Under these pressures, the nuclear family became less integrated, even as frantic mobility undermined the extended family. Of course, the nuclear family (and other versions of families) still usually live together to the extent that they sleep under the same roof and feed out of the same refrigerator. But the living arrangements are often a matter of convenience and financial dependence rather than affection or commitment. Although they have their own bedrooms and bathrooms, children still need their parents to foot the bill. Television, telephones, iPods, and computers in the bedrooms make it possible for children to sequester themselves away from their parents and siblings. The mutual dependence of a family that owns and operates a small business or a family farm (or even a garden) is replaced by the mutual independence of the well-heeled consumer. Whereas in the former, parents often depend on their children to aid in the family business, in the latter, the dependence is one way—as long as the allowance keeps flowing, no one has to talk to anyone else.

In truth, the industrial family, characterized by ever-expanding desires and bereft of gratitude, is the striking antithesis of the agrarian family characterized by an awareness of limits and well seasoned with gratitude. What separates them is not the possession of land but a way of seeing the world, for an agrarian mind is possible whether one lives on a farm or on Park Avenue.

FAMILY AND NATURAL WORLD

The industrial family has very little interest in the natural world. They might, to be sure, take a keen interest in "the environment" and carefully recycle their plastic, glass, and newspapers, but such an effort too often only represents a kind of self-satisfied attempt to soothe the conscience of a consumer who refuses to acknowledge the limits inherent in human existence. They might wring their hands over global warming and cheer when the government cracks down on the industrial polluters, but the SUV remains in the driveway, the frantic driving to and fro goes on, plenty of bottled water is consumed along the way, and the family vacation will surely include a long drive or flight.

The technological fun house that is the modern home makes the great out-of-doors pale by comparison, if, that is, the expectation is immediate and constant bursts of electronic stimulation. Indeed, enjoying the outdoors requires a willingness to submit to the pace, scale, and vocabulary of the natural world. One cannot step outside and expect the world to present itself as a video game, a music video, or even as reality television. The vastness dwarfs the narrow confines of prepackaged entertainment in which the channel or the volume can be changed in an instant and at a whim.

In his book *The Last Child in the Woods*, Richard Louv quotes a child whose frankness makes his words all the more troubling. "I like to play indoors better 'cause that's where all the electrical outlets are."[9] Now aside from the occasional current bush, the kid is dead on, but what does it say about our children that they would rather engage with an electronic screen than with the blumin', buzzin' confusion outside their doors? Is it any wonder that child obesity is at all-time highs? Is it any wonder that the passivity inculcated by hours of electronic media every day would fashion children into consumers who are all too happy to feed at the public trough, as long as it doesn't hurt or pull them away from *The Simpsons* reruns?

Only a short while ago I looked out the window and saw my three boys playing in the creek. Shoeless and up to their knees in water and mud, they had made their own fishing poles and were attempting to catch the tiny fish skittering about in the small pools. As hard as it is for me to admit, I'm fairly certain that if I had called them and offered them an hour on an Xbox, they would have jumped at the chance. I like to think they would have shaken their heads and gone back to their fishing, but they have tasted, at the home of friends, the intoxicating flavor of this form of entertainment (or enervation) and they like it. My hope is that having tasted both, they will at least be equipped to choose between the two ways of life. It is my intention to help them experience the wonder of the natural world and to be dissatisfied with an abstract life mediated forever by a screen (I write this fully aware of the irony that I am doing so using a computer).

Separation from the natural world is a kind of self-imposed isolation from reality. This isolation is made possible by the technologies we embrace with unreflective enthusiasm. The transportation, refrigeration, and preservation technologies that make the supermarket possible simultaneously make it possible for us to ignore reality in favor of convenience, simplicity, and thoughtlessness. Entertainment and communication technologies have had the same effect. The advent of the Walkman in the 1980s brought this sort of isolation to a new level. Individuals could choose to hear nothing but their own music regardless of where they went. The iPod is only the latest instantiation of this trajectory in which the world of choice opens up even as the external world is shut out by a self-selected soundtrack. When each family member is tuned in to the music of separate iPods, they are necessarily tuned out from the common world that they all could share. The same dynamic occurs when, as is increasingly the case, there is a television in every bedroom of the house, and children, as well as adults, can retreat from the common world to flip endlessly through the multitude of channels, flitting from one program to another, without the need or the desire to consider the preferences of anyone but the self.

In such a world, is it any wonder that narcissism is the natural outcome? As the echo chamber of the self is continually reinforced by the individuating technologies we embrace, we become less attentive to the people around us, to the common lives we lead, and to the natural world of which we are a part. The irony is that people can spend hours every day watching television programs about the natural world and never once escape the air cycling through their climate-controlled cocoons.

Consider, in the same vein, the family trip to Disney World, which has come to symbolize the pinnacle of family vacations. Advertisements describe it as "the happiest place on earth," but scratch beneath the cheerful music, bright colors, and smiling cartoon characters, and one finds artificiality and mechanized dullness. People can stroll down Main Street, USA, peering into the windows of shops, nodding at other strollers, and attempt to imagine that this is truly an image of community. But there is no community here. It is a stage show that is successful because it taps into our longings for the ability to stroll down a sidewalk in a familiar place among familiar people. We pay good money to pretend and then return to the land of strip malls and freeways, where strolling down the street would be unpleasant at the least and perhaps even dangerous.

After passing through Main Street, USA, one can experience a variety of thrilling rides. One can stand in line (often for an hour or more) for Space Mountain or the Matterhorn, and the ride will last a minute or two at the most. The fear riders experience may be real, but it is artificially induced. Like everything else, the risk is not real. If the lines for the roller coasters are too long, one can go to a variety of attractions featuring such things as grunting jungle animals or singing bears. But once again, the mechanical sameness lingers just below the happy veneer. Why take the trouble to go to the wilderness to see a real bear if one can see a troupe of singing and dancing mechanical bears in Orlando? Real bears, after all, are unpredictable, sometimes unpleasant, and often elusive. And they don't sing.

A family oriented toward the natural world might find it more appealing to hike through the forest, to camp beside a mountain stream, or to climb a mountain and experience the thrill of authentic risk rather than settling for the artificial experiences that we too easily accept as substitutes, and even as preferable, to the real thing. If living a life connected to the natural world is somehow important, then it might be preferable to smell like a campfire and pine needles rather than automobile fumes and stale hotdogs. It might be preferable to grow tomatoes than to buy them at the Super Mart. It might be preferable to raise real chickens for eggs and to milk a living goat rather than pay hard cash (or credit) to gaze blandly at mechanized creatures pretending to be something they are not. It might, in short, be preferable for families to encounter the natural world—where the beauty and mystery of creation induces one to contemplate the meaning of existence and perhaps even the nature of the creator. There is no room for God in Disney World.

FAMILY AND RELIGION

When we step back from all this, it seems clear that the life of the industrial family is a life tending toward self-absorbed consumption, and as such, it is a life characterized by ingratitude. It is a life of unbounded appetites in which the propriety of scale has been lost. Such individuals and families are fiercely mobile in their rush to acquire more, and they readily sever connections to their homes and extended families in order to better satisfy their ever-expanding desires. Driven by appetite, convinced that happiness can be achieved with just a little more, the pursuit has no terminus except the grave. When people come to think and act primarily as consumers, they lose sight of their own creatureliness, they lose a proper orientation to other people and to the world around them. The obvious question that emerges from all of this is, what can be done?

The first and perhaps most obvious step is to recover an orientation toward something above and beyond the self. An awareness and acknowledgment of God's providence reminds us simultaneously of our creatureliness along with the debts of gratitude we owe for our very lives and the good things we encounter each day, from the food we eat to the love we share and the beauty of the first tulips in spring. A proper orientation to God serves to counter the hubris that lies at the root of so many of our troubles. And when hubris is defused, we will find ourselves more capable of contentment and less intent on expanding our powers and our desires in ever increasing circles. The scale proper to humans will seem more attractive when we recognize what it means to be a human. We are not gods; neither are we beasts. We are creatures, made by God and in His image, who owe debts of gratitude to Him and to others, for we are not solitary creatures who can survive, let alone thrive, on our own. We flourish as human creatures when we inhabit the stories of other humans, when we embrace family members who give to us stories as our inheritance—stories of our family's past, stories that identify us, teach us, mark us as members who belong. This, of course, is most naturally and fully accomplished in the context of a particular place where our gratitude is worked out in the lives we live in the company of others who are committed to the same community.

The narrative life of a religious community incorporates our individual and family stories into a larger drama that extends back into the dawn of memory and forward into eschatological expectation. The Christian story, for example, consists of a narrative structure moving from creation to fall to redemption. When believers learn to see how their own stories fit into this larger story, membership is realized, for a sense of belonging emerges in the contours of the stories we inhabit.

A commitment to a religious community is, it would seem, a natural and fitting way to live out our creatureliness with gratitude and propriety. Partaking of the sacraments, corporate worship, the bearing of one another's burdens serve to temper the spirit of consumerism that haunts our age. They bind families together even as they bind generations of believers in a union of the living and the dead. Sacrifice, voluntary simplicity (which in our age of indulgence may look like asceticism), service, meditation—all of these serve to put our focus on God and others and in so doing temper the spirit of narcissism that walks hand in hand with consumerism.

FAMILY AND WORK

Work, especially manual labor, can also contribute to a proper grasp of one's place in the world. Why is that? After all, didn't we only recently escape the life of drudgery that manual labor represents? Isn't manual labor the sign of economic failure rather than success? Isn't it rednecks and other unfortunates who work with their hands and by the sweat of their dusty brows? Won't progress eventually deliver to us a world in which no one is required to do such work? After all, machines have relieved us of much manual labor and eventually they will do it all.

What this line of thinking neglects, though, is that humans are not simply minds who happen to possess bodies. We are not merely things that think or things that can be entertained. Our bodies are not simply the means of transporting our brains from the cubicle to the recliner and back again. Humans are embodied souls, whose bodies are as integral to our existence as our souls. To neglect the body by abuse is clearly wrong. But so too is neglecting the body by creating a world in which physical work can be avoided and its meaning denigrated. When we work with our hands, we engage the world in a way that intellectual work cannot duplicate. Both are good, and while specific individuals will engage one type more than the other, it is probably also the case that a life devoid of any physical work is lopsided in the same way that a life given merely to physical labor without thought is less than it could be.

Creative physical work cultivates the idea of production. When we learn how to make things, we simultaneously learn the value of those things. When we grasp the value of things, we will be reticent to use them carelessly or consume them wastefully. Physical work, then, might serve as a means of cultivating the virtue of thrift. It will certainly cultivate an appreciation for the work that stands behind handmade homes and furniture, a home-cooked meal, a flourishing garden, and a straight fencerow.

The family is the chief venue for teaching children the goodness of work. If children learn to work well and not to shun difficult physical labor, they will be better for it. They will be more comfortable in their own skins, as it were, knowing how to actively engage the physical world to preserve it or even improve it. Children who have learned to appreciate physical work occupy the world in a way that the passive video-child never can. They are not afraid to touch, to bend, to fashion, and to alter their surroundings. They possess a self-confidence that allows them to imagine possibilities latent in the creation and then to set out to bring those possibilities into existence. Work teaches children to imagine the end product as well as the means to achieve the end and the ability to bring the two together.

Physical work can help jar one out of the solipsistic world of narcissism. When one feels the sweat trickle down the back, one is reminded that hard work demands something of us. So too when we feel the ravenous hunger at the end of a long day or fall into bed with aching back, legs, and hands. When we work hard, we give of ourselves to the task at hand. And in the giving, we feel the vitality surge and ebb away as we near the end of our task or the setting of the sun or sheer exhaustion. Physical labor can connect us to the world around us by virtue of the fact that we labor on something. We direct our attention onto something beyond ourselves. We spend our energy on something not directly related to entertainment or diversion, although one who loves work can find both therein.

Obviously, in physical labor one can develop skills by working shoulder to shoulder with another who possesses hard-won abilities garnered by years of experience. One can learn to frame a house, build a fence, or tend a garden, each requiring skills that can be acquired and then passed on. Trades, of course, survived for generations by means of apprenticeships whereby willing beginners submitted themselves to the instruction of a master. Are we doing a disservice to ourselves, our children, and our society if we fail to learn and teach useful skills? Should we prize the ability to fix, mend, build, and cultivate? Does our personal and corporate security decrease as we become less capable of performing tasks that were once routine but are now beyond the ken of many?

I have spoken already of gardens, and at the risk of belaboring an obvious point, I will return again to the backyard. Not so long ago, many Americans kept large gardens and depended on them for a significant proportion of their food. They ate what they could and preserved the rest. They kept fruit trees and livestock even if they didn't live on a farm. Homeowners associations did not exist to demand conformity to artificial standards of beauty or hygiene. People knew how to take advantage of even small plots of land and, from them, bring forth a bounty of food.

Today, less than 1 percent of Americans live on farms, and suburbs are more notable for their wide swaths of yard than fruit trees, vegetable gardens, and chickens. But it is not simply the absence of these that is a problem, for even if the homeowners associations stepped out of the picture, many Americans lack both the desire and the skills necessary to construct a viable garden. We have become dependent on distant food producers we don't know and who don't know us. This has worked well for some years, but in times of crisis (which, if human history is any indication, will surely return) we may come to recognize that our security is better achieved when we can produce at least some of our own food. Skills have been allowed to atrophy just as we have allowed our muscles to atrophy as we drive our cars once again to the Super Mart to buy strawberries in December.

Cultivating a garden requires skill. A "green thumb" is a whimsical way of acknowledging that some people have cultivated a practical understanding of the way plants grow. This is only acquired through experience, and although one can muddle toward competence via the painful process of trial and error, one can achieve proficiency much sooner under the tutelage of a master. In addition to skill, a flourishing garden is the product of hard work. One must stoop and dig and pull and hack and all the while consider with care the health of the various plants. To cultivate a successful garden requires a union of backbreaking work and thoughtful attention to each plant. And of course, a successful garden attracts visitors: Japanese beetles, cut worms, slugs, rabbits, deer, and small children. Learning how best to control six legged pests and four-footed nibblers is all part of learning how to keep a garden. Teaching the small children to love working in the garden is a task no less important. This, it would seem, is an especially good way to help children gain an appreciation of the natural world; of the pleasures, pains, and rewards of hard work; and of the taste of a job well done.

When the crop is harvested, more work yet awaits, for if the harvest is plentiful, not all of it can be eaten fresh. The hard but satisfying work of preserving food for the winter again depends on skills that must be learned. Canning, freezing, drying, curing, pickling—these skills have been largely forgotten by those who have shunned the garden for the Super Mart. One advantage that our forebears had over us is that they knew how to feed themselves. We have forgotten and have grown dependent on a food industry founded on cheap oil (for fertilizers, pesticides, and transportation) and whose lines stretch around the globe. As long as conditions remain stable, this system will work fine, but if the price of oil increases dramatically or political unrest threatens food lines, then more local food production will become a necessity. The family garden will once again emerge as an important part of the family economy, and the skills and habits of our forebears will suddenly be sorely wanted. If for no other reason than insurance, we should make a determined effort to learn what most Americans once knew and pass those skills on to our children.

THE FAMILY MEAL

It seems that the family meal represents, in important ways, the culmination of many of the themes of this book. This is especially true when at least some of the food on the table has been grown, raised, canned, frozen, hunted, or slaughtered by members of the family. When we eat food we have worked to produce, we experience in a tangible way the fruits of our labor. We can recall the hours of toil that we invested, hours of our lives poured into the endeavor, and when we eat, the circle is closed. The life we put into the labor is replenished by the fruits thereof. We work so that we may eat, and we eat to revitalize our bodies for the tasks ahead.

The skill needed to produce the food is matched by the skill necessary to prepare it well. Eating fast food on the run in the solitude of an automobile or before the glaring eye of the television teaches us to feed like animals rather than to dine like human beings. When we eat at a table together, when the food has been prepared with care and skill, when attention is paid to the setting and to the presentation of the food, the occasion is dignified in a way that the solitary or rushed consumption of calories never can be.

An important part of a culture is its cuisine. Stories are transmitted through the foods we prepare and eat. Memories are invoked. Family ties are strengthened by the passing of familiar dishes around a table and through the hands of the generations: "This is just how your great-grandma used to make it. Now she was quite a woman. Let me tell you about her." We come to know ourselves through the stories we inhabit as a family, and the family table is a prime location for telling stories. A good meal induces conversation, for it brings relaxation, satisfaction, and affords a time suited to reminiscing. Given all this, the imposition of the television at so many family meals is a tragic development, for rather than talking to each other our attention turns to the incessant blare projected over all, and we end up listening to the stories of others rather than our own.

If the family meal represents the culmination of many themes we have discussed, perhaps the saying of grace prior to the meal encapsulates, in the fullest way, the thrust of all I have been trying to express. When we say a prayer of thanksgiving to God as we sit around the table laden with food, as a family joins hands, bows together, and takes a moment to return thanks, they are acknowledging their creatureliness. They are acknowledging that the bounty of the harvest required more than their labor and love. They are acknowledging that the food they are about to eat represents the provision of a God who brings the gentle rains upon a thirsty land and causes the sun to warm the soil. The prayer is an expression of gratitude in which each person acknowledges the grace of God from whom all blessings flow. When we, following Christ, utter the words "give us this day our daily bread," we acknowledge that it is fitting to pray for sustenance, but that it is not fitting to ask for food enough to last a lifetime. The manna in the dessert appeared daily as faith is a daily exercise of dependence. There is a scale fitting to our gratitude, for we acknowledge that we cannot possess the world but that we are children of a loving Father who knows our needs. As a family says grace around the table, there is an exclusive element, for the whole world cannot fit around that table. Family and friends can bow together, but there are limits, perhaps not of love but of capacity, propriety, and practicality. These limits are also the contours of the stories we tell, for families tell their own stories; they tell of their own memories and their mutual past as a way of preserving that which is good, of forgiving that which was not, and of coming to terms with happiness and loss. All this is done around a table. A family meal is necessarily located some place, and when that place is known and loved by those joined in prayer, gratitude, and feasting, it is enriched and becomes a home.

9

Education: The Place of the Liberal Arts

'Tis education forms the common mind,
Just as the twig is bent, the tree's inclined.
Alexander Pope, "To Lord Cobham," 1734

Nothing in education is so astonishing as the amount of ignorance
it accumulates in the form of inert facts.
Henry Adams, *The Education of Henry Adams*

All sensible people agree that education is important. Such a general claim is impossible to oppose. It is when we descend from the lofty heights of abstraction and begin to talk about the content, method, and purposes of education that the sparks begin to fly. In this chapter, I want to discuss education in the context of our four principles. When viewed in their light, does a particular conception of education emerge? Are some approaches to education disqualified out of hand? Ultimately, I want to defend the idea of liberal education, but with a twist, for liberal education too often amounts to little more than an overpriced means of creating cosmopolitans of the worst sort: people who have little interest in or concern for local communities, customs, stories, or places.

Any discussion of liberal arts education must begin with at least a cursory definition, for although the term "liberal arts" is frequently employed, there exists a fair bit of ambiguity about what exactly it means. Of course, "liberal" is derived from the Latin *liberalis* from which we get our word "liberty." The etymology is tied closely to the history of the concept, for in the classical world, education liberalis was an education suited to cultivating free citizens capable of self-government. In contrast, education *servilis* was the sort of education suited to slaves.

What, specifically, was the difference between education liberalis and education servilis? Plato's definition of a philosopher helps give us a sense of the contours of an education suited to free citizens. According to Plato, the philosopher is concerned with the whole. He seeks to grasp the way various disciplines are connected. He asks the big questions in his attempt to understand the highest things, and his education prepares him for this lifelong task. A servant or a slave, on the other hand, needs to understand only the information related directly to his appointed tasks. He may be highly skilled, but his concerns do not extend beyond his specialization. In fact, it would be undesirable, perhaps even dangerous, for slaves to begin asking ultimate questions about truth and justice. In short, the free man should be equipped to grasp not only the means but also the ends for which a task is undertaken whereas a servant or a slave should concern himself only with the means to accomplish the immediate task at hand. A liberal education is one that equips free citizens to integrate the various aspects of their experience into a coherent whole. In a democratic society, where citizens rule, it would seem that a liberal education of some sort cannot be the privilege of only a few.

For Plato, education is a matter of shaping the soul in a particular way. It cultivates the right tastes and distastes, which will complement the rational faculty as it seeks truth. According to Plato, the highest reality, the most real thing that exists, is what he calls the Form of the Good. Thus, the most real is also the most true and the most good, and their harmony is, of course, beautiful. For Plato, to grasp these highest ideas (or this one complex though unified idea) is the task of the philosopher, and such an undertaking is possible (though there are no guarantees) only if the right kind of education precedes it.

Education is about grasping reality. This assumes, of course, that an objective reality exists and that human beings are capable of grasping it, however incompletely. Human beings are creatures comprising both a body and a soul, and these twin facets of human existence are important. Because humans possess a soul, they are capable of striving outward from themselves. They are capable of attempting to grasp the whole. They are suited, and even spurred, to pursue the transcendent, which is beyond the capacity of the five senses. Humans, unlike other terrestrial creatures, are capable of seeking God, beauty, and the good.

Yet humans are not simply disembodied souls free to wander the interstices of reality, sliding around the nooks and crannies of existence, in search of truth, justice, and diversion. In addition to being a soul, humans are bodies. This means, among other things, that humans are relegated to a particular place and a particular time. We are placed creatures by virtue of our bodily existence. Therefore, the knowledge we acquire through education should, if it is suited to human beings, be oriented to the particulars out of which it emerges and into which we bring it. This is not to say that the content of education does not include that which aspires to the universal. Indeed, the *Iliad* can touch a reader today because it somehow transcends the particulars of its historical and cultural setting and points to something universal that all readers can recognize. At the same time, an education that focuses only on the directional movement from particulars to universals is incomplete, for we live and move and have our being in the concrete world. A properly conceived liberal education must equip humans to live well in a particular place, for if it merely suits them to live *anyplace*, they are ill equipped to be at home in *someplace*. Education, in short, must never find itself so attracted to the abstract universals that it neglects the concrete particulars of human life.

Before we develop an account of liberal education that does justice to both the universal and the particular, it might be helpful to consider briefly some of the challenges besetting liberal education today. For in identifying the various ideas that undermine liberal education, we might find hints of a properly constituted solution.

MODERN CHALLENGES

The first challenge is the *fragmentation of knowledge*. We are today awash in information, yet we find ourselves ill equipped to arrange the multitude of pieces into a coherent whole. There is an irony here, for as the so-called information age has opened up an unprecedented flow of information, it has not simultaneously equipped us with the ability to process it.

One can see the results of this fragmentation in the typical university, where academic disciplines are too often hermetically sealed worlds in which occupants of one universe are incapable of, much less interested in, conversing with one another in a way that would link their various disciplines into a hierarchically ordered whole. As has been frequently remarked, the modern university is more accurately dubbed a "multiversity," for the aspiration underlying the word "university" is a connected universe of knowledge, and that aspiration has in many quarters disappeared.

The rise of *secularism* is one of the chief culprits responsible for this modern fragmentation of knowledge. In an age of theistic belief, the idea of God provided the orienting framework around which knowledge could be arranged. Holy Scripture, a tradition of interpretation, and the church all served to create a context that gave meaning to the various disciplines, which were arranged in an ascending order with, of course, theology occupying the highest place and philosophy, theology's handmaiden, standing one rung below. But as skepticism replaced belief, the centripetal force of theology was replaced by the centrifugal force of unbelief. No longer were the various disciplines ordered in reference to each other and to God. Instead, each discipline tended to become a universe unto itself without reference to other disciplines or to a reality that precedes and transcends any one discipline. In short, theism provided a unifying truth, and when that was lost so too was the unity. Only fragments remained.

Another challenge to a liberal education today is *specialization*. Of course, specialization of a sort is entirely desirable. We want our brain surgeons to be specialists, so too our airline pilots and bridge builders. But there is a specialization of another sort that is related to the problem of fragmentation. This is the sort of specialization in which the concerns of the specialist become so focused and narrow that he has no concern for the larger context within which his specialized work resides. This sort of specialization is apparent when, for example, a physician is interested only in his patient's body but has no concern for the person of whom the body is a part; or when a legislator is so focused on staying in office or seeing that a bill is passed that he fails to concern himself with the ultimate reason for seeking office or passing a bill, which is to say, justice. Ultimate ends or purposes are ignored and proximate ends and means become the exclusive object of attention.

Richard Weaver, in his book *Ideas Have Consequences*, argues that specialization fragments individuals, competencies, and societies. This fragmentation, at the level of individuals, produces a character that is not compatible with wisdom and is therefore not capable of self-government, much less the government of others. As Weaver puts it, "Specialization develops only part of a man; a man partially developed is deformed; and one deformed is the last person to be thought of as a ruler."[1] This sort of deformation by specialization is clearly exemplified, according to Weaver, in the Manhattan Project. Thousands were employed in the undertaking, yet to maintain secrecy, each person focused on his or her specialized task without knowledge of the end toward which everyone was working. But, Weaver asks, should not the end of a project be the concern of all involved? The result of this isolation by specialization is that each individual, unaware of and unconcerned with the ends to which his or her labors were directed, became, in Weaver's words, "ethical eunuchs."[2] People of this sort are competent in one specific task or field. They are completely focused on mediate ends and the means by which to achieve those ends. The whole remains beyond the purview of their concern, and as a result, their perceived responsibility ends at the frontiers of their respective specialties.

Another problem that challenges liberal education is *professionalization*. If you asked the average aspiring college student (or her parents) why she wants to go to college, invariably the main—if not the sole—reason is some version of "so I can get a job." Now, getting a job is not a bad thing. In fact, it is a very good thing, but the primary purpose of a liberal arts education is not job training. In fact, in the classical world, education that did nothing more than equip a person for a specific job was what constituted education servilis. A liberal arts education, however, shapes the soul in a certain way. Through serious and sustained engagement with such disciplines as mathematics, geometry, astronomy, music, history, literature, philosophy, and theology, the student was inducted into a world of ideas where that which is good and true and beautiful reign supreme. Such cultivation of the soul requires time, a good teacher, and a student who is at least open to the prospect of sojourning into a strange and wonderful land where eternal verities present themselves to the constant delight and amazement of those who enter that domain.

This is not to say that a liberal arts education will not assist one in securing a job. In fact, I would argue that at least at the undergraduate level, a liberal arts education is better preparation for most jobs than any other degree program. A rigorous liberal arts education will require that the student read many difficult texts, compare them with each other, and seek to find points of contact and difference. Reading sophisticated, well-written language will attune the reader's ear to good writing and help to develop an expansive vocabulary, and a strong writer is a coveted commodity in the professional world. Furthermore, a good liberal arts education will include discussion of the ideas encountered in the texts. Civil discussion in which opinions can be aired, reflected upon, countered, and perhaps even altered is a wonderful training ground not only for a professional career but for life in general. Finally, a liberal education exposes the student to the sweep of human civilization. A person thus educated is oriented toward grasping the big picture. Such a perspective provides a person with the resources and imagination to grasp a problem as part of a larger whole. A liberally educated person, then, will be more valuable to an employer for reasons that are a direct result of the kind of person a liberal education develops. The irony is that all this can best be accomplished if job training is not the primary goal.

Another challenge to liberal education is the *abuse of technology*. Today we are flooded with technological devices that easily distract our minds from the hard work that a liberal education requires. It is far easier to turn on the television than it is to read the *Iliad*. And even when no television is available, we have our cell phones, e-mail, and iPods to keep us occupied with the urgent as well as the trivial. To possess the mental habits and tastes to generally prefer Homer to Homer Simpson is no easy or quick task.

The word, written and spoken, has always been at the heart of a liberal education, despite the importance of mathematics and music in the curriculum. A liberal education is logocentric. Words speak to the rational faculty of the mind and can be evaluated according to their reasonableness. The image, which is to say, the television picture, is primarily nonlinguistic and intrudes into the mind, bypassing the rational capacity and appealing directly to the appetites. This is, of course, not to say that television does not include language, but the language is usually secondary and is not required by the logic of the medium. Consider, for example, the emphasis on images in commercials. If the medium were naturally suited to language, automobile commercials would consist of scrolling text or a voice listing the attributes of the particular auto. Instead we get "zoom zoom" and flashy images of beautiful people and sleek cars doing things for which the average driver would be arrested. In short, modern electronic technology distracts from serious concerns and tutors the mind to prefer the trivial and transient over the serious and the permanent.

The final challenge to a liberal education is *progressivism*. As we have already seen, the rise of the new science, driven by the scientific method, presided over a burst of scientific and technological advances that, when compared with previous centuries, is simply stunning. The thrill of progress in a limited, though important area bred the belief that progress was sweeping all aspects of human endeavor. As humans were learning to control the natural world, so too, it was believed, they would eventually learn to control society and even human nature itself. A perfect world populated by perfect people was on the horizon, and through hard work and perseverance that new world could be realized.

The effect on liberal arts education was, predictably, not good. Liberal arts education is predicated on a respect for the past. Progressivism looks on the past with disdain, for the past was a benighted place, occupied by backwards people who were superstitious, religious, and conservative in their ways. At best, for the progressive, the past can be mined for tidbits of useful information that might come in handy as the world is remade. The progressive is unwilling to submit to the authority of the past (or any authority for that matter) as the best means to acquire a soul that is oriented toward the truth. Progressive education is characterized by its utilitarian flavor, for only if something is seen as immediately useful in the practical world is it considered of value. Liberal education, at least on the surface, fails on this score and is therefore despised as the province of romantics and misfits.

INGRATITUDE AND DESIRE

These modern challenges to liberal education have emerged in a society of individuals who are characterized by their ingratitude. Indeed, as José Ortega y Gasset noted, the modern "mass man" possesses "two fundamental traits: the free expansion of his vital desires . . . and . . . radical ingratitude towards all that has made possible the ease of his existence." The result, according to Ortega, is the psychology of the spoiled child. Although such a man is "heir to an ample and generous past—generous both in ideals and in activities—the new commonality has been spoiled by the world around it." Ortega briefly summarized what this spoiling produces: "To spoil means to put no limit on caprice, to give one the impression that everything is permitted to him and that he has no obligations."[3]

Richard Weaver noted that modern humans are all too often characterized by this "spoiled-child psychology." He argued that the expansion of science and technology and the resulting separation from the natural world has caused people to become "forgetful of the overriding mystery of creation."[4] When we come to believe that the human condition can be overcome by the miracle of science, we blind ourselves to the fragility of our own existence, to the many debts we owe to fathers long dead, to the mystery of life itself. According to Weaver, this psychology of the spoiled child inculcates in the modern mind the love of comfort above all else. But, "we need earnestly to point out that there is no correlation between the degree of comfort enjoyed and the achievement of a civilization. On the contrary, absorption in ease is one of the most reliable signs of present or impending decay."[5]

The twin maladies of secularization and fragmentation do not only change the way we view education. Even more fundamentally, they change the way we conceive of ourselves as human beings and thereby aid in the ingratitude of our time. No longer are humans understood to be unified and integrated beings, embodied souls, with a specific nature and ends that are common to all other human beings. Instead, the human person is seen primarily as the product of material causes— both genetic and environmental. Each person is merely a bundle of desires, and he who is most successful in fulfilling those desires is de facto the best human being. Of course, the term "best" in such a scenario means merely "most effective" or "strongest" or perhaps "cleverest." It can never mean morally superior or noble or anything else that stands outside a pragmatic or utilitarian calculus.

When we add professionalization, pervasive electronic media, and progressivism to the mix, it is not difficult to see how the characteristics of unlimited desire and ingratitude are given free reign. If humans are merely a collection of desires seeking satisfaction, then clearly the sole reason justifying spending years in college (not to mention thousands of dollars) is to get a high paying job so that one's manifold desires can be more readily sated. When our lives are dominated by the sight and sound of electronic media, which are so well suited to stimulating desire, then the hard work and difficult-to-quantify rewards of reading Shakespeare will be most unattractive. Finally, if we succumb to the cult of progress, we convince ourselves that our future comfort is the goal of history. Rather than expressing profound gratitude to generations past to whom we own so much, those infected with the idea of progress will see the past as merely the relics of those who did not survive to see how wonderful we turned out to be. In this light, liberal education suffers multiple blows. Many are potentially fatal.

A properly conceived liberal arts education cultivates a love for the past, which in turn shapes a proper love for the present as well as a sense of duty to the future. We ought to feel a great degree of affection for the past and recognize the debt we owe to those we can never thank. We must recognize that many of the best human things have been cultivated gently and passed down through many generations. It is, then, a high duty to tend the gifts of civilization as best we can and transmit them to our posterity with the hope that generations hence will enjoy the benefits of this gift even as they, in turn, feel the burden of its responsibility. In short, a proper love for the future requires a proper love for the past, and to love the future but disdain the past is to destroy the future with carelessness, ineptitude, and pride. Furthermore, ostensibly loving the future while despising the past is, in reality, only a futile exercise in loving the present, for such a love is without historical context and therefore is only a facile love of the self.

Ultimately, properly ordered loves unify our debts of gratitude. Our sense of gratitude will extend from God to the natural world of His creation, and we come to recognize that apart from the natural world we cannot survive, much less flourish. Furthermore, while civilization and the natural world can be conceptualized separately, they are intimately connected. Civilization cannot exist in a disembodied state separated from a physical place. That is, towns, schools, churches, and markets all must be situated in some place, and if these good things are to thrive, the places they inhabit must be healthy. The riches of civilization, so fragile and delicately wrought, cannot be fully realized or enjoyed in a wasteland. The relationship between culture and the natural world must never be ignored. Edmund Burke, in this regard, recognized the essential and perhaps obvious connection between conservatism and conserving: "I do not like to see any thing destroyed; any void produced in society; any ruin on the face of the land."[6] A proper sense of gratitude induces responsible actions while pervasive ingratitude will invariably yield actions that are irresponsible and destructive.

STEWARDSHIP

When we speak of proper care for the natural world, the word that best describes our efforts is stewardship. Stewards are caretakers. They lovingly guide, protect, and cultivate that which is under their care. In the language of stewardship the concepts of creatureliness, gratitude, scale, and place all find their proper home. But it is not only in the context of the natural world that the concept of stewardship, has meaning. In the context of liberal education, the idea of stewardship is indispensible. For as inheritors of a civilization, we are its stewards. And because the gifts of civilization are tender plants requiring constant nourishment, our task as stewards requires perseverance, courage, and ultimately, faith that succeeding generations will take up the mantle when we are no longer able to bear it.

Liberal education, in one sense, can be seen as the stewardship of civilization. But what does that mean? It sounds so grandiose, abstract, and perhaps even vain. What is it precisely that liberal education should attempt to steward? First, speaking of liberal education in terms of stewardship implies that there is a specific content to liberal education. This flies in the face of some notions of the liberal arts that place the ability to question at the center. Consider this description: "a liberal education will induce in the student a disposition to question received truths and the critical thinking abilities necessary to evaluate various standpoints in light of his or her personal convictions." Such a conception of liberal education puts the individual learner at the center and assumes that by an act of judgment and will, each individual can and should develop a set of personal beliefs by which to grasp the world. However, in asserting that there is a specific content at the center of liberal education, I am claiming that the first disposition is not dubiety or suspicion but submission and trust. One must submit to the authority of a master in order to fully appreciate the subject matter at hand. One must enter into the world of the past to understand it, and to enter the past is to submit, at least temporarily, to its prejudices and demands. Understanding requires, in the first instance, sympathy. Criticism comes later, after sympathetic understanding has been achieved.

What is it we are attempting to grasp? To whom must we submit in order to understand? Broadly speaking, the content of a liberal arts education is the great tradition of the West. To understand it, we must submit to the works represented therein. The content matters, for the end of a liberal arts education, rightly conceived, is the formation of a soul. Its goal is the inculcation of certain tastes, whereby a person comes to prefer good things over the bad just as a connoisseur of wine comes, by virtue of an education in wine, to prefer good wine to bad. The inculcation of tastes, directed toward the good, entails a reorientation of loves. The person who has never experienced the sublime will not realize what is lacking in the pedestrian stream that flows all around.

In concrete terms, the great tradition includes the essays, treatises, dialogues, plays, and novels that constitute the development of creative and analytic thought from the ancient world to the present. Most people would agree that works by such writers as Homer, Sophocles, Plato, Aristotle, Moses, Virgil, St. Paul, Augustine, Aquinas, Chaucer, Dante, Shakespeare, Milton, Locke, Rousseau, Kant, Austen, Dostoyevsky, and Einstein are properly seen as necessary and integral elements of a liberal education. To know at least some of these authors and their works is to encounter the best that has been thought and written. To wrestle with them is to strive with the mighty to grasp perennial truths. To understand these works requires the reader to submit, at least temporarily, to their authority and learn from them as an apprentice submits to a master. Therein the soul is shaped by the imaginations of great men and women who have gone before and left a record of their lives and thoughts.

At the same time, anyone who seriously engages the works of the great tradition will soon come to realize that those works do not form a seamless and coherent account of reality. In fact, if one thing is clear about the tradition it is this: the various authors often find themselves in direct conflict with each other. They are striving to know, but they often come to different conclusions. It seems that if we must submit in order to understand, we must also move from understanding to critical reflection. All the great works cannot be correct. Yet, we can learn from them all, for even those we ultimately disagree with can teach us much about the pursuit of knowledge and the pitfalls that are strewn along the way. Thus, while a serious engagement with the works of the great tradition requires submission to their authority, critical engagement implies that the process ends with personal responsibility. One must learn to exercise judgment, choose wisely, and proceed with self-control.

Here we can see how a liberal arts education is one means of preparing an individual for self-government, which is a necessary condition for a free society. It inculcates mental habits without which liberty is license. Through it, we come better to understand human weaknesses and temptations as well as the possibility of noble deeds and greatness. We can learn by the example of great men and women that self-sacrifice is commendable and avarice base; we can come to imagine ourselves treading paths forged by giants and sung by poets; we can come to realize that love moves mountains and hatred leads only to destruction. In short, a serious engagement with the great tradition gives us the ability to see the possibilities and the dangers latent in human nature. It inculcates a taste for the noble and a distaste for the ignoble. It orients our souls toward that which is highest and best in human history.

At the same time, there are no guarantees. Liberally educated people have been behind plenty of horrific acts. One thing to which we must never succumb (although the temptation is great) is the notion that there is a simple and unimpeachable method by which we can ensure that people behave well. A liberal education can aid in the cultivation of the virtues necessary for self-government, but other things are needed as well, not the least of which is good fortune or what those who know better might call grace.

PLACED EDUCATION

There is at the heart of much writing about liberal education a sort of cosmopolitan temptation that does a disservice to the concept of stewardship. When proponents of liberal education describe it as the attempt to grasp the whole, they are correct.

If, however, we do not continue with the acknowledgment that the whole is grasped via particulars and that, as human creatures, we necessarily inhabit only a small and particular part of the whole, we are missing something crucial.

If a liberal education teaches a person to love abstraction, to relish the exchange of universal ideas of justice, charity, and beauty, yet to be inattentive to the neighbor down the street or the beauty of the first buds in spring, then something has gone wrong. Such an education is suited to abstract beings who naturally belong in no particular place and have none of the senses by which particular beauty or empathy can be experienced. Such an education is, in other words, not fit for human beings.

The word "cosmopolitan," as I am using it, implies a sort of universal at-homeness and a corresponding reluctance to commit to one particular place to the exclusion of all the rest. A liberal arts education can inculcate such a sensibility, for one learns to be comfortable engaging such disparate figures as Homer, Dante, Shakespeare, and Austen. One can, if the mood strikes, do this all before lunch, as it were. A liberally educated person can flit from place to place, age to age, with the freedom of one who has been given the keys to the kingdom. One can cultivate a bird's-eye view of the world, a view that seeks continually to see the forest but that neglects the gnarled oak in the field with the initials carved in the trunk or the listing pine in the park around which the children play. In such a condition, one imagines it possible to be at home anywhere, yet actually, concretely, making a home nowhere. Such a world is one of perpetual possibility, yet it is never consummated in the particulars wherein we must live.

In such a context, stewardship suffers, for the mind given to abstract universal concepts will readily gravitate toward saving "the world" or "ending hunger" but will find it less natural to consider how to preserve a local community or care for the poor widow around the corner. If a liberal arts education makes it more difficult for human beings to live lives suited to human beings, then it has fallen victim to the temptation of abstraction. A properly conceived liberal education must include an appreciation of abstract universal principles. At the same time, it must include resources that equip the student to return to the particulars better suited than before to engage his local community.

What, then, is stewardship in the context of the liberal arts tradition? What are the key elements of a liberal education by which the student learns to appreciate the necessity of grasping for universal verities yet remains anchored to the earth, firmly rooted in the soil of one's community? Before attempting an answer, it is important to note that up to this point I have focused primarily on books and, more narrowly, on subjects that are generally thought to belong to the liberal arts: history, philosophy, and literature. But it is essential to grasp that the great tradition includes these subject matters and far more besides. Theology, science, law, music, architecture, the plastic arts, agriculture—all comprise various aspects of the whole of human existence. Each plays an important part of that many-headed thing we call "culture." To approach the whole, it is necessary to have some knowledge of various aspects of many of these areas. To live well in a particular place, one must, of course, have some knowledge of the particular history and literature of that place. So too is it important to know something of the art, architecture, law, local music, and methods and products of the local agriculture. An adequate liberal education should, in other words, help to form students to be better neighbors, better caretakers, and better citizens of the places they call home.

I want to suggest five aspects of education that while certainly not exhausting the possibilities, do get at the heart of much that needs to be said. These can, I think, help provide the contours for an approach to liberal education that exemplifies the notion of stewardship as it applies to the great tradition in the context of local communities.

Participation: First, and perhaps most obviously, we must attend carefully to that which we have inherited. We must seek to know and understand the books, the art, the architecture, and the music that has been entrusted to us by our collective fathers, for only by knowing and understanding them can we preserve them and perhaps create lasting works of our own.

Because our Western tradition places so much emphasis on the written word, it is essential that we take books seriously. This is increasingly difficult when there are so many alternatives to distract us. The habit of reading requires years of habituation; it requires practice over time, and ultimately, it requires serious engagement with the best books our tradition offers. Allan Bloom noted with acuity and sadness that "our students have lost the practice of and the taste for reading." The implications extend far beyond the mere covers of particular books, for an unread person is substantially cut off from other elements of the tradition. Bloom continues,

> Imagine such a young person walking through the Louvre or the Uffizi, and you can immediately grasp the condition of his soul. In his innocence of the stories of Biblical and Greek or Roman antiquity, Raphael,

Leonardo, Michelangelo, Rembrandt and all the others can say nothing to him. All he sees are colors and forms—modern art. In short, like almost everything else in his spiritual life, the paintings and statues are abstract. No matter what much of modern wisdom asserts, these artists counted on immediate recognition of their subjects and, what is more, on their having a powerful meaning for their viewers.[7]

Reading is an essential habit without which the task of stewarding our civilizational gifts is impossible. Novelist Walker Percy once asked an audience of professional educators to imagine a scenario in which a class of students and their teacher were shipwrecked on an island. The buildings, schools, and libraries were intact; only the people had been removed by some cataclysm. Percy further imagined that he could put a message into a bottle that would make it to this small band of survivors.

So what would my message in the bottle be? It would be very simple. One word, in fact. *Read!* Read: this word is really intended for the students, because it is a secret the teacher probably already knows. The message would be expanded to say something like this: "If you do not learn to read, that is, read with pleasure, that is, make the breakthrough into the delight of reading—you are going to miss out." And I don't mean you are going to miss out on books or being bookish. . . . You are going to miss out, not only on your profession, but on the great treasure of your heritage, which is nothing less than Western civilization.[8]

Stewards of the liberal arts tradition must be serious readers. And this reading must be done with a particular disposition, for reading merely to debunk is to approach a text with arrogance and pride. Good readers are humble readers who approach great texts critically, to be sure, but also with the humility of the learner, for great books invariably have much to teach us. To understand a book, one must inhabit it, and to inhabit a book is to submit to its shape and structure. One enters the verdant garden only by passing through the low gate of humility.

The principle of humility applies not only to books but to the other expressions of thought and creativity of our heritage. We must seek to understand the paintings of Raphael, the music of Bach, the architecture of Washington, D.C. The riches are breathtaking, but the rewards are not automatic nor can they be harvested without labor. The diligent will reap riches, while the casual observer will be met with complex sounds and colors but will not be able to glean the meaning therein.

Memorization: Second, stewards of the liberal arts tradition should, I think, seek to restore the practice of memorization. Extolling the virtues of memorization in the age of the iPhone is, if not quixotic, at least odd. Why memorize when virtually any fact we could desire is only a click away? Why clutter our brains with information that we can easily store and retrieve in seconds from the external brains we carry in our pockets? Memorization, it seems, is an outdated mode of education that was, perhaps, necessary in the past, but we now can devote ourselves to more interesting and creative pursuits, which, incidentally, do not take nearly the sustained effort that memorization requires. Literary critic George Steiner suggests that the stakes are higher than we might imagine: "The catastrophic decline of memorization in our own modern education and adult resources is one of the crucial, though as yet little understood, symptoms of an after-culture."[9] If this is the case, memorization is as necessary—and perhaps even more necessary—today as it ever was. Because of the decline in memorization, direct and internal contact with the best of our civilizational inheritance has diminished. When we memorize something, we internalize it; it becomes part of our mental furniture, as it were. Obviously, then, one must take care what one commits to memory, but there is no better way to get inside an idea or a poem or a dialogue or a piece of music than to commit it to memory and subsequently meditate upon it. This is a natural practice in oral societies, but today we must intentionally develop the habit of memorizing elements that form the backbone of our tradition.

Imitation: Third, stewards of the great tradition must be imitators. This, of course, flies in the face of our modern sensibilities that tell us that creativity is the aim of intellectual achievement and, consequently, imitation is to be avoided at all costs, or at least cleverly disguised so no one notices. In the classical world, one was encouraged to seek out a master and strive to imitate him. If one wanted to learn the art of rhetoric, for example, one went to Cicero's works. Through careful and diligent study the student would seek to make his writing and speaking conform to the style and standards established by Cicero. An element of competition was present as well, for even in seeking to imitate the master, the student was aspiring to best him. And though this rarely occurred, an especially talented student might in fact achieve such a singular distinction.

This emphasis on imitation harkens back to Plato, who, in his *Republic*, argued that humans are essentially mimetic creatures, and children most of all. A child will imitate the models that he observes, and what he imitates he will eventually become. As a result, Plato spent considerable time discussing the importance of models. Stewards must have good models, for they will eventually be models themselves. It takes only one careless generation to jeopardize centuries of careful stewardship.

Even the innovator must have one foot firmly planted in tradition if he or she is to have any hope of meaningfully responding to it in a way that will be recognized as creative and innovative. To rebel in any coherent way against tradition requires a deep understanding of the tradition against which the rebellion takes place. In other words, the rebel is formed and guided by the tradition even when denying it or attempting to escape its bonds. The most successful innovators understand the debt they owe to the past and move into uncharted territory from the tradition in which they have been inculcated. In this light, it becomes clear that true innovators are first of all imitators who submit to the contours of the tradition in a process of learning that, ultimately, makes possible the innovative movement.

Instantiation: Next, a properly conceived liberal education should seek to bring the abstract ideals extolled in various works to a concrete realization. As long as the ideals remain abstractions, the process is only half complete. While the souls of learners may be drawn upward toward eternal verities, they will not be suited to living a specifically human life unless those truths are embodied in particulars with reference to the history and stories of some place. When a schoolboy reads of General Washington's bitter winter at Valley Forge, he can better know how to live a life of sacrifice as he attends Maple Grove Middle School. When a child learns to appreciate the exacting language of Cicero and seeks to speak in imitation of him, he learns to be a better citizen and public advocate of issues bearing on his hometown. When a young girl learns to love the inventions of Bach, she brings joy to her family and neighbors as she plays with precision and feeling. To understand the methods and goals of classical architecture is to become equipped to see how our public buildings can and should ennoble the public realm even as they inspire citizens to acts of public virtue.

In other words, a liberal education should teach students how to be human beings and how to live in some place. If a course of education cultivates a hatred for home, it has failed. If it cultivates a dissatisfaction with the local, particular, and provincial in favor of distant, abstract places where cosmopolitanism drowns out the loveliness and uniqueness of local customs, practices, stories, and songs, then the education has failed. To be well educated is to be educated to live well in a particular place. It is to acknowledge the creatureliness of one's existence and thereby recognize the lines of gratitude and the scale proper to a human life.

Transmission: The final, and perhaps obvious, step in this discussion proceeds naturally out of a love for that which has been inherited. Once one has learned to love, one will want to show others the object of that love. This is true for two reasons. First, when one's soul is moved to love, it is moved by the truth in the object of that love. When one encounters truth, it is natural to want to show it to others. The missionary has this zeal for his faith. The receiver of a liberal education will be moved by similar impulses, though, to be sure not animated by the weight of eternity that hangs over religious conversion. Nevertheless, the beauty and truth one encounters in a liberal education will give birth to a desire to share those things with others. Second, an adequate liberal education will constantly remind the receiver of the fragility of one's inheritance and the need to teach others to love it lest it be forgotten. A liberal education, in short, cultivates a deep sense of responsibility in the learner, which induces a desire to show others the loveliness, truth, and goodness in that which has been acquired. Love and responsibility give birth to acts befitting stewards: the learner becomes the teacher; the receiver becomes the giver; the cultivated becomes the cultivator.

Wilhelm Röpke recounts a touching scene in which an old man lovingly passes on a precious inheritance to a young girl:

> Many years ago I visited a second-hand bookshop in Istanbul. It was run by a Greek, and I found him immersed, together with a young girl, in the study of a book. I asked him not to let me disturb him, but while I was browsing among the dusty shelves, I could not help overhearing some of the remarks passing at the table. Soon there was no doubt: they were reading and discussing the *Odyssey*. It seemed to me that there could hardly be a more touching sight than that of this Greek, here, in a dark corner of ancient Byzantium, handing down to his daughter the eternal beauty of Homer, still a living heritage after three thousand years, while outside the trams rattled past and the motorcars hooted.[10]

The obvious point is that unless the possessors of the great tradition believe it to be worth preserving, it will slowly disappear as memory fades and people die.

Unless the tradition remains alive in the hearts, minds, and lives of those to whom it has been entrusted, it will be lost, for only a living and vibrant reality will be seen as worth passing down. Parents, teachers, aunts, uncles, grandparents, and neighbors can all participate in this cultural transmission. But one cannot transmit what one does not possess. A parent cannot look to a child and say "taste and see" if the flavor is not fresh on the parent's tongue. One will not be able or even inclined to transmit what one does not love.

There exists, then, a delicate chain of reception and transmission that can be broken with one generation of inattentiveness. The responsibility placed on each generation is daunting. That we as a society have lost a sense of stewardship to the past as we embrace the promises of progress portends the loss of culture. Fortunately, as always, there is a remnant. There are children and adults who are learning to love the great tradition and together tending its delicate flame. There are adults who, having been raised on the soporific gruel of television and comic books, have been inspired to take up the mantle and, by sustained effort, enter into the tradition late yet fully. There are teachers that remain in the classroom, sustained over the years by the small handful of students whose eyes brighten and pulse quickens at the poetry of Milton or the struggles of Aeneas. While these remain, there is hope, for the truths embodied in the great tradition reach out to those who will but stop to listen; there are beauties that set the heart to singing if only one pauses to hear the notes; there are virtues that cut like cold steel and can inspire acts of nobility and sacrifice if only one submits to their authority.

The great tradition is a gift, handed down to us from our collective fathers and mothers, and as grateful children, we owe them the duty of preserving their gift. In the process, we will find that we are the beneficiaries of a way of life that, when fully instantiated in a particular place, will reveal what it means to live well.

Several years ago when I was away at a conference, my wife took our three young sons out to eat. This was a family restaurant, and apparently so families wouldn't have to talk with each other, televisions were positioned at strategic points around the room. Now children who don't watch much television seem almost hypnotized when they encounter it. It is extraordinarily difficult for them to ignore. So with the television hovering overhead, my wife struggled to maintain a conversation with three young boys who were craning their necks to see the screen.

At some point in the course of dinner, an episode of *The Simpsons* came on, and this episode just happened to include a spoof on Homer (the Greek poet, not Bart's dad). Our oldest son, Seth, who was six at the time, soon pointed and exclaimed, "Mom! That kid is pretending to be Odysseus!" He didn't know Bart and company, but he did know Homer. I pray that one day he feels the burden of responsibility even as he delights in the beauty and truth of his inheritance.

CONCLUSION

The Neighborly Arts

What life have you if you have not life together?
There is no life that is not in community,
And no community not lived in praise of GOD.

T. S. Eliot, "Choruses from 'The Rock'"

Stewarding the many good things we have inherited is the task of a lifetime. Simply learning the art of stewardship requires, for many of us, a radical change of mind and direction. Living a life of gratitude is no easy task. Admitting the various ways we are limited and dependent requires humility, that most shy of all virtues. Learning to appreciate the aesthetic of human scale requires a willingness to submit to standards not of our own making. Living contentedly in a place, at peace with the natural world and in community with neighbors, is not simple in a world that entices us constantly to move, to acquire more, to live for the fleeting pleasures that are offered on every hand.

Nevertheless, the stakes are high. But then again, they have always been high. The burden of stewardship is a crucial task—perhaps the crucial task—of each generation. It is a responsibility that falls on each of us even as it will fall to our children where we leave off. We gratefully receive, carefully tend, and pass our inheritance on in hope. The good things need preserving, not because they will necessarily cease to exist if we fail, but because if we lose contact with them we will find ourselves disoriented by the blinding glitter of the transient and temporal.

Stewardship is never a static act of passing on an inheritance unchanged. Our lives are dynamic interactions with history, with nature, and with events beyond our control or even our understanding. When we care for the good things we receive, we change them in the very process of our care. And they, in return, change us. That which we have inherited becomes a transformative part of our lives even as we tend it in trust for those who will come after us.

The challenges faced by every generation are both unique and the same. There are, to be sure, similarities with times past. We can develop an awareness of the ways our predecessors both succeeded and failed in their efforts to thrive and even survive the many difficulties that confront human beings. But the general similarities are accompanied by significant differences in the particulars, and a solution that proved effective in one generation might be quite meaningless in another. Stewarding the old things requires creativity.

Today, because many of our problems loom so large, it is tempting to think in terms of centralized, top-down fixes. Global financial failures, international terrorism, nuclear proliferation, deforestation, and pollution are problems that do not seem well suited to modest solutions. After all, big problems seem to require sweeping policies of a national or international scope. We need to take care at this point, for it may often be that our attempts to address various problems will merely facilitate more political, economic, and cultural centralization, all of which represent serious threats to freedom even as they promise security, stability, and peace.

Once, when asked for practical advice about ways an individual could make a difference, E. F. Schumacher suggested that people plant a tree. A curiously modest act, to be sure. But that is precisely the point. Because of the scope of the problems we face, it is easy to become discouraged and perhaps paralyzed by the enormity of the task. Schumacher insists that we must recover the idea of human scale, for it is only then that we can wisely engage the problems besetting us. When we plant a tree, we are caring for a small part of the creation. Such an act is inexpensive and can be done in the company of friends and neighbors. A tree will last for years. It will likely outlive the person who planted it. Planting a tree, therefore, is an act born of hope. When we plant a tree, we put something back into the system. We consciously act as a cultivator rather than merely a consumer. When we plant trees, literally and figuratively, we rise out of our complacency and take the initiative in a context that is manageable and imaginable. Such an act is, then, an act performed on a scale suited to human beings.

As we seek to cultivate lives characterized by the ideals expressed in this book, it quickly becomes clear that compromise is unavoidable. It is impossible, for example, to enjoy the benefits of a mixed-use walkable neighborhood and to live on a piece of land with chickens, three goats, and a cow. Both settings can provide many of the elements necessary for human flourishing, yet a person cannot have everything. Living well requires choosing, and often our choices are between two competing goods.

More significantly, it is no small task to live in our contemporary world and consistently remain faithful to the ideas of limits, gratitude, human scale, and place. Simply by participating in the global economy, we find ourselves implicated in practices that are antithetical to those things we hold as good. But we should not let a vision of perfection keep us from making strides toward the things we cherish. Demanding perfection of ourselves or the world is succumbing to the old temptation to expect more of this life than it can give. Perfection is not the lot of mortals. We are called to strive, to live wisely, and to carry out our duties as best we can. We can exercise faithfulness without perfection. We can practice contentment in the face of struggles and hardship. We can exercise the virtue of hope even when goodness appears only as a flicker in the dark.

Ironically, our very affluence can contribute to the problem. Our affluence is a product of the freedom we enjoy, but at the same time, affluence can breed a false sense of independence that serves to separate us from each other and from the natural world as well. When this independence is combined with a manner of thinking that tends to reduce every transaction to a cost-benefit analysis, important things drop away in the process.

Several years ago, I had dinner with a group that included a well-known economist. It soon became apparent that this man was a lover of wine. His tastes were refined, he possessed a broad knowledge of the subject, and he relished talking about the various facets of wine production. Sometime over the course of the evening, I mentioned that I have a small vineyard on the hill behind my house. He gave me a quizzical look and then shook his head. "I believe in specialization," he said. The obvious implication was that he would leave the wine-making to the specialists, for they would produce a better product than he could as an amateur. Likely he was right on this score. But is anything gained by doing something yourself? Is anything gained by sinking one's hands into the soil, carefully tending young vines, and gaining the specific knowledge of soil types, grape variety, and climate? Do careful attention, diligent work, and long months of patience impart a flavor note to the final product that is acquired in no other way?

In January 2010, the *Wall Street Journal* ran a piece on the way economists think. One example: two economists gave a friend $150 to hire movers instead of helping him themselves.[1] Of course, few people relish moving, and most care even less for helping someone else move. There are innumerable ways most people would rather spend their time. Yet, by simply giving a friend the money to hire movers, are the obligations of friendship discharged? When we send strangers to do the work of friends, we are outsourcing camaraderie. We are denying the friendship times of mutual discomfort that can draw the bonds tighter even as the difficulty is lightened by sharing it. Lost is the face-to-face interaction between people that adds another small layer solidifying the friendship.

Wilhelm Röpke recounts a conversation he had with a prominent economist in the aftermath of World War II. As they strolled along the streets of a German town, Röpke pointed, with satisfaction, to the many small vegetable gardens kept by the residents of city. The prominent economist shook his head disapprovingly and grumbled. "A very inefficient way of producing foodstuffs." Röpke quickly responded, "But perhaps a very efficient way of producing human happiness."[2] This rejoinder takes us to the heart of the matter. Happiness is the proper end of life. By happiness I do not mean the glib and transitory pleasure that so often is confused with happiness today. Happiness, as described by classical thinkers, is a life of excellence in accordance with goods and standards that are suited to human beings. This sort of happiness is not achievable in isolation, for humans are creatures fit for community.

Here we can begin to see the connection between what might be called the "neighborly arts" and a life well lived. When we make it a point to learn various skills, we become better equipped to help our neighbors. When we are able to grow a tomato, we can then share it with others. When we know how to build a fence, install a light fixture, or repair a carburetor, we cannot only take better care of ourselves and our families, we can better serve our neighbors. Learning to tend livestock, cultivate fruit trees, and keep bees provides the satisfaction of doing for oneself, but we can also share the bounty. When times are hard, the neighborly arts are at a premium. In times of affluence, they can atrophy under the illusion that specialization is all we need. But if we fail to cultivate these practical arts, the hard times will be harder and the opportunity to help our friends and neighbors in practical ways will be diminished. The bonds of community will be attenuated even as our collective need for a strong and energetic state correspondingly increases.

Could the neighborly arts be one facet of the art of freedom Tocqueville describes? Could these practical skills expand our opportunities to engage others in the associational life that is the best bulwark against the nanny state Tocqueville feared? Could these skills serve to bind families together even as they facilitate one aspect of economic independence? Could the neighborly arts provide the opportunity for healthy interaction with the natural world unencumbered by the weight of institutions and expectations that distort reality by virtue of their scale?

Recently several young women asked my wife to teach them to make bread. They knew that homemade bread tastes better than much of the stuff on the shelves at the grocery store, they knew it was healthier to eat, and they knew that my wife likes to bake a variety of loaf and artisan breads. So for several hours on a Saturday in the spring, our kitchen was full of sifting flour and questions as my wife instructed these young women in the art of bread making. Perhaps one day these young women, now grown older, will teach their own children or a neighbor how to make bread. In the ensuing years, those same children and neighbors will no doubt refine their skills, adding particular nuances and flourishes of their own, so that when they pass on the knowledge to others, it will be what they received but different nonetheless. In such a manner is any living tradition passed from one generation to the next.

The neighborly arts, like all arts, are cultivated in practice and passed on from one person to another in a particular place and time. The neighborly arts are placed arts, for they are embodied in the particulars of a local community. They are the humble arts born of people living in proximity and sharing particular knowledge in a way that improves the lives of family, friends, and neighbors. The neighborly arts bind people together in mutual help and affection.

The neighborly arts begin at home, extend outward in service to others, and return in the form of gratitude, friendships, and commitments born of practical skills shared and received. In this sense, perhaps, the art of hospitality represents in a concrete and intimate way how the neighborly arts can foster good will, good conversation, and good times (not to mention good food). Ultimately, a life together in the presence of extended family, friends, and neighbors is more possible, more durable, and more enjoyable when the bonds of nature, proximity, and affection are strengthened by the mutual assistance born of the neighborly arts. True happiness begins at home.

NOTES

1. Creatures: Limits and Dependence

1. See, for example, Richard Dawkins, *The God Delusion* (Boston: Houghton Mifflin, 2006); Sam Harris, *Letter to a Christian Nation* (New York: Alfred A. Knopf, 2006); and Christopher Hitchens, *God is not Great: How Religion Poisons Everything* (New York: Twelve, 2009).
2. Hannah Arendt, *The Human Condition* (Chicago: University of Chicago Press, 1958), 248ff.

2. Gratitude: A Creature's Love

1. José Ortega y Gasset, *The Revolt of the Masses* (New York: Norton, 1964), 58.
2. David Hume, *Essays, Moral, Political, and Literary* (Indianapolis, IN: Liberty Fund, 1985), 479.
3. Immanuel Kant, *Metaphysics of Ethics*, trans. J. W. Semple, ed. Henry Calderwood (New York: T. and T. Clark, 1886), 273.
4. Friedrich Nietzsche, *Human, All Too Human: A Book for Free Spirits*, trans. Marion Faber with Stephen Lehmann (Lincoln: University of Nebraska Press, 1984), § 323, p. 180.
5. Aristotle, *Nicomachean Ethics*, trans. Martin Ostwald (Englewood Cliffs, NJ: Prentice Hall, 1962), 1120a 12–13.
6. Marcus Tullius Cicero, *Treatise on the Laws*, Bk. I, sec. 43 (London: E. Spettigue, 1842), 56.
7. Luke 17: 11–19 (King James Version).
8. Cicero, *Treatise on the Laws*, Bk. II, sec. 16, 87.
9. I Thessalonians 5:17 (KJV).
10. Psalm 100 (KJV).
11. The Anglican Book of Common Prayer, 1928.
12. Virgil, *The Aeneid*, trans. Robert Fitzgerald (New York: Everyman's Library, 1992), II 826–32.
13. Ibid., 921–24, 932–41.
14. Kant, *Metaphysics of Ethics*, 274.

15. George Washington, *George Washington: A Collection*, comp. and ed. W. B. Allen (Indianapolis, IN: Liberty Fund, 1998), 96.
16. Edmund Burke, *Reflections on the Revolution in France* (Indianapolis, IN: Liberty Fund, 1999), 192.
17. Ibid.
18. Wendell Berry, "The Peace of Wild Things," *The Selected Poems of Wendell Berry* (Washington, DC: Counterpoint, 1998), 30.
19. Matthew 18:23–34 (KJV).
20. George Washington, letter to Governor Dinwiddie, May 29, 1754, in *The Official Records of Robert Dinwiddie: Lieutenant-Governor of the Colony of Virginia, 1751–1758* (Richmond: Virginia Historical Society, 1883), 176.
21. Thomas Aquinas, ST II.II 107.1
22. Kant, *Metaphysics of Ethics*, 278.
23. Dante, *Inferno*, in *The Divine Comedy*, trans. Allen Mandelbaum (New York: Everyman's Library, 1995), cantos XXXII–XXXIV.
24. John Milton, *Paradise Lost* (New York: Mentor Books, 1981), IV 42–57.
25. Deuteronomy 8:10–17 (KJV).
26. Wendell Berry, *Sex, Economy, Freedom and Community* (San Francisco: Pantheon Books, 1992), 103.
27. William Shakespeare, *King Lear* (London: Arden Shakespeare, 1997), 1.1.77–78.
28. Ibid., 1.1.95–104.
29. Ibid., 1.4.251–3.
30. Ibid., 2.2.366–368.
31. Ibid., 2.2.467.
32. Ibid., 1.2.117.
33. Ibid., 1.5.36–42.

3. Human Scale: Propriety in Our Lives

1. Wilhelm Röpke, *The Social Crisis of Our Time* (New Brunswick, NJ: Transaction Publishers, 1992), 66–67.
2. Friedrich Nietzsche, *The Gay Science*, trans. Walter Kauffmann (New York: Vintage Books, 1974), § 125.
3. Ibid., § 343.
4. Aleksandr I. Solzhenitsyn, *The Gulag Archipelago*, abridged by Edward E. Ericson Jr. (New York: Harper Perennial, 2002), 312.
5. Bertrand de Jouvenel, *On Power* (Indianapolis, IN: Liberty Fund, 1948), 378.

4. Place: The Allure of Home

1. Simone Weil, *The Need for Roots* (New York: Routledge, 1995), 41.
2. Ibid., 43.
3. T. S. Eliot, "Tradition and the Individual Talent," in *The Sacred Wood* (London: Faber and Faber, 1997). Eliot was, of course, referring specifically to innovation in poetry, but his insight applies across the board to all areas of discovery.
4. Burke, *Reflections on the Revolution in France*, 182.
5. G. K. Chesterton, *Orthodoxy* (Wheaton, IL: Harold Shaw, 1994). Chesterton remarks, "Tradition may be defined as an extension of the franchise. Tradition means giving

votes to the most obscure of all classes, our ancestors. It is the democracy of the dead. Tradition refuses to submit to the small and arrogant oligarchy of those who merely happen to be walking around. All democrats object to men being disqualified by the accident of birth; tradition objects to their being disqualified by the accident of death. Democracy tells us not to neglect a good man's opinion, even if he is our groom; tradition asks us not to neglect a good man's opinion, even if he is our father" (47–48).

6. Michael Polanyi and Alasdair MacIntyre both argue persuasively for this conception of tradition. See Polanyi's *Personal Knowledge: Toward a Post-Critical Philosophy* (Chicago: University of Chicago Press, 1958) and MacIntyre's *Three Rival Versions of Moral Enquiry* (Notre Dame, IN: University of Notre Dame Press, 1990).

7. Psalm 8:5 (KJV).

8. Berry, *Sex, Economy, Freedom and Community*, 119–20.

9. Ibid., 168, 169.

10. Ibid., 173.

11. Wallace Stegner, *Where the Bluebird Sings to the Lemonade Springs* (New York: Modern Library, 2002), xxvii.

12. Booker T. Washington, "Atlanta Compromise Speech," September 18, 1895, transcript, HistoryTools.org, University of Wisconsin–Green Bay, http://www.history tools.org/sources/Washington-Atlanta.pdf.

5. Politics: The Art of Freedom

1. Alexis de Tocqueville, *Democracy in America*, trans. George Lawrence, ed. J. P. Mayer (New York: HarperCollins, 1988), 508.

2. Ibid., 673.

3. Ibid., 673.

4. Ibid., 681.

5. Ibid., 670.

6. Ibid., 691–92.

7. Neil Postman, *Amusing Ourselves to Death* (New York: Penguin, 1985), viii.

8. Aldous Huxley, *Brave New World* (New York: Harper, 1950), 264, 284.

9. Tocqueville, *Democracy in America*, 509.

10. F. A. Hayek, *The Road to Serfdom* (Chicago: University of Chicago Press, 1994), 257–58.

11. Tocqueville, *Democracy in America*, 167.

12. Quotations from *Quadragesimo Anno* (May 15, 1931) taken from *The Church and the Reconstruction of the Modern World: The Social Encyclicals of Pope Pius XI*, ed. Terrence P. McLaughlin (Garden City, NY: Doubleday, 1957), § 78.

13. Ibid., § 80.

14. Ibid., § 79.

6. Economics: Private Property and the Virtues of Freedom

1. Hilaire Belloc, *The Servile State* (Indianapolis, IN: Liberty Fund, 1977), 107.

2. G. K. Chesterton, *The Outline of Sanity* (Norfolk, VA: IHS Press, 2002), 42.

3. Hayek, *Road to Serfdom*, 214, 215.

4. Karl Polanyi, *The Great Transformation* (Boston: Beacon, 2001), 145.
5. Ibid., 147.
6. Ibid., 155.
7. Stephen A. Marglin, *The Dismal Science* (Cambridge, MA: Harvard University Press, 2008), 9.
8. Edward Copleston, *A Reply to the Calumnies of the Edinburgh Review against Oxford: Containing an Account of Studies Pursued in That University* (London: P. Cooke, P. Parker, and P. Mackinaly, 1810), 174.
9. Marglin, *Dismal Science*, 37.
10. Ibid., 14.
11. Robert Nisbet, *The Quest for Community* (Richmond, CA: ICS Press, 1990), 215.
12. Frank H. Knight, *Risk, Uncertainty and Profit* (Chicago: University of Chicago Press, 1971), 77.
13. Ludwig von Mises, *Socialism*, trans. J. Kahane (New Haven, CT: Yale University Press, 1951), 485.
14. Wilhelm Röpke, *A Humane Economy* (Wilmington, DE: ISI Books, 1998), 164.
15. Joseph A. Schumpeter, *Capitalism, Socialism and Democracy* (New York: Harper and Row, 1950), 158.
16. Ibid., 161, 160.
17. Bill Clinton, George Bush, and Ross Perot, Second presidential debate, moderated by Carole Simpson, October 15, 1992, transcript, Commission on Presidential Debates, Washington, DC, http://www.debates.org/index.php?page=october-15-1992-second-half-debate-transcript.
18. Schumacher, *Small Is Beautiful*, 51.
19. Ibid.
20. Ibid.
21. Bernard Mandeville, *The Fable of the Bees; Or, Private Vices, Publick Benefits*, ed. F. Kaye (Indianapolis, IN: Liberty Classics, 1988), 1:18, 24.
22. John Maynard Keynes, *Essays in Persuasion* (New York: Harcourt, Brace, 1932), 367.
23. Ibid., 369.
24. Ibid., 372.
25. Röpke, *Humane Economy*, 281.
26. Ibid., 128.
27. Ibid., 138.
28. Ibid., 35.
29. Hilaire Belloc, *The Restoration of Property* (Norfolk, VA: IHS Press, 2002), 75.
30. Schumpeter, *Capitalism, Socialism and Democracy*, 142.
31. Thomas Jefferson, *The Life and Selected Writings of Thomas Jefferson*, ed. Adrienne Koch and William Peden (New York: Modern Library, 1944), 337.
32. Röpke, *Humane Economy*, 99.
33. Wendell Berry, *Home Economics* (New York: North Point Press, 1987), 189.

7. The Natural World: Living in a Creation

1. Wendell Berry, *Citizenship Papers* (Washington, DC: Shoemaker and Hoard, 2003), 64.

2. Polanyi, *Great Transformation*, 48, 60.
3. Wendell Berry, *The Unsettling of America* (San Francisco: Sierra Club Books: 1997), 58, 56.
4. Ibid., 76.
5. Ibid., 74–75.
6. Berry, *Home Economics*, 54–55.
7. Ibid., 57.
8. Ibid., 64–65.
9. Berry, *Citizenship Papers*, 144.
10. Ibid., 146.
11. Ibid., 147.
12. Ibid., 118.
13. Ibid., 117.
14. Berry, *Sex, Economy, Freedom and Community*, 34.
15. Genesis 3:17–19 (KJV).
16. Lewis Mumford, *Technics and Civilization* (New York: Harcourt, Brace and World, 1934), 10–11.
17. Psalm 46:10 (KJV); Psalm 121:1 (KJV).
18. Associated Press, "What's the Stench? A Pile of Cow Manure," MSNBC.com, January 28, 2005, http://www.msnbc.msn.com/id/6879097/.
19. Le Corbusier, *The Radiant City* (New York: Orion Press, 1967), 74. The same piece of propaganda includes an homage to consumption: "We shall use of tires, wear out road surfaces and gears, consume oil and gasoline. All of which will necessitate a great deal of work; there will be a titanic demand for labor; enough for all; no threat of unemployment looming in the future."
20. Andres Duany, Elizabeth Plater-Zyberk, and Jeff Speck, *Suburban Nation* (New York: North Point Press, 2002), 11.

8. Family: The Cradle of Gratitude

1. Allan Carlson, *From Cottage to Work Station: The Family's Search for Social Harmony in the Industrial Age* (San Francisco: Ignatius Press, 1993), 10–15.
2. Ibid., 14.
3. Wendell Berry, *What Are People For?* (New York: North Point Press, 1990), 158–59.
4. Berry, *Unsettling of America*, 41.
5. Tocqueville, *Democracy in America*, 62–63.
6. NAHB Public Affairs and NAHB Economics, "Housing Facts, Figures, and Trends," SoFlo.org, March 2006, http://www.soflo.fau.edu/report/NAHBhousing factsMarch2006.pdf
7. U.S. Bureau of the Census, "Median and Average Sales Prices of New One-Family Houses Sold," New Residential Sales—Characteristics of New Housing, http://www.census.gov/const/C25Ann/soldmedavgprice.pdf. Accessed June 11, 2012.
8. U.S. Census Bureau, "No. HS-12: Households by Type and Size: 1900 to 2002," *Statistical Abstract of the United States*, 2003, http://www.census.gov/statab/hist/HS-12.pdf
9. Richard Louv, *The Last Child in the Woods* (Chapel Hill, NC: Algonquin Books, 2006), front matter.

9. Education: The Place of the Liberal Arts

1. Richard Weaver, *Ideas Have Consequences* (Chicago: University of Chicago Press, 1948), 56.
2. Ibid., 65.
3. Ortega y Gasset, *Revolt of the Masses*, 58–59.
4. Weaver, *Ideas Have Consequences*, 115.
5. Ibid., 116–17.
6. Burke, *Reflections on the Revolution in France*, 241.
7. Allan Bloom, *The Closing of the American Mind* (New York: Touchstone, 1987), 62–63.
8. Walker Percy, *Signposts in a Strange Land*, ed. Patrick Samway (New York: Picador USA, 1991), 356.
9. George Steiner, *In Bluebeard's Castle* (New Haven, CT: Yale University Press, 1971), 107.
10. Röpke, *Humane Economy*, 60.

Conclusion. The Neighborly Arts

1. Justin Lahart, "Secrets of the Economist's Trade: First, Purchase a Piggy Bank," *Wall Street Journal*, January 2, 2010, http://online.wsj.com/article/SB12623885 4939012923.html.
2. Röpke, *Social Crisis of Our Time*, viii–ix, 224.

BIBLIOGRAPHY

Adams, Henry Brooks. *The Education of Henry Adams*. New York: Library of America, 1983.

Aquinas, Thomas. *On Law, Morality, and Politics*. Translated by Richard J. Regan. 2nd edition. Indianapolis: Hackett Publishing, 2002.

Arendt, Hannah. *The Human Condition*. Chicago: University of Chicago Press, 1958.

Aristotle. *Nicomachean Ethics*. Translated by Martin Ostwald. Englewood Cliffs, NJ: Prentice Hall, 1962.

Associated Press. "What's the Stench? A Pile of Cow Manure." MSNBC.com, January 8, 2005. http://msnbc.msn.com/id/6879097.

Belloc, Hilaire. *The Restoration of Property*. Norfolk, VA: IHS Press, 2002.

———. *The Servile State*. Indianapolis, IN: Liberty Fund, 1977.

Berry, Wendell. *Citizenship Papers*. Washington, DC: Shoemaker and Hoard, 2003.

———. *Home Economics*. New York: North Point Press, 1987.

———. *The Selected Poems of Wendell Berry*. Washington, DC: Counterpoint, 1999.

———. *Sex, Economy, Freedom and Community*. San Francisco: Pantheon Books, 1992.

———. *The Unsettling of America*. San Francisco: Sierra Club Books, 1997.

———. *What Are People For?* New York: North Point Press, 1990.

Bloom, Allan. *The Closing of the American Mind*. New York: Touchstone, 1987.

Burke, Edmund. *Reflections on the Revolution in France*. Indianapolis: Liberty Fund, 1999.

Carlson, Allan. *From Cottage to Work Station: The Family's Search for Social Harmony in the Industrial Age*. San Francisco: Ignatius Press, 1993.

Chesterton, G. K. *Brave New Family*. Edited by Alvaro de Silva. San Francisco: Ignatius Press, 1990.

———. *Orthodoxy*. Wheaton, IL: Harold Shaw, 1994.

———. *The Outline of Sanity*. Norfolk, VA: IHS Press, 2002.

Cicero, Marcus Tullius. *Treatise on the Laws*. London: E. Spettigue, 1842.

Clinton, Bill, George Bush, and Ross Perot. Second presidential debate, moderated by Carole Simpson, October 15, 1992. Transcript, Commission on Presidential

Debates, Washington, DC. http://www.debates.org/index.php?page=october-15 -1992-second-half-debate-transcript.

Copleston, Edward. *A Reply to the Calumnies of the Edinburgh Review against Oxford: Containing an Account of Studies Pursued in That University*. London: P. Cooke, P. Parker, and P. Mackinaly, 1810.

Dante. *The Divine Comedy*. Translated by Allen Mandelbaum. New York: Everyman's Library, 1995.

Duany, Andres, Elizabeth Plater-Zyberk, and Jeff Speck. *Suburban Nation*. New York: North Point Press, 2002.

Eliot, T. S. "Choruses from 'The Rock.'" In *The Complete Poems and Plays 1909–1950*. New York: Harcourt, Brace and World, 1971.

———. "Tradition and the Individual Talent." In *The Sacred Wood*. London: Faber and Faber, 1997.

Hayek, F. A. *The Road to Serfdom*. Chicago: University of Chicago Press, 1994.

Hume, David. *Essays, Moral, Political, and Literary*. Indianapolis, IN: Liberty Fund, 1985.

Huxley, Aldous. *Brave New World*. New York: Harper, 1950.

Jacobs, Jane. *The Death and Life of Great American Cities*. New York: Modern Library, 1993.

Jefferson, Thomas. *The Life and Selected Writings of Thomas Jefferson*. Edited by Adrienne Koch and William Peden. New York: Modern Library, 1944.

Jouvenel, Bertrand de. *On Power*. Indianapolis: Liberty Fund, 1948.

Kant, Immanuel. *The Metaphysics of Ethics*. Translated by J. W. Semple. Edited by Henry Calderwood. New York: T. and T. Clark, 1886.

Keynes, John Maynard. *Essays in Persuasion*. New York: Harcourt, Brace, 1932.

Knight, Frank H. *Risk, Uncertainty and Profit*. Chicago: University of Chicago Press, 1971.

Lahart, Justin. "Secrets of the Economist's Trade: First, Purchase a Piggy Bank." *Wall Street Journal*, January 2, 2010. http://online.wsj.com/article/SB1262388549390 12923.html.

Le Corbusier. *The Radiant City*. New York: Orion, 1967.

Louv, Richard. *The Last Child in the Woods*. Chapel Hill, NC: Algonquin Books, 2006.

Mandeville, Bernard. *The Fable of the Bees: Or, Private Vices, Publick Benefits*. Edited by F. Kaye. Vol. 1. Indianapolis, IN: Liberty Classics, 1988.

Marglin, Stephen A. *The Dismal Science*. Cambridge, MA: Harvard University Press, 2008.

Milton, John. *Paradise Lost*. New York: Mentor Books, 1981.

Mumford, Lewis. *Technics and Civilization*. New York: Harcourt, Brace and World, 1934.

NAHB Public Affairs and NAHB Economics. "Housing Facts, Figures, and Trends." SoFlo.org, March 2006. http://www.soflo.fau.edu/report/NAHBhousingfacts March2006.pdf.

Nietzsche, Friedrich. *The Gay Science*. Translated by Walter Kauffmann. New York: Vintage Books, 1974.

———. *Human, All Too Human: A Book for Free Spirits*. Translated by Marion Faber with Stephen Lehmann. Lincoln: University of Nebraska Press, 1984.

Nisbet, Robert. *The Quest for Community*. Richmond, CA: ICS Press, 1990.

Ortega y Gasset, José. *The Revolt of the Masses*. New York: Norton, 1964.

Percy, Walker. *Signposts in a Strange Land*. Edited by Patrick Samway. New York: Picador USA, 1991.

Pius XI. *Quadragesimo Anno*. In *The Church and the Reconstruction of the Modern World: The Social Encyclicals of Pope Pius XI*. Edited by Terrence P. McLaughlin. Garden City, NY: Doubleday, 1957.

Polanyi, Karl. *The Great Transformation*. Boston: Beacon, 2001.

Pope, Alexander. "To Lord Cobham." In *Epistles to Several Persons*. 1734.

Postman, Neil. *Amusing Ourselves to Death*. New York: Penguin, 1985.

Robinson, Marilynne. *Home*. New York: Farrar, Straus and Giroux, 2008.

Röpke, Wilhelm. *A Humane Economy*. Wilmington, DE: ISI Books, 1998.

———. *The Social Crisis of Our Time*. New Brunswick, NJ: Transaction Publishers, 1992.

Schumacher, E. F. *Small Is Beautiful*. New York: Harper Perennial, 1989.

Schumpeter, Joseph A. *Capitalism, Socialism and Democracy*. New York: Harper and Row, 1950.

Shakespeare, William. *King Lear*. London: Arden Shakespeare, 1997.

———. *Twelfth Night*. London: Arden Shakespeare, 2009.

Solzhenitsyn, Aleksandr I. *The Gulag Archipelago*. Abridged by Edward E. Ericson Jr. New York: Harper Perennial, 2002.

Stegner, Wallace. *Where the Bluebird Sings to the Lemonade Springs*. New York: Modern Library, 2002.

Steiner, George. *In Bluebeard's Castle*. New Haven, CT: Yale University Press, 1971.

Tocqueville, Alexis de. *Democracy in America*. Translated by George Lawrence. Edited by J. P. Mayer. New York: HarperCollins, 1988.

Turgenev, Ivan. *Fathers and Sons*. Translated by Alexandra Tolstoy. New York: Bantam, 1959.

U.S. Bureau of the Census. "Median and Average Sales Prices of New One-Family Houses Sold." New Residential Sales—Characteristics of New Housing. http://www.census.gov/const/C25Ann/soldmedavgprice.pdf. Accessed June 12, 2012.

———. "No. HS-12: Households by Type and Size: 1900–2002." *Statistical Abstract of the United States*, 2003. http://www.census.gov/statab/hist/HS-12.pdf. Accessed March 26, 2010.

Virgil. *The Aeneid*. Translated by Robert Fitzgerald. New York: Everyman's Library, 1992.

Von Mises, Ludwig. *Socialism*. Translated by J. Kahane. New Haven, CT: Yale University Press, 1951.

Washington, Booker T. "Atlanta Compromise Speech." September 18, 1895. Transcript, HistoryTools.org, University of Wisconsin–Green Bay. http://www.historytools.org/sources/Washington-Atlanta.pdf

Washington, George. *George Washington: A Collection*. Compiled and edited by W. B. Allen. Indianapolis, IN: Liberty Fund, 1988.

———. Letter to Governor Dinwiddie, May 29, 1754. In *The Official Records of Robert Dinwiddie: Lieutenant-Governor of the Colony of Virginia, 1751–1758*. Richmond: Virginia Historical Society, 1883.

Weaver, Richard. *Ideas Have Consequences*. Chicago: University of Chicago Press, 1948.

Weil, Simone. *The Need for Roots*. New York: Routledge, 1995.

Further Reading

Abbey, Edward. *Desert Solitaire*. New York: Touchstone, 1990.

Adams, Henry. *Democracy, an American Novel*. New York: Penguin Books, 2008.

Agar, Herbert, and Allan Tate, eds. *Who Owns America?* Wilmington, DE: ISI Books, 1999.

Aristotle. *Politics*. Translated by C.D.C. Reeve. Indianapolis: Hackett, 1998.

Augustine. *City of God*. Translated by Marcus Dods. New York: Modern Library, 1993.

Berry, Wendell. *Jayber Crow*. New York: Counterpoint, 2001.

———. *Life Is a Miracle: An Essay against Modern Superstition*. New York: Counterpoint, 2001.

Bess, Philip. *Till We Have Built Jerusalem: Architecture, Urbanism, and the Sacred*. Wilmington, DE: ISI Books, 2006.

Carlson, Allan. *American Way: Family and Community in the Shaping of the American Identity*. Wilmington, DE: ISI Books, 2003.

———. *Third Ways: How Bulgarian Greens, Swedish Housewives, and Beer-Swilling Englishmen Created Family-Centered Economies—And Why They Disappeared*. Wilmington, DE: ISI Books, 2007.

Crawford, Matthew B. *Shop Class as Soulcraft: An Inquiry into the Value of Work*. New York: Penguin, 2009.

Dawkins, Richard. *The God Delusion*. Boston: Houghton Mifflin, 2006.

Dreher, Rod. *Crunchy Cons: The New Conservative Counterculture and Its Return to Roots*. New York: Three Rivers Press, 2006.

Eliot, T. S. "Four Quartets." In *The Complete Poems and Plays 1909–1950*. New York: Harcourt, Brace and World, 1971.

———. *Notes Towards a Definition of Culture*. Boston: Faber and Faber, 1973.

Harris, Sam. *Letter to a Christian Nation*. New York: Alfred A. Knopf, 2006.

Hitchens, Christopher. *God is not Great: How Religion Poisons Everything*. New York: Twelve, 2009.

Homer. *The Odyssey*. Translated Robert Fitzgerald. New York: Farrar, Straus and Giroux, 1998.

Ikerd, John E. *Crisis and Opportunity: Sustainability in American Agriculture*. Lincoln: University of Nebraska Press, 2008.

Kass, Leon R. *The Hungry Soul: Eating and the Perfecting of Our Nature*. Chicago: University of Chicago Press, 1999.

Kauffman, Bill. *Ain't My America: The Long, Noble History of Antiwar Conservatism and Middle-American Anti-Imperialism*. New York: Metropolitan Books, 2008.

———. *Bye Bye, Miss American Empire: Neighborhood Patriots, Backcountry Rebels, and Their Underdog Crusades to Redraw America's Political Map*. White River Junction, VT: Chelsea Green Publishing, 2010.

Kohak, Erazim. *The Embers and the Stars*. Chicago: University of Chicago Press, 1987.

Kunstler, James Howard. *Geography of Nowhere: The Rise and Decline of America's Man-Made Landscape*. New York: Free Press, 1994.

Lasch, Christopher. *The Revolt of the Elites and the Betrayal of Democracy*. New York: W. W. Norton, 1996.

Lewis, C. S. *The Abolition of Man*. New York: Collier, 1962.

Lynn, Barry C. *Cornered: The New Monopoly Capitalism and the Economics of Destruction*. Hoboken, NJ: John Wiley and Sons, 2010.

MacIntyre, Alasdair. *After Virtue*. Notre Dame, IN: University of Notre Dame Press, 2007.

———. *Dependent Rational Animals*. La Salle, IL: Open Court, 2001.

———. *Three Rival Versions of Moral Enquiry*. Notre Dame, IN: University of Notre Dame Press, 1990.

Médaille, John C. *Toward a Truly Free Market: A Distributist Perspective on the Role of Government, Taxes, Health Care, Deficits, and More*. Wilmington, DE: ISI Books, 2010.

Oakeshott, Michael. *Rationalism in Politics and Other Essays*. Indianapolis, IN: Liberty Fund, 2001.

Percy, Walker. *Lost in the Cosmos*. New York: Picador, 2000.

Pieper, Josef. *Tradition: Concept and Claim*. Wilmington, DE: ISI Books, 2008.

Pipes, Richard. *Property and Freedom*. New York: Vintage, 2000.

Plato. *Republic*. Translated by C.D.C. Reeve. Indianapolis: Hackett, 2004.

Polanyi, Michael. *Personal Knowledge: Toward a Post-Critical Philosophy*. Chicago: University of Chicago Press, 1958.

———. *Science, Faith and Society*. New York: Maugham Press, 2007.

Pollan, Michael. *The Omnivore's Dilemma: A Natural History of Four Meals*. New York: Penguin, 2006.

Postman, Neil. *Technopoly: The Surrender of Culture to Technology*. New York: Random House, 1992.

Salatin, Joel. *Everything I Want to Do Is Illegal: War Stories from the Local Food Front*. Swoope, VA: Polyface, 2007.

Sale, Kirkpatrick. *Human Scale*. New York: Perigree Books, 1980.

Schlosser, Eric. *Fast Food Nation*. New York: Harper Perennial, 2005.

Thoreau, Henry David. *Walden*. New Haven, CT: Yale University Press, 2004.

Voegelin, Eric. *The New Science of Politics*. Chicago: University of Chicago Press, 1987.

INDEX

ABOUT THE AUTHOR

Mark T. Mitchell teaches political theory at Patrick Henry College. He earned his PhD at Georgetown University. He is the author of *Michael Polanyi: The Art of Knowing* and coeditor of *The Humane Vision of Wendell Berry*. In 2009, he co-founded the webzine *Front Porch Republic*, which brings together a variety of writers, from across the political spectrum, to advance the ideas of limits, human scale, sustainability, and care for the natural world. He lives with his wife and four children on a small farm in Virginia.